Exposing
DARWINISM'S
Weakest Link

Exposing
DARWINISM'S
Weakest Link

KENNETH POPPE

HARVEST HOUSE PUBLISHERS

EUGENE, OREGON

Cover by Dugan Design Group, Bloomington, Minnesota

Cover photos © iStockphoto

EXPOSING DARWINISM'S WEAKEST LINK
Copyright © 2008 by Kenneth Poppe
Published by Harvest House Publishers
Eugene, Oregon 97402
www.harvesthousepublishers.com

Library of Congress Cataloging-in-Publication Data
Poppe, Kenneth, 1948-
Exposing Darwinism's weakest link / Kenneth Poppe.
    p. cm.
ISBN-13: 978-0-7369-2125-1 (pbk.)
ISBN-10: 0-7369-2125-7 (pbk.)
   1. Evolution (Biology)—Religious aspects—Christianity. 2. Creationism. I. Title.
BL263.P66 2007
233.'11—dc22
                                                            2007019257

Printed in the United States of America

08 09 10 11 12 13 14 15 16 / LB-SK / 11 10 9 8 7 6 5 4 3 2 1

To the many actively faith-based people who inherently acknowledge the presence of God, especially those precious souls who teach others to do the same. Learn the Lord's science well, for it will defeat the faithless, convict the passive believers, and build your own faith with incredible consistency.

Acknowledgments

If the art of creativity is adapting what you steal, then my appreciation is extended to all those whose thoughts and comments shaped the bulk of this writing. It is truly your work more than mine.

I also want to thank my wife and children (all six of them), and my immediate and extended family for their solid support, and for forgiving the many ways I limp through life. Also worthy of mention are Blessing Ranch (Livermore, Colorado) and LifeBridge Christian Church (Longmont, Colorado), which have served as my dual church homes for many years. If the world loses your savor, how will it be salted again?

From a professional standpoint, I owe much to the members of the Phylos Network, whose collective wisdom is beyond compare, and the people at the Discovery Institute in Seattle, who are a beacon of scientific truth in an otherwise dim world. I would also like to honor the many school board members, administrators, principals, and teachers (such as in the Grantsburg, Wisconsin, school district) for showing us all that evolution can be critically and legally examined without giving leverage to even the most aggressive Darwinists.

Finally, my thanks again to editor Paul Gossard for his expertise, patience, and insightful guidance, and to editor Terry Glaspey, who opened so many doors. Also I greatly appreciate the supportive staff at Harvest House Publishers, who strive, above all else, to enlarge the Kingdom.

Contents

PART FOUR
Conclusion

For Further Consideration

The Nature of This Special Debate

I want to know God's thoughts. The rest are details.

—ALBERT EINSTEIN

Imagine if every devout Darwinist who proclaims, "Life made itself by itself," would conversely say with equal confidence, "However, when it comes to human life, well, that was a miraculous product of God Almighty." With such an admission by an evolutionist, there wouldn't be much of a debate left on origins, would there?

Enter *Exposing Darwinism's Weakest Link*. This self-explanatory title forthrightly posits that we are not here by some random mistake but by the intentional act of a supernatural intelligence carrying out a divine purpose. Moreover, this book specifically examines the special provisions for humans in our planetary backdrop—as well as family trees, prehistoric hominid evidence, human vestigial structures and behaviors, the origin of speech, good versus evil, values and morals, and the nature of transmitted information. However, regardless of these specifics, the tie that binds the book's overall message is,

> We humans are in no wise products of accidental forces. Instead, our special planetary backdrop, plus all special aspects of humanity in this backdrop, makes us unique among life-forms in the way we were designed and placed by the intention of a supernatural Being. However, this Being's every scientific creative act preceding our arrival was also intended just for us—making humans the

crowning achievement of an entire plan existing before
time itself.

And the overall message doesn't stop there. This book will continually reaffirm that this Being who created us has not left the scene, fallen
asleep, or perhaps even died. And it will refer to this monotheistic
Being as "God" with a capital "G," though He goes by other names
in other cultures—Jehovah, Allah, Manitou, and so on—names that
indicate man's historically diverse attempts to reach out to the same
Being.

To sum it up, I wrote *Exposing Darwinism's Weakest Link* to be a
book about the designed science producing and governing the human
condition. And unlike my approach in my previous book, *Reclaiming
Science from Darwinism*, I will be delving into much more than evolutionary problems in macromolecules, cells, and organ systems—I
will be examining our spiritual nature itself.

To fully understand *Homo sapiens*, you need to grasp the spiritual
aspect—an aspect that does not apply to any other animal. And you
also need to understand that at present humans have to deal with the
limitations and urges of the biological container where the spirit temporarily resides. Therefore, my content will examine not just instinct
but intuition, not just survival but service, not just chances but choices,
not just compost but consequences. If we are to come to grips with the
totality of our existence, we must not only understand the biological
side measured best by instrumentation, but also the spiritual side best
measured by abstraction.

———

So…are you intrigued by the monkey-to-man concept? Do your
senses go on alert when you hear or read about how your body parts,
behaviors, and communications are simply natural reflections of your
prehistoric past? (When you put on your best dress or tuxedo, are you
acting out just another form of the courtship that has been part of the
animal world for millions of years?) Are you intrigued by discussions
over whether any values transcend humanity itself because they are

found in all cultures? (Is stealing *always* wrong regardless of the situation?) Are you curious about your true spiritual nature, and whether you have been placed here for a reason? (Like those certain events in your life that, deep down inside, you know just couldn't be happenstance?) For answers to these and other questions, read on.

PART ONE

THE STARTING GROUND

The majority is not trying to establish a religion or to teach it—it is trying to protect itself from the effort of an insolent minority to force irreligion upon the children under the guise of teaching science.

—WILLIAM JENNINGS BRYAN

BRYAN WAS THE ATTORNEY FOR THE PROSECUTION AT THE 1925 "SCOPES MONKEY TRIAL" IN DAYTON, TENNESSEE THAT MADE EVOLUTION A HOUSEHOLD TERM. THE ABOVE WORDS ARE FROM HIS WRITTEN CLOSING STATEMENT, WHICH WAS NEVER READ IN COURT.

1

Examining Your Family Tree

A Monkey for an Uncle?

Consider your biological father. He is responsible for half of the genetic codes that shaped your body, and probably some of your personality as well. Now consider his father, your grandfather. If typical, I would guess at least a couple of your body traits are more grandpa's than dad's—having somehow skipped a generation. And how about your great-grandfather? Were you lucky enough to know him, even if just like me, through those vague and shifting memories as a very small boy? Dare I throw in a great-great-grandfather—in my case known only through legend and those grainy black-and-white photos of a roughly dressed man beside a horse and buggy?

Consider that when your great-great-grandfather was your age, for surely he once was, he could try to reconstruct his lineage just as you have done. What names and faces would he have recalled? And if you could piece great-great-granddad's and your recollections together, that would create a timeline taking you back eight generations—perhaps 250 years or so! Where would you find your ancestors then? In my case, I'm told, the Hamburg, Germany, area. And would my ancestors then be traced to the nomadic Gaelic stock that inhabited Western Europe before formal countries were established there? And then to where? Ancient Phoenicians, Sumerians, Egyptians? And how about yours?

Now to get to the main point. If you kept traveling back in time in this manner, generation after generation, where would you end up? Where would your dad's ancestors have been living 1000 years ago? 2500 to 5000 years ago? And so on? Those who believe in strict Darwinism would say an extended family schematic would show your ancestors going back several million years ago where they first evolved on the African continent. And on this reverse journey you would see slowly reappearing total body hair, steadily shrinking brains, increasingly sloping foreheads and jaw protrusions, and extending arms whose knuckles would eventually be dragging the ground, assisting a clumsy, bent-over gait. In other words, strict evolutionists say if you could backtrack your family tree for, say, 5 million years, your ancestors would now be closer in appearance to a chimp than a human. And if you continued farther back in time, the coccyx bone at the bottom of your pelvis would extend into a prehensile tail, and the reappearing grasping toes on your feet would send you back to swinging in the trees from whence you came some 10 to 15 million years ago.

Stop and ponder your supposed family tree in this way—a videotape in rewind. Is this really how it went down? Did humans come from monkeys? (Often a Darwinist will answer no to this question by saying it wasn't a direct path of evolution. But monkeys have to be on the path before apes, right? And apes would have to be on the path before humanoids, right? So it most absolutely is, in theory, "monkey to man"—no matter how crooked the line.) Now if this isn't the truth, what's the alternative? Unless you consult primitive worship superstitions, I've stated before that the world's five major religions give you one origin—Genesis—and it includes a tantalizing tale of an innocent man Adam and his companion woman, Eve, in a pristine garden. But for so many, that's a fairy tale of bigger proportions than monkeys becoming humans. So what is the truth?

Here's my response. Regardless of which religious view(s) might supply the answer(s), I will stand firmly on this:

> There is absolutely no scientific support for the monkey-to-man scenario—absolutely none.

On the contrary, science, and even philosophy, validate the title of this book and its overriding message as stated a few pages ago.

Either-Or

If there is an alternative answer to the totally unscientific view that monkeys slowly turned into people, ostensibly it is one of the religious variety. But before we tackle the idea, let me first share the concept I find continually bubbling up from the origins cauldron: Almost every major issue concludes with just two choices—*either* it could have happened this way, *or* it couldn't. So grab a writing instrument and check your choice of one of two for each of the ten statements below.

It Could Happen   **It Couldn't Happen**

_____ _____ 1. The most violent accidental explosion ever, the big bang, was sufficiently self-appointed to create the largest and most fine-tuned object ever known, the universe.

_____ _____ 2. The sheer number of planets in the universe, and the number of years these planets have existed, give us a mathematical chance that at least one would become a fully interactive biological world—ours—by accident.

_____ _____ 3. Blind luck had the ability to construct the approximately 80,000 different life-required protein chains of specifically sequenced amino acids (from an "alphabet" of 20 different amino-acid choices)—even those proteins 10,000 amino acids long.

_____ _____ 4. The RNA/DNA molecules, containing information equivalent to all the books in 20 standard libraries, suddenly appeared by chance in the "primordial soup" before the first cell was a reality.

_____ _____ 5. Almost as soon as Earth's conditions permitted, a functional cell appeared, self-prepared with a wide array of metabolizing and reproductive mechanisms.

_____ _____ 6. A half billion years ago, in the blink of an evolutionary eye, the Cambrian explosion self-generated the completely interactive gene pool of all 32 animal phyla with complex organ systems. Once complex life didn't exist, then it was all there.

_____ _____ 7. After the Cambrian explosion, random scramblings of genetic information kept producing improved genetic codes. This allowed life to surge forward as animals kept giving rise to improved offspring with which, suddenly or eventually, they could not mate.

_____ _____ 8. These accidental genetic surges adequately explain a whole host of large-scale advances—for example, straight bones in fins turning into jointed bones in legs, reptile scales turning into bird feathers, photosensitive cells turning into eyes, births from amniotic eggs turning into births from a placenta, and chordates like cows or hippos going back into the ocean to become whales.

_____ _____ 9. While animals randomly surged forward within 32 phyla from sponges to mammals, plants accomplished a similar advance in complexity from moss to cacti, but did it in only 8 steps, often called divisions instead of phyla.

And central to this book:

_____   _____   10. Primates like monkeys left the trees and
kept getting bigger, stronger, and smarter.
About 5 million years of natural selection
was sufficient time for hominids to adapt to
walking on their hind legs, learn to use tools,
fashion clothes to wear, master fire, develop
first spoken and then written communication, and finally organize societies in cave
homes among maple groves that eventually
became cottage homes on Maple Street.

So how did you score on this checklist? The two most extreme
scores would be to have *all* ten checks in the right column of "it
couldn't happen"—like me—or all ten checks on the left column of
"it could happen." Of course, you realize that *one single check* in the
right column dooms Darwinism to immediate failure. All it takes is
one legitimate "couldn't" check in this either-or set-up and natural
evolution has no chance to produce me the writer, or you the reader.
If you can, actually imagine trying to agree with all ten statements as
checked on the left, and I'll wager you'll feel the full weight of the
folly of "self-made" life. Therefore, if you find evolution insufficient *in
even one instance,* you need to consider a bigger-than-science connection—unless, of course, you want to remain apathetic. So, if evolution
or apathy is not the answer, I suggest you begin a quest to come to
grips with the "God" who engineered this miracle.

Rejecting statement #10 above reflects this chapter's opening rejection of the idea that all our ancestral lines slowly become more stooped
and stupider as we observe the reverse of totally natural processes. If
the world generally rejected that notion and stood on the "God alternative" with confidence, it would dramatically change the debate on
the other nine statements. And yet if monkeys are not our uncles then
how *do* you explain human origin? How do you explain the master
plan of God the Designer?

2

A Masterful Plan

We Are Here by Design

Building on the previous chapter, strict Darwinism (completely natural evolution without the need for God) is an idea for the scientific and philosophic scrap heap. So how did it get started? History now shows evolution to be an idea that originated about 150 years ago when Charles Darwin wrote *The Origin of Species,* first published in 1859. History also shows that evolution got a huge boost in public awareness from the Tennessee "Scopes Monkey Trial" in 1925.* And yet the bulk of evolutionary theory got rolling so many years ago when, compared to today, so little was known about the science of our world—especially our micro (invisible) and macro (celestial) worlds. That is why so many scientists today with the most impeccable credentials in all fields see natural processes as completely inadequate to produce life, such as Frances Collins, the man of strong faith who led the impressive worldwide team that decoded the entire human genome in 2000. It is also why such scientists, and a snowballing number of common people, see so much merit in movements such as Intelligent Design, which do not even need a religious component.

---

* See the appendix of my previous book, *Reclaiming Science from Darwinism.*

My opinion? The entire faulty premise of Darwinism had to sit atop a steaming pile of faulty theories until science, not religion, finally shoveled it out of the barn. In fact, if Charles Darwin or Clarence Darrow tried to introduce strict evolutionary theory today, it wouldn't sell. Therefore, even if only by default, we are left with a "God" behind it all—and an all-powerful monotheistic type, unless those religions with a bona-fide origins explanation are all wrong.

An Alternative Explanation

How about a scenario that would necessitate a "master plan" explanation? It would read something like this:

1. The big bang was a planned and directed creation of energy and matter that also produced the physical laws governing our expanding universe. In a series of controlled unfolding steps—some very short in duration and some very long—the basic atomic elements formed all celestial objects, which eventually took on their intended and stable configurations. God was "monkeying" with physics.

2. The Earth was placed at the perfect orbital location in the solar system, along with other perfectly placed planets around a star of perfect diameter and intensity in the perfect location of the galaxy. Furthermore, our Earth is the perfect size with the perfect tilt, and has the perfect temperature ranges, water content, atmospheric balance, soil mixture, terrain variations, weather patterns, and mineral content to support life. The mathematical probability of randomly getting such a complete and fully interactive backdrop for life is *zero*.

3. The probability of generating one small cellular protein of 100 amino acids in the correct sequence (from an amino-acid "alphabet" of 20 choices) is one chance in 10^{130} random tries. If life appeared in the first two billion years of Earth's existence as evolution often says—that's 10^{16} seconds of total time—nature would have to be testing 10^{114} new combinations every second to have the necessary odds for

success. In that there are "only" an estimated 10^{80} atoms in the universe, the odds of getting that one protein are *zero*. Furthermore, since there are some 80,000 other proteins to generate, some 10,000 amino-acid chains long, blind luck has a "zero to the infinity power" chance to produce organic molecules without intelligent assistance.

4. RNA/DNA, the most complex organic molecules of all, have no natural explanation, and cannot exist before the less complex proteins they produce in statement 3. Therefore, this blueprint for life that ensures species reproduce "after their own kind" *has* to be a product of design.

5. Molecular biologists say getting that first metabolizing and reproducing cell was a bigger probabilistic barrier than that cell eventually evolving into a human. Cells are not blobs of jellied homogenous protoplasm, but individual ultracomplex factories with highly technical components utilizing a fantastic number of *predesigned* molecular machines—each machine having no use alone because "nothing works until everything works."

6. The Cambrian Explosion—biology's big bang—has no natural explanation for the sudden creation of so much new genetic information. The only alternative is intelligent assistance.

7. The scrambling of any information—genetic or otherwise—always leads to degradation. Yet Darwinism is completely dependent on "good mutations" that constantly provide new and improved genetic information to the tune of an estimated 30,000,000 species worldwide. Believing that creatures were constantly giving birth to an innumerable number of slightly improved species—or a fewer number of greatly improved "monsters" with which they cannot mate—is bad science that forces one to look elsewhere.

8. There is no scientific explanation for the overall large-scale advances in animal complexity. Environmental factors

cannot cause genetic changes—like cows living too close to water to eat the most lush grass and eventually becoming whales, or monkeys learning to walk on flat land because they had to leave trees that were disappearing due to environmental changes. Such common explanations are also completely untenable because there are virtually no significant transitional fossil forms left behind to document step-by-step such natural changes. Instead, the Designer has been at work even in the latest of times introducing new genetic information.

9. Plants have the additional difficulty of bridging the same range of complexity seen in animals in about 8 jumps instead of 32. The larger the jump, the higher the requirement for intelligent input.

And central to this book:

10. Monkeys could never, ever evolve into humans by totally natural processes.

Do a short survey. Try statement #10 above on a few average people, and see how often you get agreement. Since any poll will show that a great majority of Americans believe in some form of God, surely they tie their own existence at least in part to the presence and activity of this God. I will also say that since Darwinism was born 150 years ago, people have always been naturally resistant to the notion that monkeys are our uncles, usually for religious reasons. However, in the last decade or so, science—from physics to chemistry to biology—is convincing people from all walks of life that someone's "master plan" has been implemented. Another telling earmark of the paradigm change is that as the old Darwinists are passing away, no young brilliant minds are currently coming out of science to carry evolution forward with new details on the mechanisms of self-made. It is truly a dead theory with no place to go, and the current responses of Darwinist temper flashes and name-calling lend further proof of evolution's failure.

Science in the System

If you still wonder if strict Darwinism is valid, consider the simplest definition I have for natural evolution. It's the straightforward one I often share with students to reveal its overriding flaw: *The science in the system is sufficient to create the system.* If you need a personal example, try to imagine the system where you work—the shelves, the books, the tables, the tools, the appliances, the computers, the machines, whatever—being able to generate and organize its components, and then operate itself, without the need of intelligent input from outside the system. I would call that notion preposterous.

I suspect *Exposing Darwinism's Weakest Link* will join *Reclaiming Science from Darwinism* and so many other volumes that show beyond a *scientific* doubt that natural evolution can only be a philosophic construct—philosophic because, like other open-ended concepts, it can be debated in any direction, and involves comparison of opinions rather than pursuit of proof. Darwinism must release the science it has held hostage for over a century. Therefore, while additional books will continue to flesh out a few more details about the collapse of evolution, I say scientific publications, laboratory research, and especially science education need to be dramatically overhauled *right now* to not exclude the idea of a "Master Plan" and its various definitions and mechanisms that are totally scientific—*intelligent design, specified information, irreducible complexity, information theory,* and so on.* And again, if it can be proved that at least the human life here must be a product of God Almighty, debate on the rest of evolution is likely to become moot.

———•◦•◦•———

Again, I say, your uncle was not a monkey but the culminating product of God's Master Plan. But before Part Three goes into the undeniable reasons that humans were designed, let's first have a little fun in Part Two investigating the amazing backdrop of the planet on which we live.

---

* Let me offer you a ready resource for people and materials to help you counteract the "evolution only" view that infuses society—especially science education. The International Foundation for Science Education by Design at www.IFSED.org offers non-Darwinian consultants who will publicly present on this topic, as well as offer the best in science and math teaching materials that do not have that subtle, or sometimes not so subtle, evolutionary spin. See page 299 for more information.

PART TWO

SPECIAL-ORDER
SCIENCE AND MATH

As we look out into the universe and identify the many accidents of physics and astronomy that have worked together for our benefit, it almost seems as if the universe must in some sense have known that we were coming.

—FREEMAN J. DYSON

DYSON IS PRINCETON PROFESSOR OF PHYSICS, HOLDS 21 HONORARY DEGREES, AND IS THE WINNER OF THE YEAR 2000 TEMPLETON PRIZE FOR HIS WORK IN BLENDING SCIENCE AND THEOLOGY.

3

OUR BACKDROP

A Scientific Garden of Eden

The Garden of Eden. Paradise. Has a nice ring to it, doesn't it? Let's have a little fun with the tale. According to the Bible story, a man and a woman in pristine surroundings with nothing to do but enjoy. And Adam wasn't stuck with someone he couldn't get along with either. His mate, Eve, was picked by a divine dating service that has, shall we say, an incredible knack for compatibility.

Paradise had to be beautiful—like the inside of a moist and lush greenhouse full of diverse and exotic plants, only much bigger. (Everything was watered by a heavy dew, and God Himself enjoyed a quiet stroll among its beauty—Genesis 3:8.) Water everywhere, but protected where never a storm, flood, or drought was known. Genesis says all that water from the Garden produced four rivers, and this abundance of water grew all types of vegetation to enjoy, especially trees both beautiful and good for food. This means Adam and Eve could be vegetarians without nosy people asking too many questions.

I wonder how old our couple was? Surely not retirement age, but not children either. Probably young adults at the zenith of vitality. Illustrated children's Bibles, like the one I had as a kid, always made them look like they were in their mid-20s. Works for me. That means bodies not too young or too old for prime physical activities, and no struggles with either going through puberty or dealing with aches and pains and sagging body parts. And—a key point here—they both were getting no older.

And of course the pictures showed them correctly naked. Was nakedness an embarrassment? No pretense—no problem! Their innocence knew no shame or guile, like when very young children happily run around unclothed in public. (With my six kids, that practice always stopped around age four or so.) With all that abundance of gratis material provisions and no need to impress anyone with a spiffy wardrobe or fine jewelry, there was no envy, so no strife or quarreling. Like I said, Paradise.

Intimacy in Paradise

Before the Fall, when God put the first couple in the Garden, He had already charged them to be "fruitful and multiply" while still in their sinless state—Genesis 1:28. So Eve never had headaches and Adam never needed any enhancement products.

But more importantly—much more importantly—Adam was surely tender and considerate with his wife's physical safety, which would make Eve feel so protected and valued that she would respond freely. And as we all inherently know, a married couple with sizzling and respectful monogamy has something for which the deprived in the world would exchange all their material possessions.

Not only that, the pair had no task but to enjoy their surroundings and each other because they didn't have to do a lick of work. All their food grew automatically, unless like me they enjoyed raising a few home-grown tomatoes. But unlike my tomatoes, they did not have to work up a sweat tilling and digging because there were none of those infernal weeds. And since I guess there were no other botanical drawbacks, no poison ivy or fear of stepping on a cactus with bare feet, then there must have been no zoological irritations either, such as biting flies or mosquitoes, no wasps, no skunks (except perhaps the de-scented kind), no leeches, and so on.

In fact, if there were no unpleasantries of any kind, I assume there would be no natural violence going on such as predation. Does that mean no animals then, since they seem predisposed to kill and eat each other? Not necessarily. In Paradise, the "lion lay down with the lamb" (Isaiah 11:6-7). It must have been like one large petting zoo with free snacks, and only one rule for the couple, later stolen by the creators of George of the Jungle—"Watch out for that tree!" Perfect couple, perfect backdrop, perfect physical and mental states, and all the time in the world—once again, literally—to enjoy it.

It's great to have a tale like that to tickle our imagination. To the majority of people I've ever met, the Adam and Eve story is just that—one big fairy tale. You know, like the Bigfoot and Loch Ness Monster legends such as are found in every culture. Some have said that like other legends, perhaps there was a grain of a story surrounding an advent couple, but as the story grew through telling and retelling, there is now no separating fact from fiction. Others have told me instead that the story is an outright fabrication that someone wrote as an object lesson, and it caught on. I will examine these legend claims in chapter 12, but first let's see if the basic Garden of Eden story line can be compatible with science in any way.

Genesis says the Garden was separated from the rest of the world, so ostensibly it had boundaries. For example, the four rivers originated there, but flowed *out* of it, meaning it had finite borders you could cross over, I assume. Also, when Adam and Eve sinned and were sent out, an angel with a flaming sword turning in every direction guarded the way back *in* (Genesis 3:24). Personally, I've always envisioned some sort of invisible but semipermeable barrier where predatory animals surrendered their instincts and other biological necessities when they went inside and temporarily joined Adam and Eve in that ageless condition. How do you see it?

So then, if Paradise existed in protected isolation, it was isolated from—from what? Well, the rest of the world was already created, I suppose. And what might have been going in the rest of the world beyond the Garden's secure borders? Science as per normal is my guess.

Imagine that the Garden of Eden—where normal rules certainly did not apply—was cordoned off from all other terrestrial activity while the rest of the world recycled through its ebbs and flows. And for how long? Well, since our couple and their surroundings were in sort of a divinely sustained time warp, how long do you want? A few thousands of years? How about the millions of years science needs for its version of geologic time? Why not? When I mention this scenario, sometimes I get asked that if Adam and Eve were virile and inclined, how did they avoid kids for even a few years? It could go back to the time concept. If we cannot free ourselves to see a day and a thousand years as equal measures (2 Peter 3:8), we cannot grasp the eternal nature of God—conferred at least for a time on our couple.

Other skeptics sometimes ask how the Garden avoided millions of years of climate changes such as ice ages, droughts, and comet strikes. This could go back to the power concept. The wording above uses terms such as *separation, barrier, protected isolation, normal rules did not apply, cordoned off, divinely sustained time warp.* Allowing God could create the universe by speaking words, let's assume He has enough power to specially protect a minuscule portion of it.*

Balance and Beauty

In this view, beyond the Garden's boundary all the rest of the activity on the planet is bedlam, right? On the abiotic side, geologic forces such as volcanoes, earthquakes, lightning, floods, forest fires, continental drift, cooling/warming/cooling trends, tornadoes, hurricanes, and other windstorms are constantly hammering the Earth. On the biotic side, it's "dog eat dog" where in the competition for limited resources in food webs, one minute you get lunch, the next minute

---

* If you still have trouble with the omnipotent aspect of monotheism, try 2 Peter 3:5. Or, if you want to see how the ability of omnipotence to create with spoken words directly applies to the debate on Darwinism, read chapter 24, "The Answer," from *Reclaiming Science from Darwinism.*

you are lunch. In fact, the more plants and animals are eaten by other species, the more they must grossly overproduce just to survive.

Here are some examples of the extent of consumption. Of two expected polar bear cubs, one doesn't make it to adulthood. Of twelve newborn baby ducks, only three become parents. Of 5000 salmon fry, only one becomes a breeder. If you consider mice and worms, the former are eaten by the thousands and the latter are eaten by the millions in a single ecosystem. Tragic? In the minds of some people, I guess. But remember, the myriad of animals that depend on mice and worms received their sustenance, and you still have enough mice and worm survivors to make thousands and millions more.

And plants, of course, are the megaproducers that get devoured in incredible quantities. Imagine if 1000 corn plants grow to maturity in a given year, but 999 get eaten. No problem. Another 1000 corn plants can be regrown the following season if only one kernel from one cob on that uneaten cornstalk germinates and matures. That's because when planted, that one seed can produce the customary two cobs with 500 seeds apiece. (That's right. You should average around 500 kernels per cob. Try counting them.) And if those 1000 plants each produce two cobs, that's 1000 x 2 x 500 = 1,000,000, a million potential corn plants the next year from your one surviving seed. Such is the tremendous reproductive power of DNA, especially in primary producer plants that must generate sufficient food-web biomass so all consumers—including we humans—can kill and eat.

Yes, it's a battle out there. And because the competition is this keen, science says many life-forms throughout time lost their survival struggle and went extinct, such as the dinosaurs. By a common estimation 99 percent of all species that have ever lived—the dodo bird and passenger pigeon being two modern-day examples—are gone forever. But science says the fossil record shows new species continually replacing the lost, and the battle continued. This is "survival of the fittest" in action—adapt and out-produce your competition or die. It's the Darwinist's view of the life through which even *Homo sapiens* must struggle, lest we also perish like the Neanderthals. Hmm. I think I'd prefer the safety of the Garden, wouldn't you?

And yet the biologist in me still sees sustaining balance and tremendous beauty all around. If you want a negative temporal view of our world, define life according to the futility of the two previous paragraphs. However, if you want a positive spiritual view, a view that this world was designed just for the likes of us, keep reading.

Earlier this summer I called my son Caleb over to view the activities of an ichneumon wasp who had stung and paralyzed a sphinx moth larva—a larva better known as that "blankety-blank tomato worm" that strips your tomato plants of leaves overnight. The "worm" had to weigh four times that of the wasp, so the wasp was dragging it along heading to her nearby nest hole in the ground. We quietly followed her to a pencil-sized hole a few feet away, and after determined exertion, she managed to pull that fat worm underground until both disappeared.

But here is the rest of the story. First, the wasp probably found the larva because the tomato leaves give off a certain attractive scent when attacked. So after the locating, stinging, dragging, and stuffing process, the wasp lays her eggs on the paralyzed but still very much alive worm, and then departs with her mission accomplished. Later her baby larvae hatch. Yes, the young wasps are unparented, but they are protected underground with a living food source to consume on their way to pupation. Wow! Tough luck for the tomato worm (in my estimation, poetic justice), but an ingeniously designed system for making offspring nonetheless.

Incredible Harmony

This is the incredible harmony I've enjoyed seeing in nature all my life—the beauty of which I've always hoped to instill in my biology students. Because of this cannibalism, the wasp benefits, the tomato plant benefits, animals that feed on the wasps and ripe tomatoes benefit, other plants that get aerated roots from wasp holes benefit, and nutrients from all recycled bodies benefit the next growing season. Even sphinx moths benefit, as they are not allowed to overpopulate and consume their food supply. It's precision of the highest order, and we all need to recognize that.

Credit the wasp? Though clever, she and her kind are only rigidly programmed with no thought beforehand. Credit the worm? Not a chance. How about the other plants and animals involved in the drama, or even the nutrients? Do we take the primitive route and worship the air, water, or sun? How about the modern agnostic route of passing it off to Mother Nature—or the atheist route of crediting blind luck?

Yet there is that third option—crediting a Designer I choose to refer to as "God." So when I would teach my biology students of these magnificent arrangements and someone would invariably ask, "How did all this come about?" my oft-used line was, "Great idea. I wonder who thought of it?" Remember, we're talking public school here, and I had to be very careful in sharing my opinion. But later, when these same students saw monkeys turning into humans in their textbooks, they saw my one-liner "great idea" deflection as totally inadequate. Therefore, great discussions would ensue, and I was once again outside the comfort zone of public-school curriculum. Though the risks were great and the chastisement sometimes painful, the gains were greater, in that these discussions are a major influencer of my writing.

Permit me another story of the graceful balance in nature that we get to enjoy—a scientific report my students just love to analyze. A recent study by biologists found that when timber wolves were reintroduced to Yellowstone Park where they once thrived, fish populations—if you can believe it—went up. That's right, more wolves meant more trout—but how can that be possible? The connection was a mystery until the following relationships were discovered.

The normal routine for deer and elk when predators such as wolves are about is to only drink and feed along the riverbanks early and then late in the day. This exposes them briefly to the wolves, but then once filled, the big game animals retreat to the safety of deeper timber between feedings. (I hunt big game, and everyone who does knows the age-old pattern of hunting early and late in the day.) But without wolves, deer and elk began to just to hang around riverbanks all day long. "Eating trout?" my kids would ask. No, continuously grazing or browsing while breaking down riverbanks as they walked in and out.

This created two problems. First, with so much dirt kicked into the rivers, the mud would silt over rocky streambeds and trout couldn't lay their eggs in the needed gravel. Second, deer and elk were spending an unnatural number of hours eating bank saplings to the ground that were supposed to grow into tall trees and bring cooling shade to the river. If you know your trout habitat, you know optimum water temperatures for these fish have tight tolerances, and the warmer unshaded water caused significant fish numbers to migrate away seeking cooler water. So see if you can follow this. Trout populations dropped because there was too much mud in the spawning beds; and the river got too warm because the banks and trees were being destroyed, because the deer and elk were wearing them down, because there was no need to hide from wolves, because the wolves had been exterminated. (Whew!) But when the wolves returned, the ecosystem repaired itself in a handful of years.

Precision

And that's called *specified complexity*—the intentionally designed beauty of the biology that sustains us in our surroundings. Even people with a modicum of scientific knowledge know that such symbiotic relationships in our ecosystems are innumerable, and many are more incredible than the stories of wasps and wolves. And even allowing that geologists are right about the "old earth," many of these relationships, accurately described as "delicate" and "susceptible to disaster," have been operating with such precision for millions of years.

Hmm. Perhaps the Earth doesn't seem so "violent" anymore. Then what about the havoc wreaked by earthquakes, tornadoes, and such from which our couple in Paradise would need to be protected? Well, we all need to realize as well the indispensable biotic roles played by these abiotic geologic forces. We get mountain and valley habitats from volcanic activity. We get rivers, streams, and lakes from earthquake activity. Our major climatic biomes now sustained by jet streams and ocean currents were produced by continental drift caused by violent forces that separated the single Pangaea landmass into smaller pieces.

In similar fashion, our precious topsoil is produced by the erosion process where floods, storms, and freezing/thawing cycles break up rock. For example, those river floods, though initially devastating, sweep away accumulated branches and silt that clog up the watercourse and degrade the environment. In fact, massive releases of water from beneath huge dams are done intentionally as periodic cleansing to rejuvenate the rivers below. Even forest fires, at least the natural ones, are well-known for bringing renewal to old-growth forests where biologic activity is greatly reduced in the darkness under the canopy. (People criticized the U.S. Forest Service for not aggressively fighting the massive Yellowstone Park forest fires of 1988. Yet despite the initial damage, visitors now see more big game, and the grasses and flowers are more beautiful than ever.) Yes, the orchestration of the intertwining of the mechanisms that make our existence possible only gets more mind-boggling the deeper you dig.

Two points need to be stressed here. First, despite how you think it got here and how long it's been here, nobody can argue that the Earth is not incredibly fine-tuned. All plants, from the least to the greatest, have specific roles. All animals, from the dumbest to the smartest, fill their niches masterfully. And they work together, along with the planet's natural forces, to make beautiful music. Consider my words from *Reclaiming Science from Darwinism:*

> The rhythm of life is not a cacophony of random and banging noises that somehow fell together, but a symphony by a Master Composer where all players are unfamiliar with the composition and their assigned instruments, and yet never miss a note.

Relative Stability

In my opinion, we find ourselves pretty much at scientific ease in this relatively stable planet governed by God's natural laws and under His watchful eye. In fact, the music only seems to get out of tune when we humans act as if we don't have to abide by these laws. Yes, it's not the Garden of Eden. Plants and animals have to die to make the system work—sometimes in huge quantities. Also, old age, disease, accidents, and natural disasters take their toll as part of the sustaining and renewing process. But these plants and animals are all part of the *nefesh* of life—not the *neshama*—and their passing is totally natural and necessary to maintain this amazingly beautiful scientific backdrop in which we live. (For now, let's consider *nefesh* vs. *neshama* as the *general spirit of life* vs. the *eternal spirit of life*—the "spark." (I will say much more about *nefesh* and *neshama* in chapter 12.)

How fine-tuned is our planet? Allow me to give you a personal example. Back in the year 2000 I worked on a bioremediation project out of Colorado State University in Ft. Collins, Colorado, related to all this discussion on ecosystems. Colorado was just coming out of a drought cycle. Because of the tinder-dry conditions, there were devastating forest fires in the state the two previous years, said to be unnatural in intensity because of the increased fuel load caused by the policy of immediate repression of even small fires. When spring rains finally came following the "scorched earth" fires, an inordinate amount of soot, ash, and mud was washed into rivers and streams. Because of this toxic runoff, some riparian ecosystems, especially those around small creeks, were generally destroyed.

Our research team was investigating how to speed up nature's restoration of this destruction, especially of trout populations that support much of the state's draw for tourist dollars. And yet going back to food webs, the stream would first have to have established trout *food* before fish could return. Trout food in this case are *macro-invertebrates*—the small aquatic insects and worms you find under an upturned rock—such as mayfly, caddis fly, and stone fly larvae that had been pretty much wiped out. Our hypothesis was, "When the earliest pioneer macroinvertebrates reappear, are they hardy survivors of the remnant population that withstood the disaster, or are they imports from undamaged streams farther away?" (The answer to this question obviously would have a bearing on artificial efforts to ameliorate the health of a stream.)

Our team's job was to test this hypothesis through DNA analysis of local and neighboring larvae populations. So one minute we were running around in the wild with hipboots, nets, and buckets catching little bugs, and the next we were pureeing them in a blender and analyzing the contents with multimillion-dollar genetic analysis equipment. Our results? We found that, indeed, hardy survivors of the local populations from within each stream were the first to reestablish viable populations. So the next question was, "Is it feasible to throw a bunch of money into an artificial breeding program with these 'super bug' survivors, and will they also withstand and repair damaged streams in different ecosystems?"*

So without further damage, nature (God's natural forces) would repair the stream in time, and it wouldn't cost the public a dime. Or you could spend millions of dollars in a super-bug research project in hopes of getting your money's worth in more rapid stream restoration. These are questions for ecology specialists and government agencies to decide. Now, keeping these issues in mind, let's take a look at the challenge in Biosphere 2.

Biosphere 2 was the early 1990s project where eight people spent two years in a completely enclosed three-acre glass dome compound in the Arizona desert with no contact with the outside world. The project was designed to study environmental stability in a closed facility, and to investigate the possibility of artificial habitats for space colonization. Within the dome, all products were grown and recycled—food, water, waste, soil, carbon dioxide, oxygen, plant and animal byproducts, and so on. The cost of Biosphere 2—an attempt to simulate Earth's natural provisions—was $9 million per person per year. If the Earth has about 6 billion people, it would cost us $540,000,000,000,000,000 (540 quintillion dollars) annually to do what our planet does for free. Our home planet, "Biosphere the Original" if you will, is fully equipped to take care of us (if we just stay within the ecological rules), and operates—as Freeman Dyson said—almost as if it were expecting us.

More Fine-Tuning

That's point one—that our planetary backdrop is perfectly fine-tuned to meet our *biological* needs. The second point is much more personal. Consider how our world fully accommodates all our special *personal, emotional,* and *psychological* needs as well—needs that are not shared by any other creature on Earth. So what are the ways human

---

* Are you are tempted to jump up and say, "Evolution in action! Natural selection produces improvements in survivability of aquatic insect species!" No. These hardy survivors already possessed that rare survivability gene sequence heretofore not needed. View it as something like that deep red hair color in humans, already sprinkled throughout the population, suddenly preserving these people's lives while others perished. This is a simple gene sort, not a mutation. The key in both the new bug and the red hair predominance analogy is to realize we are dealing with a mere shift in gene frequency. There is *no new genetic information* here—the heart of Darwinian theory—as the repopulating species are no different from their ancestors.

needs are supplied beyond the very basic physical necessity of the very air we all breathe?

- *Water?* Just wait until you get a dose of chapter 6.

- *Food?* We join a few other omnivores like hogs and raccoons in our ability to feed on a variety of substances, and I suppose we are lucky that we didn't evolve into a one-diet creature like the koala, stuck with eucalyptus leaves. But we are free to sample food worldwide from the highest mountains to the deepest oceans. Furthermore, when we sit down to those fancy banquets or quiet meals with loved ones, the special feeling of the experience goes way beyond the intake of calories.

- *Shelter?* Humans can build structures out of useful plant materials like maybe the Neanderthals did—branch lean-tos, sod huts, and so on. But we can go way beyond with materials that bring versatility, richness, and warmth to our homes.

- *Mobility?* We have the musculature to walk or run, even the ability to domesticate and train a horse. But we also have incredible fossil fuel resources the world over, and the ability to design and build vehicles to drive or fly using this fuel. (In the obscure 1983 movie *Local Hero,* two men muse about the vagaries of the oil industry and one says, "Can you imagine a world without oil? No motor cars!" Yes, I can imagine a world without oil, and so can you—every other planet in our solar system, galaxy, and universe.)

- *Expression?* We can make facial gestures and use body language to communicate like other advanced animals. But we also have the materials, the dexterity, and the *imagination* to create poetry, draw pictures, write literature, and compose and sing or play music, as well as design and build the instruments that accompany them, as additional means to try to capture and express what we are really feeling inside.

- *Relaxation?* Animals take a break, get necessary rest, even "chill out" as they observe their world. But humans have a dizzying myriad of hobbies and pastimes that take up innumerable hours, and we have the unique capacity to not only stare—but gaze and wonder.

- *Recreation?* Animals get necessary exercise in a variety of ways, such as swimming. (If you haven't ever heard this, all animals naturally know how to swim.) But we go beyond that to make swimming a sport—even a precision Olympic event—and even ski on that water in both liquid and frozen form. And would anyone care to list all the forms of recreation we enjoy—the importance of which to us no animal on Earth could begin to comprehend?

- *Beauty?* The sun is driving the water cycle while dust particles in the sky called *condensation nuclei* are allowing the Earth to receive sustaining rains, and the refraction effect produces rainbows whether humans see them or not. But the same forces also cause those magnificent sunrises and sunsets recognized by even the most impassive and uninspired among us. And how many natural sights in our world do animals daily fail to contemplate that cause every human to stop and savor?

- *Comfort?* Your best friends could be seen as just additional biological life forms and members of your local clan. But when you are hurting, they can actually understand your anguish (anguish, not simply pain), and can come alongside and help you through with love, even though there is no evolutionary reason to be so sacrificial.

I could go on with this list ad infinitum, but I hope the point has been made:

> Our world, though perhaps not Paradise, undoubtedly provides for us way beyond our survival needs as mere animals. Furthermore, we are unique among all life forms in our ability to interact with these provisions.

The way I see it, the above list considered in total makes a strong case that humans—and the backdrop in which we live—can in no wise be defined strictly by laws of nature whose origin would otherwise be strictly accidental. In fact, if you want the full flavor of such a list, try to imagine any animal in our world, from protist to primate, having to understand the life we pursue as defined in these points. Then it follows that if many of our attributes are way beyond animalistic necessity but still far short of perfection, they have as their origin a source of ultimate power and unlimited bounty—rather apt descriptions for God.*

A World of Delights

Then I get to wondering. If Adam and Eve really lived in that Garden as I described earlier, they certainly got to avoid a lot of the unpleasantries of our world. But how much of the enjoyment described above did they miss also? I mean, eating, traveling, recreating, relaxing—these are pretty cool things you know. Or *did* they truly miss out? Maybe they got to avoid the crazy chase we humans get into for the nicest house, the best car, the perfect hobby, and so forth. In fact, maybe we are caught up in an endless and futile quest trying to optimize our provisions, thinking we can create heaven on earth just like they had. But we are still stuck in our ultimately imperfect backdrop that at present offers no hope of perfection.

At any rate, there is one thing I'm sure we share with Adam and Eve regardless of our surroundings—choice. Unlike all other creatures, they must have had the God-given capacity to comprehend the tremendous blessings they enjoyed, and also the heretofore unknown capacity to *choose* to pay homage to the One responsible. (And, of course, legend says they blew that choice.) Then there's us, the only other *Homo sapiens* also vested with a soul ever to walk the planet. And like Adam and Eve, we also can compare, wonder, and dream—and choose—about who or what (if anyone) gets credit for all that has come about.

---

* In chapter 10, "Vestigial Structures and Behaviors," I will share a list with you developed by my high school students called "Things Humans Do that No Other Animals Do." I think it's an eye-opener.

Once again, it's the difference between the *nefesh* and the *neshama* to be discussed later—the *general spirit of life* vs. the *eternal spirit of life*. Look at it this way. That female wasp cannot comprehend the complexity of the drama in which she participates. She earns no plaudits for her ingenuity, and the worm deserves no pity for its destruction. Similarly, the deer and elk don't consider the environmental damage they can cause, or commiserate about the cruel nature of wolves. At the same time, the wolves don't need counseling for preying on the young and infirmed, and the trout aren't petitioning the EPA for redress. None of these creatures, from the larva under the river rock to the dolphin in the ocean, think about a future lost or gained—all are just mindlessly playing their instruments to perfection.

By contrast, my son and I stare at the wasp saga and shake our heads in amazement. With the same power of choice, millions of people leave houses bigger than they need and drive or fly to places like Yellowstone not just to recreate, but to read, write, compose, and photograph—and then come home needing a vacation to recover from the hectic vacation. We also admire from afar the fury of a volcano, get transfixed at sunsets on the beach or the moon over the mountains, and muse about distant stars. Then we spend countless hours working on environmental projects that will not directly benefit us, and we do very "unanimal-like" actions such as taking our adult children back into our house to the detriment of both. Why do we do these things? Believe me, such behaviors that waste time and resources violate every tenet of Darwinism. So what is our real nature? How are we able to be first so compassionate and then so self-serving?

Some people think our world is a pretty cool place filled with wonder that brings enjoyment. Then again—based on the number of suicides perhaps—others must think our world is a dreadful place filled with confusion that brings misery. Which is it? Let me call before you two expert witnesses on the nature of our world whose opinions have to be respected. The first declares,

> This world...is very faulty and imperfect compared to a superior standard and was only the first rude essay of some infant deity who afterwards abandoned it, ashamed

of his lame performance; it is the work only of some dependent, inferior deity and is the object of derision to his superiors; it is the production of old age and dotage in some superannuated deity and, ever since his death, has run on at adventures from the first impulse and active force which it received from him. I cannot think that so wild and unsettled a system of theology is preferable to none at all.

I would call that a negative view of life, wouldn't you? The author is David Hume (1711–1776), celebrated philosopher of the eighteenth century. Then let's consider the second quote:

The scientist is possessed by the sense of universal causation...His religious feelings take the form of a rapturous amazement at the harmony of natural law, which reveals an intelligence of such superiority that compared with it, all the systematic thinking and activities of human beings are utterly insignificant reflections.

That's better, isn't it? The author—the man who spoke this book's opening quote—is Albert Einstein (1879–1955), and he needs no introduction. Permit me some reflections here. I wonder which guy enjoyed a more contented life? That seems obvious to me. I wonder why the scientist had a better outlook than the philosopher? Perhaps it's because the philosopher tried to understand people, who can sometimes be shifty, discordant, and shallow, while the scientist dealt with God's laws that are unchanging, harmonious, and profound. Furthermore, one can see both Hume and Einstein profess faith in deities—the philosopher seeing "them" as a force for mischief and the scientist seeing "Him" as a source of majesty. Finally, the philosopher seems to have an attitude of discontent, stubbornness, and defiance, while the scientist has an attitude of appreciation, humility, and respect.

But let me close this chapter by being very serious. When it comes to groundbreaking and precise thinking, Einstein's name is virtually synonymous as the best of the best. So it's no wonder that both Darwinists and Designers would claim him as one of their own. Though

Einstein was born Jewish, he generally discarded those traditional religious practices that he saw as inflexible and mechanical. However, you have read his quote above. What do you think about his level of faith, and where would he stand on the issue of, say, intelligent design? And let me add that this quote came from a series of essays written when he was 55, after most of his pivotal theories had already changed science forever. I would say this view represents wisdom that's a product of age and lifelong reflection.

Forget Hume and others like him. I'm siding with the guy with wild hair: *"God is."*

In Part Three we'll go into more detail on how modern humans fit into the world Einstein perceived. In the remaining five chapters of Part Two, we'll first cover a bit of specific science—a specific wonder from five different areas that have made our world the place we delight in.

4

DID SOMEONE DEAL THE PERFECT HAND?

Odds Are, the Deck Was Stacked

Comedian Bill Cosby, with his ability to capture the essence of life through humor, commented about trying to learn math in school as a little kid. When the kindergarten teacher pronounced, "One plus one is two," his response was something like, "Yeah man, right on, that's cool…What's a two?" Well, I can relate because math has given me my share of headaches. And yet two of Cosby's "twos" added together seem to become a "four." So you go on to subtract, multiply, and divide, hoping the answers come out right. Then before you know it you are into decimals, fractions, ratios, percents, squares, roots, and integers. Finally it gets so technical that the math needs specific names, like algebra, geometry, trigonometry, and calculus.

Even from 1 + 1 = 2, math is highly regulated. There always is the right answer even if it sometimes eludes you. For example, as a math teacher I know that for students with language barriers, or rebellious students with poor behavior records, math tended to be their favorite subject. Why? The first case is obvious. While linguistics change with locality, numerics apply worldwide, and we all "speak the same language" when doing math. In the second case, I found that students who are on a teaching staff's "blacklist" often feel they don't get any breaks on subjective grading schemes applied to such as essays, posters, and speeches. But when it comes to numbers, when you get the right answer, it has to be marked correct whether they like you or not.

This precision extends to horizons that have no limit. Using advanced math, people explore the reaches of outer space and the depths of inner space, and build gigantic skyscrapers and invisible "nanobots." Math even allows guys like our inimitable Einstein to predict nuclear power—$E=mc^2$—long before it became a reality. Did this precision, and our ability to use it, also get blown into existence by the accidental big bang and the happenstance events that followed?* Most surely the power of numbers has been there since the beginning of time, even if we puny humans have been using them for only a few thousand years. So is it all another stroke of luck?

Let's table the precision and comprehension concepts for a moment and move back into the public school classrooms, where Dr. Cosby eventually did learn his math. From both a student and a teacher standpoint, calculating probabilities is my favorite area of math to teach. You actually get to fiddle with objects, because even the most unimaginative teachers would let you do something like roll dice. And from there, you probably get to work with fractional numbers that you yourself generate. High intrigue, high involvement, high cognition—high retention.

But my favorite teaching tool for probability is using games like blackjack and poker. So allow me to share with you a lesson I've done several times with my students. It's a lesson that not only teaches the concept of calculating odds, but also shows how numbers have "magically" worked to our benefit since the beginning of time.

One day in my seventh-grade science class, I pulled out a standard deck of 52 cards (no jokers), displayed them to the class, and in theat-

---

* See chapter 13 of *Reclaiming Science from Darwinism,* where the big bang is shown to be a more mathematically precise event than a Space Shuttle flight.

rical fashion gave them three quick shuffles to assure randomization. I also showed them the candy bar, the ice-cold soda, the bag of chips, and the package of cookies sitting on the table in front of me. The students were watching closely, knowing they were about to see another one of my "dog and pony show" lessons. I dealt out a five-card hand of poker facedown and asked the students what the odds were that I had actually dealt a royal flush—a ten, jack, queen, king, and ace of the same suit.

After some strange speculations from the kids, I then asked them what the odds were that my first card would start me on the way to that elusive royal flush. If you think about it, that first card *has* to be a face card, an ace, or a ten, because if I got anything less than a ten (like, say, a four) I was done already, right? One girl correctly said the odds of success on that first card were "20 out of 52": 20/52 (12 face cards plus 4 tens, plus 4 aces equals 20 out of a 52-card deck).

So with the answer in hand, I returned the first five cards to the deck, reshuffled them, and had her come up and draw one, telling her she could have that tantalizing candy bar on my table if she drew a face card, a ten, or an ace. She was not successful—no candy bar—sit back down. So I intentionally searched out any usable card until I got the jack of hearts. With the jack of hearts on the table, I asked what the odds were of getting the next necessary card toward a royal flush. More kids were catching on, and one boy said "4 out of 51": 4/51 (ten, queen, king, or ace of hearts out of the remaining 51 cards). So I had the boy come up and draw from the deck, and I promised him the can of soda if he was successful. He was not, so I found the ace of hearts. With the jack and ace on the table, hands were already up on the odds for the third card, "3 out of 50": 3/50—3 cards left to get out of the 50 remaining. No luck again, and the bag of chips remained on the table. So I quickly found the king of hearts and placed it with the other two I had already intentionally drawn. Now there were only two more cards to go. On the fourth draw, "2 out of 49"—a different girl got a queen, but alas, not the queen of hearts, so the cookies went unclaimed. I found the queen of hearts and placed it on the table.

So far not one prize was won—candy bar, soda, chips, or cookies— and there was only one more card left to complete the royal flush, the ten of hearts at odds of "1 out of 48": 1/48. Then I revealed the grand prize from a bag, a wrapped 12-inch sub sandwich from the well-known sub chain in town. At this point the drama in the room was reaching its peak because there was an entire lunch sitting before them, and the class knows I always find a method to award all prizes. So I told them that one more person could draw for that ten of hearts, and if successful, could have the whole "meal deal." But first this person had to calculate correctly the overall odds of dealing that royal flush from five consecutive cards!

Now one boy remembered from an earlier lesson that consecutive odds are calculated by *multiplying* the fractional numerators and denominators of each individual probability, so he grabbed a calculator and went to work. Here again are the numbers he used—the fractional odds of getting each of the five required cards for a royal flush.

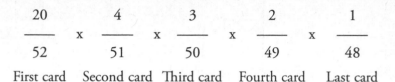

20/52		4/51		3/50		2/49		1/48
First card		Second card		Third card		Fourth card		Last card

He punched in 20 x 4 x 3 x 2 x 1 to get 480 for the numerator, and punched in 52 x 51 x 50 x 49 x 48 to get 311,875,200 for the denominator. Then he correctly announced that, "theoretically," you should get a royal flush 480 times out of every 311,875,200 hands! Good job! For ease of understanding, I reduced and simplified that answer to approximately one royal flush out of every 600,000 hands. And as you see below, you could further simplify that to "one in half a million."

$$\frac{480}{311,875,200} \approx \frac{1}{600,000} \approx \frac{1}{500,000}$$

So with the problem solved, the boy got to draw for that ten of hearts and the elusive five-course "free lunch"—his chances, at "1 in 48" being slim but certainly not impossible. Did he succeed? I'll tell you in a minute. But first, let's get more serious.

From Poker to DNA

The reason to recount these classroom events is to be sure you as the reader understand my objective—to know how probabilities govern a random selection process. Then, once you grasp the concept, you need to decide once and for all whether numbers have sufficient power within themselves to account for our existence by sheer luck, or whether some divine entity manipulated these numbers to make the mathematically impossible become possible. (It's the "either-or" thing again.) And if you decide that the numbers just don't add up without a Designer, then once again you must admit the backdrop of our world was specifically prepared for us.

The first aspect of calculating probabilities involves the indispensable concept of "randomization." Random means "the luck of the draw" must be fully operational, and intelligence can in no way be involved. (As any card player knows, a "stacked deck" instantly alters the odds.) Probabilities always are calculated comparing the desired outcome(s), like heads on a coin, with the number of possible outcomes, like heads or tails. Hence the odds of heads on a fair coin toss are "1 in 2" or, expressed as a fraction, one-half. Other factors governing subsequent probabilities are whether choices can be repeated ("no" in the card scenario because there is only one of each card in the deck), whether order is essential ("no" again, in that a royal flush can be dealt in any order) and, whether once made, the same choice can happen again ("no" once more because any cards dealt are not replaced).

With the math governing the process in hand, I then had the students apply this information to accidental construction of a protein out of amino acids. For nature to make a correct protein chain out of the necessary amino acids is in many ways like drawing random cards out of a deck. Only in the case of even the smallest necessary proteins, you need to be dealt not just five but 100 correct amino acid "cards." And instead of 52 different cards, you only have 20 choices since there are only 20 specific amino acids used in protein construction.*

Molecular biologists now know the absolute critical nature of the exact sequence of these amino acids. To omit one, use the wrong one, or even change the order is like the common frustration of not reaching a Web site because just one character in the Internet address is wrong. Therefore, drawing 20 amino acids "out of a hat," which natural evolution must do, means your odds of getting the first one right to start your protein chain are 1 in 20. If nature gets lucky on the first amino acid, and we assume its removal did not significantly change the available numbers in the "primordial soup," then the odds of getting the next correct amino acid are still 1 in 20. Therefore, once again multiplying numerators and denominators says that the odds of getting lucky on the first two are already 1 in 400, and there are still 98 amino acids left to properly sequence. Extend the math to the end, and you find the probability of constructing any one specific protein 100 amino acids long to be:

---

* For more detail, see *Reclaiming Science from Darwinism*, chapter 7, "A Sword with One Edge."

1
in
10,000,000,000,000,000,000,000,000,000,000,000,
000,000,000,000,000,000,000,000,000,000,000,000,
000,000,000,000,000,000,000,000,000,000,000,000,
000,000,000,000,000,000,000,000.

Writing those 130 zeros in scientific notation, that probability is 1 out of 10^{130}. Considering there are an estimated 10^{80} atoms in our entire universe, I'd say we are way beyond luck! And the problems increase further beyond comprehension, considering nature must make about 80,000 other proteins the body requires, some being 10,000 amino acids long.

Other factors make the odds of dealing a royal flush fade to nothingness by comparison. Unlike our hand of cards, getting one amino acid in the right place doesn't improve your odds on the next draw because one less card has to be factored in. In nature, you could get a second "jack of hearts" that might render your protein useless. Also, poker cards can be dealt in any order, for example the jack of hearts could be the last card drawn, and the hand is just as much a winner. But in proteins, each amino acid has to be in the right position to have the proper information, especially if the protein is to fold correctly.

And we are still not done. As you hold your cards, you can turn them upside down and it makes no difference to the value of your hand. You can even hold them horizontally instead of vertically—no problem—or even flip them over for the opposition to see, though that could seriously impact your winnings. But in amino acids, each has a minimum of four possible bonding sites, and yet only one site is the acceptable rotational location. Finally, amino acids are three-dimensional, and such spatial isomers can be *left-handed* or *right-handed*. But the body utilizes only what are called the L-shaped amino acids, which means fully half of what otherwise occurs in nature is immediately disqualified because those molecules are "facing the wrong way." This rotational and spatial factor, called "chemical chirality," pushes the odds of getting lucky from out of reach to out of sight to out of mind.

To put this all in perspective, let us first err on the side of caution, something proponents of Design seem to say with increasing frequency. We will ignore the rotational and spatial chirality and just hope against hope that nature can give us the right amino acids in order 100 times. Now get a standard deck of playing cards, assure complete randomization (shuffle well), and deal out five. (Please get out a deck and actually deal out those five cards. If you don't, you still may not appreciate the odds.) Now turn all five over. How close did you come to a royal flush?

Now, this may seem impossible, but the math says you will deal this many royal flushes...

100,000,000,000,000,000,000,000,000,000,000,
000,000,000,000,000,000,000,000,000,000,000,000,
000,000,000,000,000,000,000,000,000,000,000,000,
000,000,000,000,000,000,000

...(10^{125}) in the same number of probabilistic attempts it would take luck to make our *one* lonely protein of 100 amino acids. No wonder natural evolutionists are often accused of having more faith than the most religious among us!

———————

Oh, yes. The boy trying to win the entire lunch. He drew the three of clubs. You know, it looked strange to see that beautiful near straight flush—an almost perfect hand—that was now worth less than a measly pair of twos. But as molecular biologists know, "nothing works until everything works." I did give the boy the meal anyway, because I could see in his face that the lesson was well-learned. He now knew that someone rather powerful had to be manipulating the math that made our existence possible. And because of that truth, he would never be an evolutionary four-flusher. (Four-flusher? That was a name for a cheat in the Old West who tried to pass off a near-winning but actually totally useless hand as a winner. Back then, people could get shot for that.)

5

The Divine Proportion

The Pleasure of Perfect Math

*Geometry has two great treasures; one is the theorem of
Pythagoras; the other, the division of a line into extreme
and mean ratio. The first we may compare to a treasure
of gold; the second we may name a precious jewel.*

—Johannes Kepler (1571–1630)

Proving that human existence is not accidental is pretty serious work.
However, that doesn't mean that in the process you can't mix in a bit
of fun now and then—with a very serious message built in, of course.
So this chapter is about the *divine proportion,* or the *golden mean,* as
it is often called. This mathematical ratio goes by many other names,
including the *golden section,* the *golden number,* the *extreme and mean
ratio,* the *golden string,* the *medial section,* the *divine section,* the *golden
cut,* and the *mean of Phidias.*

In one sense, it's a number like the Greek letter π *(pi)* for circles—
that magic irrational number (infinite decimal) of 3.14 that describes
the ratio between any circle's circumference divided by its diameter.

However, the divine proportion uses the Greek letter φ *(phi)*, and instead of being confined to circles, it is more like duct tape. (You know, *duct tape*. The answer to that old joke, "What else besides 'The Force' in *Star Wars* has a 'dark side,' a 'light side,' and holds the universe together?") Why? Because the phi ratio actually *is* at the heart of the universe—from the biggest cosmic objects to the smallest molecules.

I have covered the divine proportion in middle school and high school math classes many times, and the kids love all the examples of phi in and around their world, especially the ones on their bodies. Even the Darwinist students are amazed, some not even realizing the heavy implications of phi in movements such as Intelligent Design. So put on your favorite music, get out an aluminum can of your favorite beverage, and open a pack of sunflower seeds (explanation to come), because some math is about to come at you. If you want to bypass this next section, okay. But don't miss the finale of the chapter.

A Beautiful Proportion

What is phi? If you want the classic definition in words, call it *the relationship that the sum of two quantities is to the larger quantity as the larger quantity is to the smaller quantity.* Or how about the classic equation for "phi"?

$$\phi = \frac{1+\sqrt{5}}{2}$$

Let me give you a simple diagram and a simple explanation.

$$
\begin{array}{c}
\qquad\qquad\text{(a)} \qquad\qquad\qquad\qquad \text{(b)} \\
*\underline{\qquad\qquad\qquad\qquad\quad *\qquad\qquad\qquad}* \\
\text{(a + b)}
\end{array}
$$

Now looking at the above picture, imagine a line divided into two sections—one bigger portion, *a,* and one smaller portion, *b*—such that the total length of the line can be expressed by the term *a* + *b*. Now look at the equation below. If your line above is divided into the proper two lengths such that *a* + *b* divided by *a* equals *a* divided by *b*, then you will always get the same value!

$$\frac{a+b}{a} = \frac{a}{b}$$

And what will that value always be? Phi—ɸ—equaling 1.618 (and the digits extend into infinity).

Phi is a value that has truly endless applications as a major designing ratio in all realms. One thing is for certain, phi always produces exactly what the title of this chapter says, "The Pleasure of Perfect Math." Just as circles have an inviolate ratio in 3.14 or pi, so do countless factors in our lives constantly mirror the 1.618 ratio of phi.

Here's an introductory example out of so many possible from which I could pick. Take a plastic credit card, or a gift card, or a driver's license and with a ruler measure the length and the width—and be sure to use as exact a unit as possible, such as a millimeter. Now divide the longer measure by the shorter, and see what value you get. I measured my supermarket member's card and got 82 millimeters high and 51 millimeters wide. (What did you get?) Then I took the 82, divided by 51, and got 1.608. Not bad! If you want a more mathematical representation of what happens with a credit card that represents a golden rectangle, look at the directions used in this construction of a 1.618 ratio.

1. Construct a unit square.

2. Draw a line from the midpoint of one side to an opposite corner ($\sqrt{5}/2$).

3. Use that line as the radius to draw a circle's arc, which defines the long dimension of the rectangle.

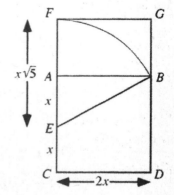

"So you get 1.618," you say. "What's the big deal? Every rectangle has to have some kind of dimensions." But the magic is that this ratio is at the heart of Pascal's triangle that produces the amazing *Fibonacci numbers*. If you look at Pascal's triangle below, you will see that the number sequence made by adding the two previous numbers produced by the triangle very soon yields phi by simple division.

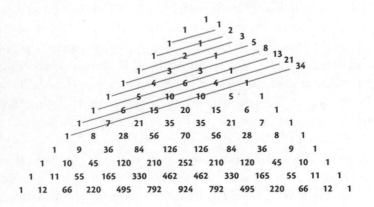

Here's the extended Fibonacci sequence produced by the triangle.

0, 1, 1, 2, 3, 5, 8, 13, 21, 34, 55, 89, 144, 233, 377, 610, 987, 1597...

Now, if you begin to divide each Fibonacci number by its predecessor, the amazing number phi soon appears.

$$1 \div 1 = 1 \quad 2 \div 1 = 2 \quad 3 \div 2 = 1.5 \quad 5 \div 3 = 1.667 \quad 8 \div 5 = 1.600 \quad 13 \div 8 = 1.625$$
$$21 \div 13 = 1.615 \quad 34 \div 21 = 1.619 \quad 55 \div 34 = 1.6176 \quad 89 \div 55 = 1.6182$$
$$144 \div 89 = 1.61797 \quad 233 \div 144 = 1.61805 \quad 377 \div 233 = 1.61802$$
$$610 \div 377 = 1.618037 \quad 987 \div 610 = 1.6180327$$
$$1597 \div 987 = 1.6180344$$
$$\text{and so on}$$

Wherever You Look...

Here's where the magic begins. The number sequence producing this ratio is, once again, found everywhere. The dimensions are faithfully rendered in the Parthenon's façade, and Euclid calculated the value of phi as early as 300 BC. Egypt's Great Pyramid of Giza approximates a golden triangle, as does Mexico's Sun Pyramid at Teotihuacán, and the divine proportion is evident in the Great Mosque of Kairouan. Furthermore, contemporary architects such as Le Corbusier, Alberti, and Botta have used the 1.618 ratio in their works. Even the United Nations Building in New York approximates phi height to width, and the floor plan for the new California Polytechnic Engineering Plaza is cleverly based on the golden spiral. Also, there is no doubt that artists have employed the divine proportion, with Leonardo da Vinci heading the list. You may not know the title, but you know the sketch below.

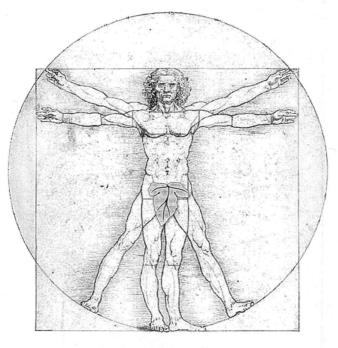

It is da Vinci's "Vitruvian Man," a drawing from around 1490 in one of his journals, based on the earlier writings of ancient Roman architect Vitruvius. In da Vinci's sketch, the arms and legs of both bodies constitute rays that form a perfect pentagonal figure based on Ptolemy's *golden theorem,* as seen below.

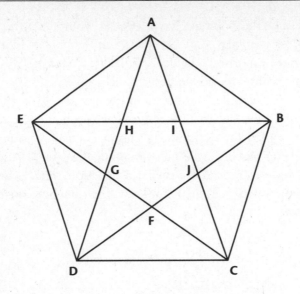

The bodies also approximate the border and radii of both a perfect square and circle that follow the dimensions of the eye-catching *golden spiral*, also constructed on the Fibonacci sequence and the phi ratio, shown below.

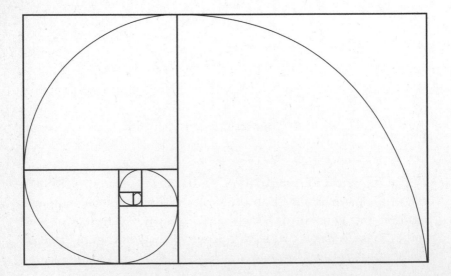

A Master of Phi

Many experts believe it was Leonardo da Vinci's understanding and use of the phi ratio that made his portraits so appealing. The dimensions of the canvas on which he painted *The Annunciation,* the sections of the picture based on the face placements of the angel and the Virgin Mary, even the masonry and tree branches in the background, can all be measured according to 1.618. Phi also appears in many of his other works like *Madonna with Child and Saints.* And in da Vinci's most celebrated work—the *Mona Lisa*—the mysterious lady's face follows the dimensions of his sketches for the human head that appeared in Luca Pacioli's journal called *De Divina Proportione—The Divine Proportion.*

You could even build a good case that da Vinci's knowledge of phi was the principle reason behind his overall success, because remember, he was not only an artist but an inventor, scientist, engineer, architect, sculptor, musician, physiologist, astronomer, geologist, and philosopher. In his own words, "No human inquiry can be called science unless it pursues its path through mathematical exposition and demonstration."

As an artist, da Vinci was hardly alone in his knowledge of the divine proportion. Salvador Dali's masterpiece *The Sacrament of the Last Supper* uses phi not only for the dimensions of the canvas, but for objects in the painting. Furthermore, other artists and sculptors past and present known to have used phi include Michelangelo, Raphael, Agesander of Rhodes, Pacioli, Dürer, Seurat, Signac, Mondrian, Rogers, Sutherland, Sudduth, van Prooijen, and May. And photographers, picture-makers in their own right, roughly follow the spirit of the divine proportion in their "rule of thirds" for placement of objects and people in their photos. Why? Because phi is just so pleasing to the eye!

Phi in Music and Literature

But we are just getting started here. One of the most cited examples of phi is in musical instrument dimensions, such as those in the design of the inestimable Stradivarius violin, where even placement of the f-holes follows the golden section. The golden spiral is also central to *fractals*—those beautiful repeating kaleidoscopic designs that turn inward and outward. Furthermore, you can find the divine proportion in cabinetry, furniture, tombstones, chimneys, book shapes, boats, electric outlet and light switch plates, and 3 x 5 and 5 x 8 note cards—actually, it seems, anywhere geometry is apparent. For example, remember in Genesis 6:15, when God told Noah to make the ark's end dimensions 50 cubits wide by 30 cubits high? Do the math of 50 divided by 30 now, and think about your answer the next time you open a "KitKat" candy bar.

Phi goes way beyond the geometric two- and three-dimensional creations of mankind. It spills over into aesthetics like literature, poetry, and music. A certain Professor George Duckworth wrote an entire book on how Virgil used the Fibonacci numbers to structure the *Aeneid;* and the syllabic stress and meter in Sanskrit poetry also follows the Fibonacci sequence. But the most astounding examples come from music. To begin with, there are 13 musical tones in the span of any 8-note octave where the fifth and third notes create the basic foundation of the chord. Also the chord is based on the whole tone that is 2 steps from the root tone, that is the first note on the scale. Also consider how the piano has 13 keys from "C" to "C"—8 white keys and 5 black keys split into groups of 3 and 2. (Review the Fibonacci numbers backward—...13, 8, 5, 3, 2, 1.) Even the wave frequencies of the notes on the western scale (we'll look much more at wave mechanics in chapter 7) follow a Fibonacci ratio with incredible accuracy! Next, it is even possible to put the golden string of numbers to music. The golden string is a fractal-like arrangement of "0"s and "1"s that grow in Fibonacci-like style where after the first two lines, all others are made from the sum of the two before it.

1

10

101

10110

10110101

1011010110110

10110101101101 10110101

When the London group Perfect Fifth put this to music, the resulting valleys and peaks in the tonal graph had definite Fibonacci-like qualities.

But I can make it less complicated than this. In so many songs, the timing of a composition generally places the climax at the phi point, as opposed to the middle or end of the song. The United States' national anthem is a case in point. Its four stanzas follow a very simple and very common pattern of A-A-B-A. In a 32-bar song, look for the climax around bar 20, which is approximately 61.8 percent of the way through. And just as with art and artists, famous composers constantly used phi whether they realized it or not. Many of Mozart's sonatas divide into two parts at the divine proportion, and in Beethoven's towering Symphony No. 5, the motto that appears in the first and last bar before the coda—bar 601—also appears at bar 372. Bar 601 divided by bar 372 equals 1.616. In addition to these two musical giants, here are other well-known composers who appear to have deliberately used the golden section to enhance their compositions—Bartok, Debussy, Schubert, Bach, and Satie. Amazing, isn't it?

Phi in the Natural World

Ever since I began to investigate phi, I was convinced something unexplainable by science was afoot. I agree with Swiss architect Le Corbusier, who described Fibonacci numbers this way:

> Rhythms apparent to the eye and clear in their relationship with one another. And these rhythms are at the very root of human activities. They resound in man by an organic inevitability, the same fine inevitability which causes the tracing out of the Golden Section by children, old men, savages, and the learned.

I've never met an evolutionist well acquainted with math, such as a geometry teacher friend of mine, who didn't also admit the uniqueness of phi. But strangely enough, the divine proportion is obviously not sufficient to get a die-hard Darwinist to admit to the divine. So what's their explanation? Probably different from person to person, and yet it was once explained to me that these were just astute people tapping into another quirk of numbers—like pi in circles—that arose when the rest of the universe made its random appearance. So like the water molecule (coming up in Chapter 6), I guess it was another place we got lucky.

Now I might buy that if the "quirk" of 1.618 wasn't vital to the assembly of living organisms, who don't need buildings or portraits, but certainly need bodies. Remember the sunflower seeds? If you take a look at the front of a sunflower, you'll see the arrangement of the seed backs placed point-first into the face.

Could you have any doubt of the mathematical precision? On large sunflowers you can count 89 spirals from the first edge, 55 spirals in the next row, 34 in the next, and so on toward the center—perfectly following the Fibonacci sequence based on phi. What is equally amazing is that if you look down on a growing sunflower plant from overhead, you will see that the leaf arrangement per clockwise "turn" follows a 2, 3, 5, 8…pattern, and not just for a pleasing appearance but for a very specific "design." Speaking partly as a biologist but more as a home gardener, I can tell you such a pattern gives each leaf maximum exposure to the sun above as well as maximum channeling of falling rainwater to the roots below.

And the sunflower is hardly unique in this pattern. Other plants that exhibit a spiral pattern based on 1.618 are cauliflower faces, bib lettuce bases, African violet leaves, cactus spines, sneezewort secondary shoots, pineapple flowers, sectioned bananas, poppies, daisies, and pine trees on their cones. (If you have a pinecone, look directly at the back and the arrangement of each blade.) In fact, one estimate is that 90 percent of all flowering plants exhibit seed or leaf patterns based on Fibonacci numbers, such as these examples:

    1:2—elm, linden, lime, some grasses

    1:3—beech, hazel, blackberry, other grasses

    2:5—oak, cherry, apple, holly, plum, groundsel

    3:8—poplar, rose, pear, willow, aster

    5:13—pussy willow, almond

But we are not yet done with plants. There is no doubt that flower petal numbers themselves hold to the Fibonacci sequence. Invariably, the number of petals will always be 3 (lily, iris, and so on), 5 (buttercups, larkspur, columbine, and so on), 8 (delphiniums), 13 (ragwort, corn marigold, cineraria, and so on), or 21 (aster, black-eyed Susan, chicory). Amazingly enough, some even jump to 34 (plantain, pyrethrum, and so on) and 55 and 89 petals (the asteraceae family)! How can this possibly be coincidence?! And if it is, why does your encyclopedia say all of these plant phenomena are covered in *phyllotaxis*—Greek for the study of "leaf arrangements"?

Animal Number Sequences

Will you find evidence of the divine proportion in the animal kingdom as well? Certainly! It has long been known that many animals produce offspring numbers corresponding with the Fibonacci sequence. For example, it was a certain Filius Bonacci, better known in Italian as Leonardo Pisano, who stumbled on the famous number sequence in the early 1200s that bears his Latin name. He began by trying to see how fast rabbits could breed under ideal conditions. Assuming no deaths and a new pair of rabbits born every two months to mature parents, he found the total number of rabbit pairs would grow thus: 1, 1, 2, 3, 5, 8, 13, 21, 34…(Because of his work with number sequences and his perfection of calculating procedures and square/square root operations, Leonardo Pisano has been called the greatest mathematician of the Middle Ages.) This ideal reproductive sequence has since been repeated with cow and honeybee mating, but the relationship of offspring growth to phi, as well as the innumerable implications of 1.618, were not well understood until long after his passing.

Beyond just counting honeybee offspring, the divine proportion is evident in many other insects. Comparing the "head to thorax to abdomen" length ratio of many hymenopterans (bees, wasps, ants, and so on) shows they follow the Fibonacci sequence. Similarly, measuring the color panel ratios of many brightly shaded male birds, the spacing of eyelike markings on moth wings, or the sections of a dolphin's body will produce the golden section.

Furthermore, counting various features in higher-order animals consistently reveals Fibonacci numbers. For example, the shells of many turtles have 13 cornea plates, 5 in the center and 8 at the boundaries, while the gavial crocodile has 55 cornea plates. In other reptiles, the body of a Caucasian viper has 55 dark spots, while the Gabon viper has 144 vertebrae. However, for just plain old beauty, I favor seashells. If you have never examined the shell of a chambered nautilus, a conical mollusk, a spiral snail, or an extinct ammonite, you are missing both beauty and precision of the highest design. Just like the 1.618 mathematics governing the design and spin of the Milky Way galaxy, so do these equiangular shells faithfully follow the golden spiral in their growth. And whereas a galaxy becomes the fascination of the most skilled astronomer, so does the shell become the favorite of the child's most modest shell collection.

I could go on and on. I could mention phi measurements done on the proportions of atoms in molecules, the curl of the ram's horn, the ratio of Earth's land to water, the ratio of oxygen in the air, the geometric faces of crystals like perovskite, laser-beam pulse compressions, the percentages of sedimentary, metamorphic, and igneous rocks, and the depths of various horizon layers of soil. But maybe it's time to fully accept the words of biomechanical engineer Vladimir Petukhov, who said, "The laws of the golden proportion determined the main schedule, the main idea of extremity design."

Phi and the Human Body

Hall of Fame baseball pitcher Nolan Ryan had a great strikeout pitch—a certain pitch he saved for critical situations when he needed the best in his repertoire. So is my last section on the divine proportion. This will be the "strikeout pitch" that leaves you no option but to acknowledge that with 1.618 there may be man-made, but there is also "made-man."

Begin by looking at your thumb. Again you are seeing the golden spiral, not on a sunflower, not in a spiral galaxy, not on a shell, but quite literally at your fingertips—your thumbprints and fingerprints! And this is the beginning of the use of the divine proportion in humans—some that are for beauty, some that are for fun, and some on which life itself depends.

Let's start with a fun measurement first. As best you can, carefully measure from the center of your navel to the bottom of your toes, and then from your navel to the top of your head. Now divide the longer measure by the shorter and see what you get. I do this in class with my kids, and of course not every child is a perfect 1.618. (Some of those little angels are quite dumpy, while others are literal string beans.) But do this. Take a whole class of kids—or better yet a whole day's worth of classes—and average all their measurements. For me it always averages so close to 1.618 that it's downright spooky! And when you do this, you have just illustrated the straightforward definition of the divine proportion—"the sum of two quantities is to the larger quantity as the larger quantity is to the smaller"—meaning your lower length divided by your upper approximates phi. Or, as a mathematical expression, again it is

$$\frac{a+b}{a} = \frac{a}{b}$$

Going back to the sketch of da Vinci's "Vitruvian Man" shown earlier, our bodies are truly what he called a "canon of proportions," because 1.618 seems to be absolutely sacred in our human dimensions. Here's a list of divine proportion candidates that is by no means exhaustive. Phi is the result of

- the height of the face divided by the width of the face
- the bottom of the chin to the bottom of the teeth, divided by the bottom of the teeth to the bottom of nose
- the bottom of the teeth to the center of the eye, divided by the bottom of the teeth to the bottom of the chin
- the bottom of the nose to the top of the head (at top of skull, not top of hair, divided by the bottom of the chin to the bottom of the nose
- looking directly at the teeth in the smile starting with the incisors, the width of each front tooth divided by the visible portion of the one behind it

- the hip to the floor divided by the knee to the floor
- the shoulder to the fingertip divided by the elbow to the fingertip
- the elbow to the wrist divided by the wrist to the fingertip
- for each of the four finger bones, the longer divided by the next shorter attached to it, three times for each ratio
- the length of each vertebra in the spine divided by the length of the next shorter one attached to it

We are quite well proportioned! And to these you can add the magic of the number 5, which can produce phi all by itself in this manner:

$$5^{.5} \times .5 + .5 = \phi = 1.618$$

The number 5 has always been the pivotal figure in the Fibonacci sequence. So many of the best examples seem to hinge on 5, and the perfect pentagon shown earlier was the first known geometric figure used to calculate phi, by the Greek mathematician Ptolemy (about AD 90–168). So it's not coincidental that we have five fingers, five toes, five appendages on the torso (one head, two arms, two legs), five openings on the face, and five senses. Now perhaps you can see why architect Adolf Zeising said that the golden section was a universal law,

> in which is contained the fundamental principle of all formation striving for beauty and completeness in the realms of both nature and art, and which permeates, as a paramount spiritual ideal, all structures, forms, and proportions, whether cosmic or individual, organic or inorganic, acoustic or optical; which finds its fullest realization, however, in the human form.

Before I close this, I want to get serious. I said earlier that some of the phi examples are actually life-critical. Blood pressure is one of those. If you take normal blood pressure, commonly designated "120 over 80," you can divide the larger by the smaller and get a modest 1.500. However, I'm convinced the 120/80 has been rounded off for ease of public memory, because when you examine an electrocardio-gram of normal blood pressure and heart rhythm—well, look below and see for yourself.

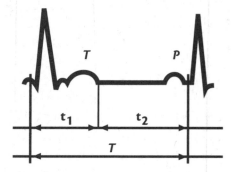

As another example of life-critical, how about the DNA molecule? The basis of life itself is perhaps the best example of phi that nature has to offer. First, a cross-sectional view from the top of the "molecule of life" reveals a decagon, which in actuality is two overlaid pentagons, one is rotated by 36 degrees. (Two pentagons. Once again 5 is the basis of phi.) If you remember from above, the ratio of the diagonal of a pentagon to its side yields 1.618. Then to seal the deal, the DNA cross section measures 34 angstroms by 21 angstroms (an angstrom being one ten-billionth of a meter—slightly less than a pepper flake), which of course are Fibonacci numbers, which approximate phi by division. There can be no doubt that DNA, *and therefore all of life,* is constructed using the divine proportion. Case closed.

To sum up all this math, you simply have to say that all life—especially human life—follows a master design. It's sobering to me to realize that here we stand in the middle of all this majesty. If you look high above you see spiral galaxies, and if you look deep within, you see spiral double helixes. If you look high above, you will find, like Russian astronomer K.P. Butusov, that the ratio of the revolution cycles around the sun of adjacent planets follow 1.618, or its square, 2.618. You will also find NASA arranging the mirrors on the *Starshine 3* satellite according to the golden section for circles ($360°/\phi = 222.5°$).

Or if you look deep within, you will find the *stoichiometry* (numer-ical relationships of chemical formulas and chemical equations) of the following molecules based on phi in some manner—benzoid hydrocarbons, methyl alkanes, butadienes, uranium and chromium oxides, and the amino-acid sequences in the proteins coded by the master information in DNA—which will be covered later in chapter 14. (Let me also add that these stoichiometry studies are chemistry pursuits of the highest order, not just people measuring objects with a ruler.)

If my book's subtitle is incorrect, then the universe blindly made man. But decide for yourself. Isn't phi an undeniable reality that existed before man? Weren't all these masters in their various fields connected to the very foundation of creation itself? If so, then the universe *was* intentionally made for man, and when we investigate this magical phi ratio, we are investigating heavenly design. It's as astronomer Johannes Kepler, a great scientist who had faith in both the divine and the proportion: "We are thinking God's thoughts after Him."

When you consider the importance of water to life, it is fair to look at the miracle that is H_2O. The content of the next chapter will involve a certain amount of chemistry. However, I think you will find that the details add up in a way that supports Design—and will further dispel the myth that our existence was accidental.

Education Without Proportions

Phi—1.618—the Fibonacci sequence, and Pascal's triangle go deeply into all higher math courses such as trigonometry and calculus. And yet a sixth-grader with a ruler can explore the fun of the divine proportion, and in doing so learn a lot more necessary basic calculation skills than through "experiencing" math the way it is being taught today—with pictures and puzzles instead of ample sets of practice problems.

So why am I the only math teacher I've ever heard about in 35 years in the education business to have taught phi publicly? Why are teachers committing the equivalent of ignoring pi in circles? Well, I know the reason, and so do you. It's the name, especially the first name—*divine* proportion—because God is not necessarily welcome in schools. And yet, phi is not even taught under its other names, like the golden mean or any other identifiers using the word "golden" because of the implications. Once again, "golden" = "divine" = "design" = God, and we just can't have that in public schools.

If you doubt this, spend a little time on a school staff. From my perspective on the inside, I can tell you with all surety that math, and especially science, are driven by the few who adamantly force a Darwinistic view on the many. These are the people who believe all is self-made, even the incredible "luck" of phi. As a Web site for mystics that investigated strange phenomena like the golden mean put it,

> Remember, however, that these "higher dimensional visions" are still self-created, not a function of a higher "god" so-to-speak, but a function of itself.

The words "a function of itself" are a perfect match to the "self-made" aspect of strict Darwinism. Once again, without a doubt, we need more academic honesty in education, as was the call in my first book, pointedly titled *Reclaiming Science from Darwinism*.

6

THE WATER MOLECULE

A Miracle in Its Own Right

If you think about it, water is one of the very, very few readily identifiable liquids found naturally on our planet's surface. (Quick—name another if you can.) In fact, water is the only compound of *any* kind that exists in normal Earth temperature ranges in all three states of matter. But the biggest miracle is that water in its several forms—solid (ice), liquid (fluid), or gas (steam)—behaves as if it doesn't have to follow the standard rules of chemistry.

The miraculous attributes of water make up an amazing list. Maybe this list alone of water's magic capabilities will leave you with the desired impression that God has been doing some amazing work on our behalf. (However, if you want the fascinating details, refer to the sections of this chapter that follow the list.)

1. Water and its components as the basis of chemistry education

2. Why two hydrogens and one oxygen make the perfectly bonded molecule

3. What makes water different from other polar and non-polar molecules

4. Water's amazing partial symmetry and its incredible ab initio state

5. Ice floats (and the profound implications)

6. Water's incredibly "lucky" melting and boiling points

7. The life-giving nature of the hydrogen bond

8. How life-forms are kept alive by the miraculous nature of cohesion

9. Hydrogen bonds in life-giving chemistry of polymer structure, buildup, and breakdown

10. Water as the indispensable universal solvent and transport molecule

11. Condensation nuclei, high compressibility, latent heat of evaporation and fusion, and so on

12. Water, the space program, and the possibility of life on Mars

1. Water and its components as the basis of chemistry education

Water is the place where chemistry education always starts, for who has not heard of the elements hydrogen and oxygen, and what other standard molecular formula would anyone learn before H_2O? Who wouldn't be able to identify the names for the H and the O on the periodic table of elements, and what better place to start explaining atomic numbers, weights, valence electrons, and bonding? Let's take a look at some information on the atoms that make up a water molecule.

1   ±1

Hydrogen   H

1

As a diatomic gas, *hydrogen* is the lightest and most common substance in the universe; highly explosive. As an atom, atomic number of 1 and weight of 1 AMU (atomic mass unit) due to the singular proton (positively charged) and no neutrons (neutral charge) in the nucleus; a lone balancing electron (negatively charged) in the 1s orbital ready to be shared (covalent) or transferred (ionic) in making a bond with another atom, giving it a valence of ±1.

	16	-2
Oxygen	O	
	8	

As a diatomic gas, *oxygen* is necessary for combustion and respiration. As an atom, required in the biochemistry of all Earth forms of multicellular life; atomic number of 8 due to its eight protons in the nucleus and an atomic weight of 16 due to the eight additional neutrons, eight negative electrons to balance the eight positive protons; two inner electrons orbiting in the first energy level ($1s^2$), and six more valence electrons orbiting in the second energy level ($2s^2\ 2p^4$); preferring to either share or borrow two more electrons to complete its outer shell, giving it a most likely valence of -2.

2. Why two hydrogens and one oxygen make the perfectly bonded molecule

Now let's talk about why atoms stick together to make molecules like water (I'll make this as quick and easy as I can). First, double-check the bonding preferences, or "valences," listed above for both atoms. Two hydrogens wanting to share one electron each, and one oxygen wanting to share two electrons. They do so, and that makes a nice arrangement in a stable molecule called H_2O, where each atom thinks its outer electron orbital is filled. As to the atomic weight, both hydrogens have one AMU apiece, and the one oxygen weighs 16 AMUs, making a total of 1 + 1 + 16 = 18 AMUs per molecule of water. All seems proper, so what is so defiant about the lowly water molecule?

3. What makes water different from other polar and non-polar molecules

It all starts, and actually ends, with the two types of designs that molecules are *supposed* to exhibit—polar and non-polar. When dealing with other simple Group I molecules under 100 AMUs, the atoms in their molecular arrangements are either asymmetrical or symmetrical.* If asymmetrical, like hydrochloric acid in the stomach, HCl (H-Cl), the one electron in hydrogen is transferred over to the chlorine to meet its need to fill its outer shell, forming an "ionic" bond. This creates a highly "magnetic" molecule—one end with a negative charge around chlorine with the extra electron, and a positive charge around the hydrogen on the other end that still has its proton in the nucleus. This makes each H+ Cl- molecule like a tiny bar magnet similar to those you play with in science, with a positive pole at one end and a negative pole at the other. And as students know, like charges repel, and unlike attract. Therefore, hydrochloric acid has the ability to react strongly with atoms of either positive or negative net charges, giving the acid its corrosive nature.

Compare that to a symmetrical molecule, like the carbon dioxide gas found in air, CO_2 (O=C=O). Here the negatively charged valence electrons in both carbon and oxygen are equally shared in a pair of double "covalent" bonds, and the positively charged protons also are evenly distributed, producing no imbalance of charges. This results in a *non-polar* molecule, one that has no electrical imbalance, and neither readily attracts nor repels other substances.

The two choices? Polar or non-polar, and the choice depends on the symmetry of the molecule.

4. Water's amazing partial symmetry and its incredible ab initio state

Enter H_2O, the "slightly polar" molecule. This renegade decides to share the best of both arrangements by being *somewhat* symmetrical. By having the two bonded hydrogens at a partial angle, this still allows the molecule two different areas of magnetic polarity, as seen below, but

---

* See *Reclaiming Science from Darwinism*, chapter 8.

only with a lesser attraction. The area of slight negativity dominated more by oxygen's unshared electrons appears in the upper left, and the area of slight positivity dominated more by hydrogen's offset protons appears in the lower right, giving each molecule a slight charge. The H_2O molecule is typically drawn in the spatial orientation seen below. In addition, some of the pertinent data on water's ab initio state is listed on the side.

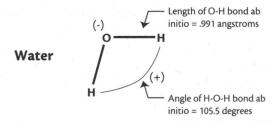

The term *ab initio* deserves explanation. It literally means "from the beginning," and the above lengths and angle measurements are based only on principles of physics as if water was in its originally made, isolated state. But because of its unique slight polarity, the water molecule is very dynamic and subject to flux. In actual conditions, water molecules are in constant contact with each other in one of three states of matter, and furthermore are often interacting with other molecules. This causes the length of the O-H bonds and the angle of the hydrogens to shift as needed. It is this flexible nature that allows water to accommodate an amazing variety of conditions and reactions, and helps create many of its magic capabilities. Though a bit technical, I find the following facts extraordinary!

Water's elasticity compared to other molecules is unparalleled. The molecular arrangement can utilize O-H lengths from .957 to 1.0 angstroms, which represents tremendous variation at this submicroscopic level. (An *angstrom* is a standard unit of atomic measure, a length of one ten-billionth of a meter, derived from the wavelength of light.) In addition, the angle of the bonded hydrogens can fluctuate from 104.45 to 109.5 degrees, again an unequaled range of separation. (Experimental values for these figures are often given for water in a vapor state, O-H bond length of .95718 angstroms and hydrogens at an angle of 104.474 degrees.) Let's investigate how such incredible dynamism allows water to break many expected chemical behavior patterns.

5. Ice floats (and the profound implications)

The first nearly unnatural trait of water is something few people ever consider. As a solid, *ice floats*. Of course it does, like the ice cubes in your glass, but only because water is actually *less* dense as a solid than as a liquid. Ice is obviously not incredibly buoyant like Styrofoam, but the fact it floats at all defies the general chemical rule that solids, being more dense than the same compounds in their liquid states, sink—not float—in that medium.

This phenomenon again goes back to the partially symmetrical configuration. As water molecules lose their kinetic energy of motion, the liquid's volume begins to contract as per normal. But at the last moment, as the molecules begin to configure in a crystalline structure at 32° F. (0 degrees C.), the partial polarity actually forces them to align in a slightly expanded pattern. This is why your car's engine block will crack open on a frigid day without antifreeze, and why the soda can explodes in the freezer—the one I put there for a "quick chill" and then forgot about. It is also the reason your tomato plants die at the slightest frost, and successful cryonics is still a hopeless impossibility. (*Cryonics* being the freezing of human remains prior to death in hopes of later restoring them to life and health.) Car radiators, pop cans, tomato plant cells, and human tissue contain large quantities of water, and when water is frozen in any closed container, the expanding ice crystals are strong enough to rupture everything from cell membranes to car engines.

Okay, so ice exhibits the curious behavior of floating and expansion. Perhaps a world produced by strictly random processes should be full of such curiosities. So just compensate by checking your radiator fluid and covering your tomato plants, right? But you have to realize this buoyancy actually prevents the complete extinction of many aquatic and marine life-forms. If ice were to *sink* as it formed (as general chemistry rules normally operate) all bodies of water—ponds, rivers, and oceans—would *freeze from the bottom up*. This would be catastrophic. Benthic (bottom-dwelling) organisms, from macroinvertebrates (insect larvae, worms, and so on) to frogs and turtles that reside or hibernate in mud could be extirpated by the first hard winter freeze, and fish would starve when frozen mud denies them winter-season bottom feed.

Another factor is that if water were even able to exist above the ice, it would be colder than tolerable for life. However, floating ice acts as an insulating blanket, allowing the water below to stabilize at a comfortable 39° F. (4° C.) so aquatic life can continue below the lethal freezing levels at the surface.

Furthermore, if ice settled on the bottom away from the rays of the summer sun, deeper bodies of water in colder climes would freeze solid after a few winters and never thaw to open waters, and this would destroy those impressive fish in wonderful cold-water food webs. (This "frozen to the bottom" lake configuration is more than speculation. In areas of ground permafrost, the ephemeral summer sun thaws only the top few inches of soil in a growing season measured in weeks, before the onrushing winter locks life back in the deep freeze.) How would an Alaskan lake with ice forming from the bottom upward not just become a partially melted ice skating rink for a few summer weeks?

Once again, just as with all the other "lucky" celestial arrangements in our solar system, it is time to celebrate our good fortune—good fortune that benefits humans more than we can appreciate. And here a cliché may be appropriate: "This is only the tip of the iceberg."

6. Water's incredibly "lucky" melting and boiling points

Already noted is the "long shot" that Earth's location produces mean seasonal temperatures perfect to accommodate water's three states of matter. Remember, water has no choice but to solidify at 32° F. (0° C.) and below, and vaporize at 212° F. (100° C.) and above. And just as frozen H_2O exhibits amazing qualities, so does water in relation to its boiling point. For a comparison, let's revisit that carbon dioxide molecule, CO_2. For carbon dioxide molecules to freeze, they must reach a temperature of -109° F., and they boil, or *sublime,* as they rise above that same temperature. (*Sublimation* means to pass directly from a solid to a vapor state, hence the term "dry ice.")

To show how small our planet's temperature window truly is, the lowest extreme temperatures reported during Antarctica's winters are about -110° F. If such extremes were sustained in the slightest as they are on every other planet, carbon dioxide would crystallize and settle out of the air, and the process of photosynthesis would collapse.

Now here is the amazing difference. Water is a *liquid* at normal Earth temperatures, while carbon dioxide is a *gas*. This should make no sense because CO_2 is over *twice* as heavy, molecule per molecule, as H_2O. (With one carbon and two oxygens, carbon dioxide has a molecular weight of 44 AMUs, while a molecule of water with one oxygen and two hydrogens weighs only 18 AMUs.) Therefore, why is carbon dioxide always in vapor form while water isn't? Or better yet, why does water conveniently stay in a glass, pond, river, or ocean, while CO_2 merrily floats through the air? By chemistry's dictates, water should immediately join carbon dioxide in the atmosphere, leaving our planet's surface completely dry. What prevents such a disaster?

The answer takes us back again to that curious partially polar molecule and the offset hydrogens that create a slightly positive (+) and negative (-) pole. As stated previously, polar molecules have strong attractions like miniature magnets. Water molecules are also attracted to each other, as shown by the arrow below, but to a lesser extent due to their partial symmetry.

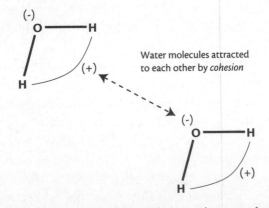

Water molecules attracted to each other by *cohesion*

Still, they cling to one another with enough strength to stay in your glass on a hot summer day. Good thing! This special attraction is called *cohesion*. But the force of cohesion is not so strong as to prevent an occasional molecule from breaking the surface of the water glass and wandering off into the air. Therefore, in a few days, all the water in your glass has escaped into the atmosphere by evaporation, along with a few trillion others, to rejoin the life-sustaining water cycle.

Of course you can accelerate the evaporation process by heating the water, but at normal Earth temperatures, water has enough "stickiness" to hold together in liquid form with impressive density, enough to float an aircraft carrier by weight displacement. (Want to give a person a challenge? Ask them to explain how water can float a ship made of tons of steel. And while you're at it, get them to explain how hot water freezes faster than cold water.) Light enough to easily vaporize, while being dense enough to float the largest of objects, while becoming buoyant as it freezes. As I seem to say regularly in my science classes, "Good idea. Wonder who thought of it?"

7. *The life-giving nature of the hydrogen bond*

No molecule besides water has these amazing properties, and if the technical chemistry escaped you, just remember it's all due to the unusual configuration producing the unique magnetic pull seen above. The attraction of cohesion is so immensely important to life that it has been given the worldwide-accepted term of *hydrogen bond,* though it is not as strong as a regular bond, either ionic or covalent. (One study estimated that a hydrogen bond is only one-twentieth the strength of a covalent bond.) And yet, would you expect this hydrogen bond to have a tremendous impact on life in ways other than maintaining proper states of matter in our limited window of Earth's temperature ranges? Of course. Read on.

Try this. Ask any person unfamiliar with general scientific principles if they can explain how water moves *up* a tree. From my experience, they are likely to say, "The tree just sorta sucks it up."

This might even be the response of students proficient in high school biology who have learned about root hairs, osmosis, xylem, and stoma in the process of transpiration. First they may quote their textbook saying, "Transpiration is that technical process where ground water enters the roots of any plant via microscopic hairs, moves to areas of low concentration within the root by osmosis, travels up stems or trunks by capillary action through specialized water carrying cells called xylem, and exits by evaporation out the underside of the leaves through microscopic openings called stoma." And after this they might still conclude, "Like it said, just sorta sucks it up."

Note, however, that we are not talking about a trace of moisture, we are talking upward of 150 gallons daily in a tree like a cottonwood. (Carrying a full pail of water a few steps will help underscore the weight of water.) At 8.3 pounds per gallon, how does a half a ton of water travel up a tree in a day? The suction explanation is out of the question. There are no pumps (like a heart) to create pressure, and no bellows-like movements from the tree's body to force it up through one-way valves. Some have supposed pressure is involved, such as the weight of the ground pushing down on the plant roots. But if you guessed it is due to water's slight polarity, the answer to every question in this chapter so far, you are right.

Imagine several gymnasts climbing up on each other's shoulders to make sort of a human totem pole. The first person stands firmly and helps the second crawl up to eventually position himself to stand on the shoulders of the first, who holds his ankles. Then comes the third, crawling up with the assistance of the first two to stand on the second's shoulders, and on up until a small tower is formed with a pretty girl on top.

If you imagine each gymnast holding on to an object like a pole to allow for greater height, that is a fair description of upward water movement in the invaluable process of transpiration. Once water is inside the roots by osmosis and then diffuses to the base of the stem, the slight charges of each water molecule cause them to piggyback upward over one another. While they cling to each other via those hydrogen bonds, they also hold to charges in the sides of the microscopically small xylem tubes of the stem.

In contrast to cohesion, this process of water clinging to other objects is called *adhesion*. If you want a personal demonstration, find a transparent straw or hollow glass tube with a small diameter and place it in a clear cup. Without question, you will see that the water level in the straw or tube exceeds the water level in the glass, and the thinner the diameter of the straw or tube, the higher the water level.

Now imagine a plant's xylem tissue in the stem, filled with microscopically hollow sieve tubes and cylindrical vessels stacked on each other, and up the molecules go, being drawn rather than pushed. The combination of cohesive and adhesive forces allow the molecules to gradually work their way up the stem or trunk, move through the branches and into the veins of the leaf, and eventually reach the stoma in the leaves. Then solar power causes them to quickly evaporate into the air, allowing others underneath to move up. Note that this requires no energy expenditure on the part of the plant. Upward water movement will even take place in cut flowers without roots, keeping them fresh for a few days until they begin to starve due to lack of photosynthetic food. But though the process may seem simple, without the weak attraction of hydrogen bonds, water molecules would never travel upward. Then the only plants capable of life on Earth would be bryophytes, those simple mosses that live close to dampness because their simple structure has no water-carrying tissues.

8. How life-forms are kept alive by the miraculous nature of cohesion

The weak hydrogen bonds make transpiration, and therefore life, possible. But that is just the beginning of the importance of these bonds. What of the evaporated water? Of course the water cycle will return it to earth through condensation, usually in the form of gentle water droplets. Enter another phenomenon, called *surface tension.* Water molecules at the edge of the fluid hold so tightly that they form a "skin," a layer that is not easy to breach. If you have never done it, see how many drops of water you can put on a penny before they leak off unto the table. Surface tension will cause the water to "mound up" until it is close to twice the thickness of the penny before it breaks free. The water molecules on the surface even hold tight enough to float a needle if it is placed gently with a tweezers. If you are an insect called a "water skipper/strider/skater," you are lucky enough to actually "walk on water" as you stand on this skin.

Here are other incredible facts about the surface tension of water. Let's say you are an essential microorganism in a food chain that lives *inside* a water drop and must complete your life cycle there before that water drop evaporates. You'd better be quick about it, right? Well, the phenomenon of surface tension holds the drop in a tighter and more rounded configuration that greatly reduces the exposed area—and greatly slows evaporation rate—giving you the precious time you need.

All in a Drop

Water's surface tension is also responsible for the "roundness" of a water drop. In the atmosphere water molecules will collect into a droplet with the perfect size and weight commensurate to the steady pull of gravity, which allows them to fall to Earth when they are just the right size. Think about the size of water droplets when they finally form. If they were too small and light, they would stay aloft. If they grew too big and heavy, they would pound down with disastrous effects. Call it "luck" again?

Then how about the combination of surface tension along with cohesion and adhesion that allow dewdrops to hold to leaves and evaporate more slowly? Imagine how fast the essential morning dew would disappear if the moisture were smeared as a thin glaze over the plant's surface. It is truly amazing how many essential biological effects come from just the concept of surface tension. Maybe you find yourself saying again, "Good idea. Wonder who thought of that one?"

Water's unique properties are perfectly tailored to living organisms. But more than that, they are responsible for Earth's climate itself. Because of these hydrogen bonds, water also has a much higher than expected "specific heat," meaning it warms slowly and then retains heat longer. Many people have entered a swimming pool after dark and are pleasantly surprised to find the water still very warm compared to the air and even the rock.

The critical application here is that Earth's surface, about 75 percent of which is covered by heat-controlling water, does not go through the tremendous daytime-to-nighttime temperature extremes common to all other planets. Not only does this moderate the Earth's overall temperature ranges, but it keeps lakes, ponds, and even puddles from day/night heat surges and crashes that would dramatically impact life. This heat-retention feature is also important in an internal sense to warm-blooded animals, which must maintain a constant body temperature. Since mammal and bird tissue approximates 70 percent water content, such life (that includes us) could not survive if this fluid did not have extraordinary temperature stability.

9. Hydrogen bonds in life-giving chemistry of polymer structure, buildup, and breakdown

Hydrogen bonds are probably held in highest esteem by a biochemist. Remember those incredibly complex proteins, the ones whose probabilities of correct amino-acid sequences exceed the math contained in the universe? Those proteins are totally unusable unless they fold correctly and stick together at all the correct junctures. And what forces cause them to attract at the proper points? The same hydrogen bonds from the water molecules formerly incorporated into their structures.

Then you can go on to investigate how monomers like amino acids or saccharides are joined together to make polymers like proteins and starches. The polymerization of life itself takes place through *dehydration synthesis,* where, as the term implies, an H_2O molecule is extracted when joining the two building blocks. And how are these macromolecules split again, as in the process of digestion? The term is *hydrolysis,* which means to "split with water" as H_2O is reintroduced to produce smaller molecules, like glucose, that can now be burned for energy in respiration.

If you need one more example, ask any geneticist what type of bonds hold the DNA molecule together at the nitrogenous base pairs in the middle, adenine to thymine (A—T) and guanine to cytosine (G—C). It is none other than the same hydrogen bonds. This makes them responsible for the very blueprint of life itself. Is there no end to the magic of water? Actually, not yet.

10. Water as the indispensable universal solvent and transport molecule

Here is another property of water that initially is simple to understand, but leads to concepts of deep complexity. Science textbooks, especially those in biochemistry, call water the *universal solvent.* As the term implies, water as a solvent is able to accommodate virtually any *solute* (dissolved substance), becoming the only life-sustaining liquid medium possible for the human body's heart-driven, water-based plasma.

The reason? That incredible partial symmetry one more time. In that the molecules have positive poles (+) and negative poles (-), water can certainly dissolve polar or ionic substances called *hydrophilic solutes*, like essential salt (NaCl), water-soluble vitamins (Vitamin C), and so on. They can also accommodate the polar end of a fatty-acid molecule (COOH) attached to the non-polar lengthy hydrocarbon chain, a description typical of any number of organic molecules that must travel throughout the body.

And what's more, water can even carry non-polar molecules called *hydrophobic solutes*, like oils and waxes. How do you overcome the old adage that "oil and water don't mix"? It is possible because several water molecules can link by their hydrogen bonds to surround an oil molecule in an envelope called a *hydration shell*. This shell can then float like a bubble in the plasma stream until it reaches its location.

In a word, blood—viewed as a highly hydrated tissue—can simultaneously carry sugars, starches, proteins, nutrients, and water-based vitamins, as well as fats, oils, waxes, and oil-based vitamins. And after these molecules are hydrolized, water in the blood can also accommodate the removal of the resulting polar and non-polar waste products of urea, carbon dioxide, and so on.

If all this was too much chemistry, just remember that water is a specially "designed" molecule—the only medium that can circulate absolutely *any* substance that animals require for life. And as you might suspect, similarly tailored organic transport processes are going on in plants with the help of water moved by transpiration.

The details of such movements throughout the circulatory apparatus of plants and animals still contain many, many mysteries. Also, what is only now beginning to be understood is how these molecules enter and leave cells once they arrive at their locations, and by what methods they cross cell membranes and cell walls. It is certainly analogous to the floor of a large and bustling manufacturing center where components, spare parts, and discardable pieces move fluidly via assembly lines, conveyor belts, and corridors to and from various departments and storage areas with the purpose of producing a product. On the manufacturing floor, intelligent directives obviously decide which items enter and exit which locations or departments.

But how does it work in living tissue, where no such "on site" intelligence is present to direct molecules to and from their proper locations? Compatible and incompatible polarities have long been the most promising answer. For example, it seems that a fatty-acid molecule is able to orient itself in a specific way with the transporting water. This in turn allows it to properly orient itself with the phospholipid molecule in the cell membrane through which it must pass. Essential proteins seem to move in and out of cells based on similar polarity mechanisms related to their water medium.

However, a composite description of how such molecules know where, when, and even why to move is far from being available. How about you? Can you explain how all these substances, fortunately afloat in their water medium, know where they are supposed to go? One thing is sure. The magic of the water molecule is at the heart of the answers.

11. Condensation nuclei, high in compressibility, latent heat of evaporation and fusion, and so on

There are many other general life-related contributions of water that could be discussed, such as its formation into snowflakes, its adherence to condensation nuclei, and its heating and cooling in the generation of wind currents and jet streams. There are other organic attributes as well, such as *high incompressibility*, which allows animals with high water content like slugs to maintain body mass; *high latent heat of evaporation*, which permits the essentials of sweating and cooling; and *high latent heat of fusion*, which keeps water from solidifying even at subfreezing temperatures, when combined with the right combinations of cytoplasmic solutes.

At a minimum, however, remember that all these properties are due to water's curious molecular structure, a unique structure that a "big banging" explosion 13 billion years ago just happened to make possible. If H_2O had gone the way of every other molecule produced by that "random" event, the probability of life would, once again, be zero many times over.

12. Water, the space program, and the possibility of life on Mars

To cap off this chapter on water, a reference to the U.S. space program is very appropriate. Since the late 1990s NASA has been launching a new series of Surveyor spacecraft probes to Mars. The missions of these Surveyor vehicles are analogous to that of the Lunar Surveyor series in the late 1960s, which eventually allowed us to land men on the moon. The sequence? First, detailed pictures are taken from orbit (already done extensively with Mars' surface), then nonmanned soft landings follow with instrumentation that can assess the actual surface (now going on), and then the eventual landing of astronauts on the surface (perhaps in 20 years) and their safe return.

But you can also add that the allure of finding water is a major parameter in current mission planning. For example, *Mars Polar Surveyor* of 1996 and *Mars Odyssey* of 2001 caused much initial excitement when they both returned extremely close-up photographs. With both vehicles using the sophisticated Mars Orbital Camera (MOC), NASA received pictures as tight as one meter wide of what looks to be large seas of frozen *water*. Of course we all know how motivated science gets about the prospect of life when water is found. Such excitement was especially high back in the 1970s just prior to the first Viking spacecraft soft landing on the Red Planet, but as is common knowledge, Viking found nothing to support the past, present, or future existence of even the simplest type of life-forms.

Still, water ostensibly provides a chance for life on Mars, and though science is now much more guarded on such speculations, water remained the focus of two Martian launches in 2004. NASA's Exploration Rover Missions successfully landed two vehicles on Mars days apart in January 2004.

Both vehicles successfully deployed mechanized rovers with the most sophisticated automated labs to date. The rover named "Spirit" was successfully deployed in Gusev Crater and was able to sample soil in what NASA scientists called a dry lakebed. The rover "Opportunity" was released in the Plain of Meridiani that was said to be once "drenched" in water, and sampled soil in an area of hematite concentrations and sedimentary rock. The automated lab on the latter rover returned detailed soil analyses on high concentrations of silicon, aluminum, and sulfur, as well as curious "berries," spherules typical of mineral concentrations left behind in porous rock now evaporated—all signs that the liquid form likely once existed. Unfortunately, no water and, more disappointing, no concentrations of carbon compounds related to metabolizing life were found.

With all this data from Mars and other locations in space, maybe it's time to call the bluff on the "water equals life" notion. Can you imagine an alien vehicle looking for our types of life-forms landing on any extremely dry lakebed on Earth, such as Death Valley, or an area of once water-soaked sedimentary rock, such as below Hoover Dam, and finding nothing to report in a soil analysis? Unthinkable. And yet, NASA's repeated answer to the absence of life on Mars is that the environment is too hostile because of temperature extremes, violent storms, toxic chemicals, and constant bombardment of lethal radiation.

But wait a minute. Aren't these the same powerful reconfiguring forces evolutionists say accidentally created life in the first place here on Earth? Why is it that violent random forces produce life only in theory, but never in practice? Besides, water does not necessarily contain life even here on Earth. The huge aquifers deep underground, like the Ogallala Aquifer that stretches from Texas to South Dakota, contain water that is completely purified by percolation action and absolutely devoid of life. Also, never forget how far removed an H_2O molecule is from one of DNA. The difference in size and complexity is a random jump of mathematical probabilities not contained in the universe.

I would say this mentality of "water equals life" has blinded natural evolutionists in their desperation to find any type of extraterrestrial life. I am convinced that if on Mars, or elsewhere, we someday find warm sandy beaches caressed by rolling waves and gentle trade winds, we still will find no life if a designing intelligence has never been present. If I am found wrong—if someday we find unmistakable proof of something as incredibly simple as a living (or dead) bacterium on Mars, which is itself an incredibly complex cellular organism—I will repudiate the contents of this book. But in all fairness, just like NASA discontinued the funding of SETI (the Search for Extra-Terrestrial Intelligence) after ten years because there were no results, so should evolutionists at some point be willing to end their speculations of life being found on Mars.

—•—

To most Darwinists, this chapter's discourse on the miracle of water will have little or no impact. Yet the story is told of a Carpenter who once gave a lesson on water to a woman beside a well—and in the end, the woman did not need instruction on the physical attributes of H_2O in order to have faith in the implications of "spiritual water." Neither did she make the mistake many Darwinists make—admiring only what was made, and not paying homage to its Maker.

Time for a shift in gears. Let's go back to physics and look at an amazing concept that is at the heart of our modern lifestyle.

Theories That Come Up Dry

Over 30 years ago I won $50 from a fellow GI named Ernie, already an aggressive Darwinist by his early 20s. As the *Viking I* spacecraft had just completed the first ever soft landing on Mars, Ernie was convinced the automated lab would at least find bacterial life and was willing to put his money where his mouth was. Well, *Viking I* landed in July 1976, but it took Ernie until May 1977 to pay up.

So now I wonder how many rovers will have to be deployed before evolutionists finally relent about life on Mars? Will it take an actual manned landing that finds nothing, or will we first have to have several domed cities full of unsuccessful researchers? Whatever the benchmark, I say they should pick a number of years after which they will finally admit that even the water on Mars was insufficient to allow the flotation of the hopeless theory of spontaneous generation. Then while they are at it, they should also admit it is impossible for a living cell to crawl out of the primordial soup here on Earth, and finally end the "wild goo chase," as techno-entrepreneur and author George Gilder called it.

7

WAVE MECHANICS

Tailor-Made Physics

If there were no humans on our planet, waves of radiated energy would still be absolutely essential to all other forms of life. Consider these examples.

- Animal eardrums, or tympani, detect sound waves at certain frequencies and amplitudes, allowing them to hear. Dogs, of course, have a wider range of receptivity and can hear pitches we can't. (Bats and dolphins, among others, also use echolocation by bouncing sound waves off objects for identification.)

- The narrow visible spectrum of electromagnetic waves, better known as *light,* can stimulate the photoreceptive cells that allow animals to see. ("ROY G. BIV" anyone? R-red. O-orange. Y-yellow. G-green. B-blue. I-indigo. V-violet.)

- When it comes to the miracle of photosynthesis, plants cannot live without sunlight. True, most plants use only a very narrow range of the electromagnetic light spectrum— wavelength distances first at about 450 nanometers and again at 650 nanometers—but for most plants that's more than sufficient energy to excite the electrons in chlorophyll.

- The heat energy from the day's sunlight properly radiates from the Earth's surface at the prescribed rate. If it didn't, climatic disasters would happen as we become too hot or too cold. (Global warming, anyone?)

- While major events like volcanoes and hurricanes play their roles in various life cycles, they also send out strong random radio waves as part of their activity.

- Finally, if you are a Darwinist, you rely on ionizing radiation above the *petahertz* range, such as X-rays and gamma rays, to fracture DNA molecules so the old genetic codes can reorganize into improved mutations and allow animals and plants to give you the needed "hopeful monsters" that drive life forward in complexity. (Don't feel bad if that last one sounded like a fairy tale. It does to me too.)

But these applications of wave mechanics are only the beginning of what makes human life so uniquely convenient.

Wave Basics

In that last paragraph there was some vocabulary thrown your way that may prove tricky if not explained. Words like *frequency, amplitude,* and *wavelength* are rather common in our language but not well understood. Here a picture or two is worth more than a thousand words.

Crest

Trough

Few waves per second   Many waves per second

Waves of energy, like the surf rolling onto the beach, come at you first in peaks called *crests* and then as valleys called *troughs,* as seen above. The crests can be extremely high and troughs can be extremely deep, such as on days when the surf is heavy. Or the crests and troughs can be low, such as in the resulting ripples when a pebble is dropped into a calm pond. Furthermore, regardless of the height and depth cycle, the waves can also be coming at you slowly or rapidly—a few per second such as in low musical tones, or millions of waves passing by in a split second, such as in gamma rays. But despite their differing heights and speeds, all waves can be quantified by their relationship to the midline as seen below.

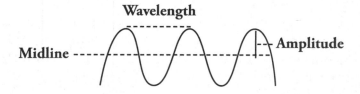

Wavelength is, by definition, the distance between two crests. For example, in a shortwave radio signal, the distance between crests is not as long as in regular radio waves—allowing them to travel farther. And as should be obvious, the shorter the wavelength, the greater the number, or *frequency,* of waves that will pass by per second. For example, 1 hertz (Hz) equals one wave per second. One of my favorite AM radio stations in the Denver area is 850 KOA, broadcasting at a frequency of 850 kilohertz (KHz). That means the waves of its signal pass by at a rate of 850,000 crests per second. Compare that to one of my favorite FM radio stations, broadcasting at 105.1 mega-hertz (MHz), KCOL, the "oldies" station. This station's signal rides on 105,100,000 waves per second, and such a high speed requires a whole new radio dial. And yet all these radio and TV communication signals are actually moving much slower than the visible light that activates the retinas of our eyes. Whew!

Some Personal History with Waves

Think of some of the ways the electromagnetic spectrum affected people's lives in the twentieth century. What would my grandparents, who lived in the southeastern Colorado plains, have done without their old AM Motorola radio in the tall wooden box? How else could they have listened to the St. Louis Cardinals play baseball on those muggy summer nights? Or how could my parents, who lived in the cracker-box house on Third Street in Wausau, Wisconsin, have watched Jack Paar on *The Tonight Show* without the old black-and-white Sylvania TV—the one whose tubes took forever to warm up?

And later, as a teenager, how could I have enjoyed the original *Mission Impossible* series without our first Zenith color TV—the one my parents scrimped and saved several months to buy? The one CBS station I grew up with—the only one our antenna could pick up—seemed to be a luxury. (To this day, some reruns of *Bonanza* are new to me because there were no stations that carried NBC programming close enough to us.)

On the other hand, *amplitude* is, by definition, the strength of the wave regardless of its wavelength. When you turn up the volume on your radio, the wavelength doesn't change, but the amplitude of the crests get higher as the power of the sound rises. So as amplitude changes, imagine the diagram above as having higher or lower crests, but crests that are still the same distance apart.

The length between each wave crest as it passes—also called an *oscillation*—is the key that determines distance traveled and penetrating power, and hence the wavelength's usefulness. (An *oscilloscope* is an instrument that measures wave frequencies.) For example, sound waves have extremely long wavelengths, and therefore a low frequency of few waves per second. So it's no wonder sound waves do not travel far but quickly dissipate, and can be easily blocked by any dense material. Conversely, gamma rays travel the length of the universe and are dangerously ionizing to cell structures, as they zip right through the body at an incredible number of oscillations per second. To see the ordering of wave mechanics that are part of nature, examine the simplified continuum below.

Frequency (hertz)

10^1	10^3	10^6	10^{12}	10^{14}	10^{17}	10^{19}	10^{22}
Sound waves	Random emissions	Radio	Infrared (heat)	Visible spectrum "ROY G. BIV"	Ultraviolet (black light)	X-rays	Gamma rays

Wavelength (meters)

10^8	10^4	10^1	10^{-2}	10^{-5}	10^{-8}	10^{-11}	10^{-14}

Waves—Suited for Human Beings

This spectrum is obviously highly suited to the needs of all life on Earth, but think of its specific wonders for us humans. And this is the central point of this chapter. How many TV stations do *you* currently receive on those many color TVs throughout your house? Programming choices in the hundreds, right? And beamed to your home by a satellite from outer space, I'll bet. Me too! Well, that's just the beginning of the electronic "bells and whistles" that somehow were there and available to our technological grasp by the time modern humans were ready to invent them. We certainly still have "ROY G. BIV"—visible wavelengths between 700 and 400 nanometers to sustain all plant and animal life—but we also have many totally human luxuries to enjoy because the electromagnetic spectrum is so wide and versatile. Since there is no possible way to include them all on the continuum above, I'll just list them below.

wireless atomic clocks: 60 KHz

AM radios: 535 to 1700 KHz (1.7 MHz)

ultrasound imaging: 1 to 20 MHz

CB radios: 26.96 to 27.41 MHz

radio-controlled toys: 27 and 49 MHz

cell phones: 824 to 829 MHz

newer cordless phones: 900 MHz

air-traffic control: 960 to 1215 MHz

radar: 1000 MHz (1 GHz) to 100 GHz

LF ham radios: 1.240 to 1.300 GHz

shortwave radios: 3 to 30 MHz

GPS systems: 1.227 to 1.575 GHz

alarm systems: 40 MHz

deep-space radios: 2.290 to 2.300 GHz

older cordless phones: 40 to 50 MHz

HF ham radios: 2.390 to 2.450 GHz

baby monitors: 49.3 to 49.9 MHz

wireless computers: 2.4 GHz

radio-controlled airplanes: 72 MHz

microwave ovens: 2.450 GHz

FM radios: 88 to 108 MHz

satellite dish TV: 3.7 to 22 GHz

VHF TV: 54 to 220 MHz

medical screening: .2 to 4.0 THz

wildlife monitors: 215 to 230 MHz

bio-imaging: 1 to 10 THz

weather satellites: 300 to 420 MHz

TV remotes: 275 THz

walkie-talkies: 450 to 470 MHz

baggage screening: 10 to 1.0 angstroms

UHF TV: 470 to 806 MHz

medical X-rays: 10 to 0.1 angstroms

pagers: 806 to 824 MHz

crystallography: 2.2 to 0.7 angstroms

And these are just extras for low-tech flunkies like me. High-tech operations like military and commercial applications have the following uses between wavelengths of about 100 meters to .01 angstroms (an angstrom being 10^{-10} meters long):

land mobile radios

tactical air/ground signals

data links

search and rescue

early warning systems

air vehicle flight terminations

anti-stealth radar

foliage penetration radar

biomedical telemetry

radio navigation

wind profiling

test-range support

drug interdiction

nuclear detection

aerospace communication

space-station communications

satellite tracking

night-vision technology

laser technology

dental-filling curing

fiber optics

PET imaging

(Why, these two lists should be enough to make even a strict Darwinist feel real lucky!)

To top this chapter off, imagine if luck gave us all other life-forms, but for some reason *Homo sapiens* had never "evolved." What I'm saying is, imagine if over millions of years random Darwinian processes successfully took us from a concoction of simple inorganic molecules all the way to something like the Neanderthal man—and stopped! Certainly this is possible because evolution can't have any idea where it is headed—specifically, nothing could have had modern humans as a goal in mind, right? So we could have just as easily stopped at cavemen—maybe even backed up.

If that had happened, then all these aforementioned electronic gadgets would forever sleep in the untapped physics of our world as technology stopped at clubs and spears. What a strange concept to get your mind around! I just don't buy it. I believe wave mechanics were invented by a Designer who fully intended them to, at first, support all life, but also preplanned them so they would later be at our creative disposal—along with the necessary minerals and electrical-power systems to fabricate and operate our toys. Furthermore, and what may be even more fantastic, this Designer also gave us what He denied all other species—the mental capacity and physical dexterity necessary to imagine and invent these devices. And if I'm right that it's ridiculous to call all this great technology a "lucky accident," that means Someone prepared all this only for us.

As part two closes, we are back to an either-or situation. Even if the whole phenomenon is a colossal stroke of luck, the math, chemistry, and physics of our planet are still well suited to our physical existence. Furthermore, our backdrop provides for our emotional and even social needs as well. All this leads us to...

- *Either* civilized Homo sapiens got here all by itself and was lucky enough to be able to take special advantage of the world it accidentally evolved into...

- *Or* God gets the credit, and His powerful hand guided the process from beginning to end—with Homo sapiens being the focus from the start and the crowning achievement.

Part three will now show in detail why the belief that human existence is accidental and not designed is truly Darwinism's weakest link.

HUMANITY,
A SEPARATE REALITY

My religion consists of a humble admiration of the illimitable superior spirit who reveals himself in the slight details we are able to perceive with our frail and feeble minds.

—ALBERT EINSTEIN

At our moon's Sea of Tranquility on July 20, 1969, Neil Armstrong was the first human to set foot on another natural object out in space. Armstrong's historic words? "A small step for man, a giant leap for mankind." In one sense it was a monumental moment, but in another sense it was just another event in space exploration, later repeated by other astronauts.

Furthermore, when the *Apollo 17* mission returned from the fifth and last landing on the moon, some people say that all we had netted from these immense efforts was about 200 pounds of rock samples— none of which were all that distinguishable from rocks you could find here on Earth. Nope, no new source of water, oil, or air for our planet. Not even any gold, silver, uranium, or precious stones to cash in to pay for all those expensive rockets. (And now NASA speaks of going back to the moon again? Whatever for? It's a totally dead rock. I say, "On to Mars!")

The Giant Leap for Mankind

But in a more distant past, the Book of Genesis says, God spoke into reality a much bigger leap—one without equal, whose importance goes beyond any mortal evaluation. Genesis 1:26 says that after everything God had made thus far, He then said, "Let us make man in our image."

Call it yet another one of these either-or choices mentioned early on in this book. *Either* we naturally changed from something like a chimpanzee and are just another installment in the panoply of evolving animals—*or* God intelligently and intentionally brought us into being through the Adam and Eve scenario. *Either* we are just an extension of an extension of an extension of a long line of evolving life-forms, and the South Beach Diet books are correct in saying our tendency to eat poorly is just another vestigial reflection of our cave-dwelling past—*or* God made us so distinct that it is futile to attempt to find true parallels in other animals, even chimps, for any number of human attributes.

Speaking of chimps, Darwinists never fail to extol their humanlike virtues. They constantly put out quotes such as, "With DNA codes 98.4 percent the same as ours, chimps have to be somewhere in our family tree!" And that frequent rallying cry is framed by such pronouncements as, "The big bang gave us a planet. Then lightning, UV rays, thermal vents, and the like created bacterial life in the ancient seas. And then natural selection eventually transformed bacteria into those chimps that became us—all by totally natural processes." *Exposing Darwinism's Weakest Link* says believing that chimps (or any other primate) could accidentally turn into humans is the biggest delusion of all.

Ask yourself this question. Is a chimp closer to a bacterium or a human? Now *biologically,* I readily admit a chimp is immeasurably closer to us than a bacterium. But God "formed man of the dust of the ground, and breathed into his nostrils the breath of life; and man became a living soul" (Genesis 2:7 KJV)—thus He made chimpanzees and all other life-forms virtual equals by spiritually vaulting humans into an existence all their own. Just to be sure you caught that, here it is in plain language:

> Considering the spiritual factor—the only one that really matters—chimps and bacteria are identical in the eyes of God, and chimps and humans are an eternity apart.

If you look at human existence, you will see this fact everywhere. And that's what the forthcoming chapters will examine with respect to our body parts and our behaviors, our language, our morals and values, and our use of information. But first, let me address the Darwinist's totally misleading theory of human evolution and migration, and set the record straight based on the fossil evidence.

HUMAN EVOLUTION

The Hopeless Fairy Tale of Origin and Migration

For most of you, this chapter may be the main reason you are reading the book. You want to hear an explanation for "monkey men" and "cavemen" and how they came about. And you are especially curious whether, back in chapter 3, I treated the Adam and Eve story as more than a fairy tale.

Darwinian Origin Tales

So let me set an unmistakable tone. I'll do it with a quote from *National Geographic* magazine's August 2002 issue, whose cover article was called "The First Pioneer?—A New Find Shakes the Family Tree." Why *National Geographic*? Because in my view this most excellent of publications does more to foster in the average person a belief in human evolution, Darwinian-style, than any other single source.

Think about it. For a magazine on "geography," *National Geographic* sure enjoys its many forays into Darwinism. It continues to print one or more major articles on natural evolution each year, covering the "non-directed" origination of fish, reptiles, birds, whales, humans.

Furthermore, in almost all of those wonderfully photographed featured articles on the world's mysterious species, references to supposed evolutionary mechanisms are nonstop. Without a doubt *NG* goes out of its way to promote a naturalistic rather than a faith-based view of the origin of our world. And considering their readership, I consider them a formidable source of evolutionary misinformation.

The quote from *National Geographic*'s "The First Pioneer" article is from a story that covers the collection of hominid bones and tools recently found in the West Asian country of Georgia. These are now called samples of *Homo habilis* by its discoverers. And here are the words, from a scientist quoted in the article who preferred not to be named: *"They ought to put it back in the ground."*

That utter confusion reigns in the attempt to prove human evolution through the fossil evidence is the case I will build in this chapter. A summary of my key points sounds like this:

> To accept that the present hominid fossil evidence supports natural human evolution requires two beliefs:
> 1) You have to have a preconceived mind-set that monkeys did indeed turn into humans by natural processes. And 2) the arrogance of the first belief gives rise to a second belief—that you never take an objective look at the fossil evidence that fails to support your first belief.

These two beliefs are necessary for this reason. Actual paleoanthropologists who dig up these bones (experts in prehistoric human remains), as opposed to Darwinists who interpret the finds (experts in philosophy), readily admit—as in the *"put it back in the ground"* quote above—that each new hominid find *muddies* rather than clarifies the evolutionary waters. I'm going to show you why this is true in numerous ways.

The Fictional Timeline

To open the discourse, let me briefly walk you through the history of the personal home microcomputer. (You'll find out why very soon.) The first home computer I ever heard about would be a strange unit called an MITS Altair 8800, introduced in 1975. It had 256 *bytes* of memory and had to be assembled from a kit. A year later, on April Fool's Day 1976, the Apple computer was introduced. It had a whopping 8 kilobytes of memory for the suspicious cost of $666.66.

However, the first microcomputer I ever saw used in someone's home was released early in 1981. It was purchased by an older colleague who, weeks earlier, had said he'd rather retire before the computer age forced him to learn the new technology. The computer he now proudly operated was the VIC 20. It cost a mere $300 and still provided a massive 5 kilobytes of memory. It also had a printer port, a joystick for computer games, and an external magnetic cassette drive that took only 20 minutes of download time for every use.

The success of the VIC 20 was obvious. Being the first microcomputer to sell over 1 million units, it sure put the squeeze on its competitors. But later in 1981 a heavy hitter entered the home computer market. IBM began marketing its first 16-kilobyte PCs using the MS-DOS operating system, designed by a bespectacled computer whiz named Bill Gates.

But before IBM assumed such dominance, the Commodore 64 grabbed a quick share of the market. Released in 1982, the "Breadbox 64"—referring to its shape and its glorious 64 kilobytes of memory—allowed both sound and color for the video games played on your TV. Though it had quality-control problems (over half of the units had defects), it became the bestselling single microcomputer of all time. But in short order, Big Blue, with its superior operating system and marketing ability, soon dominated the home computer market. However, one serious challenger arose in 1984, the Macintosh from the Apple company, and these machines became a major player by catering more to educators than business people.

So in conclusion, here's a brief list of the steps in home computer development:

MITS Altair	1975
Apple	1976
VIC 20	early 1981
IBM PC	late 1981

| Commodore 64 | 1982 |
| Macintosh | 1984 |

Hold on a minute. When you look at all the developments in mainframe computers before home computers became a reality; all the computer company names and their technologies that have since come, gone, or are still going; all those separate companies that make only components; all those incredible gadgets still on the drawing board—"brief" has got to be the mother of all understatements.

Here's the application. Evolutionary authors of science textbooks, magazine articles, and lecture notes will similarly condense the complex theory of hominid development into something as deceptively oversimplified as the six linear home computer steps above. Then, even more amazing, by using a chronological sequence akin to the below, they often convince their audience that enough of the story has been told.

Australopithecus afarensis	4.5 mya (million years ago)
Australopithecus africanus	3 mya
Homo habilis	2 mya
Homo erectus	1 mya
Homo neanderthalis	500 tya (thousand years ago)
Homo sapiens	10 tya to present

Unfortunately, the often-used fossil record of human evolution I just gave above is no more linear than my computer timeline. In both there are advances out of place and time, unexplainable regressions after obvious successes, blind alleys that fit no place in line, and many other odds and ends that defy sequencing. Hence our unnamed researcher's quote after yet another find added to the confusion: "They ought to put it back in the ground."

What Did Darwin Say?

Before we go on in regard to the impossibility of human evolution Darwin-style, let's take a look at the man himself. It is safe to say that Darwin's first book, *The Origin of Species,* published in 1859, was a landmark piece of work. In it, Charles Darwin made it clear that evolutionary processes could cause only minor alterations.

However, in 1874 Darwin published another influential book, *The Descent of Man,* in which he confines his philosophy mostly to the origin of *Homo sapiens* and its possible progenitors. There is little doubt that later in life Darwin felt the evolutionary process had much more power, enough to allow us humans to accidentally arrive on the scene. Furthermore, we accomplished this through the same gradual natural selection processes that he believed produced all other species—that is, one organism taking one gradual step forward at a time until it became a new species. And of course, one type of organism taking these gradual steps was monkeys, who became apes, who became "ape men," who became men. Consider these eight quotes from *Descent of Man* as Darwin develops his theory:

1. "The homological construction of the whole frame in the members of the same class is intelligible, if we admit their descent from a common progenitor…On any other view, the similarity of pattern between the hand of man or monkey, the foot of a horse, the flipper of a seal, the wing of a bat, and so on, is utterly inexplicable" (page 25).

2. "Monstrosities, which graduate into slight variations, are likewise so similar in man and the lower animals, that the same classification and the same terms can be used for both" (page 30).

3. "The canine [tooth] is more deeply implanted, and by a stronger fang than the incisor. Nevertheless, this tooth no longer serves man as a special weapon for tearing his enemies or prey; it may, therefore, as far as proper function is concerned, be considered as rudimentary" (page 40).

4. "If we look back to an extremely remote epoch, before man had arrived at the dignity of manhood, he would have been guided more by instinct and less by reason than are the lowest savages at the present time" (page 46).

5. "Turning now to the nearest allies of men, and therefore

the best representatives of our early progenitors, we find that the hands of the Quadrumana [a New World monkey] are constructed on the same general pattern as our own, but are far less perfectly adapted for diversified uses" (page 50).

6. "If it be an advantage to man to stand firmly on his feet and to have his hands and arms free, of which, from his pre-eminent success in the battle of life, there can be no doubt, then I can see no reason why it should not have been an advantage to the progenitors of man to have become more and more erect or bipedal" (page 53).

7. "The gradually increasing weight of the brain and skull in man must have influenced the development of the supporting spinal column, more especially whilst he was becoming erect" (page 56).

8. "The half-art, half-instinct of language still bears the stamp of its gradual evolution" (page 131).

To summarize these eight quotes in order, Darwin said,

1. We certainly look like lower animals in many ways.

2. We obviously can be similarly classified, especially with apes and monkeys.

3. We still bear vestiges of our primitive past.

4. We were no doubt once much more instinctual than rational.

5. We slowly added extremities and other human adaptations, transforming from those more primitive forms.

6. We gradually walked upright.

7. We incrementally developed a larger brain.

8. We eventually learned how to communicate with civilized language.

I would say Darwin makes his position clear. However, his entire line of thinking has been termed "philosophic" rather than "scientific," even by evolutionists as respected as the giant of American biology, Harvard professor Ernst Mayr. (Dr. Mayr will get prominent attention later, in chapter 15.) That is because Mayr reminds us that Darwin conducted *no* ongoing scientific experiments to produce data to see if his theories worked in practice.

Furthermore, unfortunately for Darwin, he had to employ a liberal amount of sup-position because the only ancient hominid fossils known in his time were the first few samples of the poorly understood Neander-thals. In fact, Darwin makes just a single prehistoric hominid reference in the entire *Descent* book. Of the Neanderthals he says on page 56,

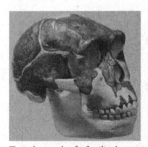

Typical example of a fossilized Neanderthal skull.

> It must be admitted that some of the skulls of very high antiquity, such as the famous one of Neanderthal, are well developed and capacious.

Had other types of hominid fossils been available, Darwin undoubt-edly would have woven them into his arguments, and would surely have added them to his already constructed evolutionary tree in some chronological manner. But despite no laboratory testing and scant evidence, his line of reasoning must have been convincing because science quickly embraced human evolution to near totality.*

Evaluating the Fossils

With Darwin's thinking in hand, the question becomes, "What does the fossil record say over 100 years later, and does it prove Darwin was right?" *Origin* and *Descent* were written in the second half of the nineteenth century. It is now the twenty-first century, and paleoanthro-pology has produced significantly more prehistoric hominid evidence,

---

* The remaining 400 pages or so of *The Descent of Man* are devoted to Darwin's idea of sexual selection. In many different ways he tried to prove that the struggle between males for the possession of the females was the driving force for all subsequent evolutionary advances. Read these chapters yourself and see if Darwin doesn't sound quite obsessive in his nonstop references to sexuality.

evidence guarded as heavily as the gold in Fort Knox. But how much more fossil evidence?

First, between what dates do the experts say we should count bones as hominid? In other words, how far back in time does evolutionary science say a bone sample can go and still bear more human features than monkey traits, and how far forward will evolutionary science allow hominids to go until they're admitted to be fully human?

Signs of Dissension

It is worth mentioning that when you begin reading material on dated prehistoric hominids written by paleoanthropologists doing actual fieldwork, you will probably detect rampant disagreement, contradictory positions, and liberal disclaimers before you hardly get into the text. There simply is no agreement on when or how even minor advances happened. For example, that six-step linear sequence of hominid development given earlier will surely draw fire from some researchers, but there is no reason to take this personally, because those researchers' timelines will not produce agreement either. And this lack of consensus is not evidence of healthy scientific exchange. Rather, it betrays a tremendous problem.

Now, back to date ranges. For a frame of reference, I am going to suggest a date of 4.5 million years ago as the earliest that paleoanthropologists would expect a sample to be sufficiently hominid. Most researchers seem to believe any earlier samples would be more *pongid* (ape) than hominid.

On the other end, I will suggest 30,000 years ago as the latest a specimen can go before evolutionary science finally would expect it to be one of us, *Homo sapiens*. That boundary is chosen because the Cro-Magnon man of the last few thousand years (a term now out of vogue with many researchers) seems presently considered technologically "stone age" but genetically 100 percent human. The Native American Indians before Columbus arrived would be fitting examples of Cro-Magnon, able to freely interbreed with Europeans so as to be fully human, yet separated by thousands of years and miles. Below, then, would be a fitting scale for a proposed hominid time frame.

Hominids appear   All other hominids extinct
4.5 million years ago   by 30,000 years ago
| . . . . |

Next, what is your guess as to how many partial skeletons, individual bones, bone fragments, and teeth now exist that are accepted
and catalogued as prehistoric hominids by paleoanthropologists, within
the time frame we've determined? (And it's all fragments, of course.
In extremely rare cases, such as "Lucy," you may have three-fourths of
a skeleton, but generally it's a bone section here, a portion of a skull
there, a single tooth, and so on.) Well, at the turn of this century, even
with the most stringent exclusionary criteria, most paleoanthropologists would agree that the number of fossil samples on which to base
human evolution is a little over 5000. And on these few thousands
we must answer the most burning question of all in natural evolution,
"How did humans get here?"

After research of available lists helped me arrive at this 5000-plus
figure, let me say I was surprised at the quantity. Over 5000 specimens was a much higher number than I had previously imagined.
Unfortunately, not many publications exist attempting to catalogue
all specimens, probably because of the absolute confusion on what
constitutes legitimate evidence. For the most respected source, I suggest the ambitious undertaking called *The Catalogue of Fossil Hominids*
published by the British Museum of Natural History. This book contains exceptional detail on pre-human bones, dividing the catalogue
by continents to separate African, American, European, Asian, and
Australian finds. It lists "only" 3998 specimens, but its latest editions
date no later than 1977, and it is safe to say hundreds more have since
been discovered.*

Why Isn't the Fossil Evidence Enough?

Collectively, we now have 5000 to 6000 hominid fossils in our
professional cache. However, I have yet to find one evolutionary scientist who feels the evidence is anything more than sketchy. Why? If

---

* If you want more updated information on hominid fossils, I suggest a creationist writer, Marvin L. Lubenow's
Bones of Contention, Baker Books, 1994; or evolutionist writers Jones, Martin, and Pilbeam's *Cambridge
Encyclopedia of Human Evolution*, Cambridge University Press, 1994.

you were an archeologist trying to validate an ancient civilization and had only 5500 artifacts, would you have a difficult task? I think not. Or if you were a historian trying to prove the existence of a defunct carmaker and had only 5500 old auto parts, would your task be difficult? No. Or if you were a detective trying to solve a murder case with only 5500 pieces of evidence (probably the most fitting analogy of the three), would a conviction of the suspect be difficult? In this case, definitely no! Then why do Darwinists always call the hominid evidence woefully insufficient?

> It is my firm belief that Darwinists call the present hominid evidence incomplete because it *refuses* to validate a theory they accept without question.

Even if you accept all the evidence supplied by paleoanthropologists as legitimate (which you will later see is a dangerous allowance), you can *still* never trace the human family tree as if it were a sequential product of natural processes. It is like trying to take your present computer or laptop and trace it backward in linear fashion to the Altair 8800—only much, much worse. Again, the only way to be a Darwinist is to stay away from the evidence—especially hominid evidence—so you can let your preconceptions imagine at will.

Imagine playing the famous Parker Bros. board game of Clue and just deciding beforehand, "Colonel Mustard did it in the dining room with the wrench." But then as the game progresses, you kept being led back to the library because everyone is seeing Miss Scarlet there with the rope. If you hold to your original theory, count on losing the game. So here on the following pages are several reasons why hominid fossils betray the predetermined belief that we evolved from monkeys.

Reason 1: Lack of continuity. With about 5500 pieces of human fossil evidence to prove monkeys turned into men, that amount should be a luxury. But like the old joke about the guy who fell in love at first sight—until he took a second look—there's much more to those numbers than meets the eye.

The first major problem is that the majority of the evidence is not where it's needed most, which is early on in the developmental sequence when "more like an ape" crossed the line into "more like a human." The percentages below may need some adjustment because, again, total agreement is impossible. But even after you alter them using any reasonable source, the point will still be made that the distribution of evidence is thinnest where the most proof is needed.

4.5 million to 2 million years ago = 4 percent of hominid samples
2 million to 1 million years ago   = 10 percent of hominid samples
1 million to 500,000 years ago   = 20 percent of hominid samples
500,000 to 30,000 years ago   = 66 percent of hominid samples

If the magical transition from ape to human did take place in that mysterious time around 5 mya, it would sure be nice to have more evidence from that latter part of the Pliocene epoch (58 to 1.8 mya). And why would that be out of place to ask? Dinosaur fossils aplenty are said to go back over 200 million years. Of course the proper evolutionary response would be that the earlier hominids weren't as numerous—as evidenced by that 4 percent above. In fact, all pictures portray them as living in very small nomadic packs, surely never even reaching 100 in a clan. (Maybe that would make them like the Sioux Indian Nation of early pioneer days. The word *nation* is appropriate for the Sioux because they were the largest of all Indian tribes, with all combined villages numbering an impressive 5000 total individuals!)

But then if you admit that the populations of Pliocene hominids had to be very small to correlate with the scarce amount of fossil evidence, then you open a whole new can of worms. Stop and think what non-Darwinistic implications come from assuming such small hominid populations—implications you have to ignore when your stance is, "Don't confuse me with the facts. My mind is made up." With populations of something like the *Australopithecus afarensis* so low—surely, like the Sioux, no greater than in the scant thousands— this severely limits the available number of live births to experience those accidental genetic improvements that magically launch the species into something like the *Australopithecus africanus.*

And there is another dicey problem arising from having only clan-size numbers for prehistoric hominids. Follow my reasoning here.

Let's say we allow a life expectancy of 50 years for "ape-men" in the first 4.5 million years before civilized man. Considering the perils of a hunter-gatherer lifestyle, this is probably quite generous. However, I'll use 50 years because that seems to approximate the life span of today's few Stone Age tribes still existing in rain forest jungles. So if a generation turns over approximately every fifty years, and it takes the *Australopithecus afarensis* about 4 million years to become a *Homo sapiens*, then 4 million years divided by 50 years says it would take the survival of about 80,000 continuous generations of hominids to reach the time of recorded civilization.

Now that's what I call optimistic! Considering their supposed tenuous lives in these small clans—what with predators, no health care, ice ages, and all—doesn't it seem like a miracle that they accidentally survived? Or if you just start with Neanderthal populations that require them to survive for about 470,000 years (500,000 minus 30,000), that 50-year life span figure would have to produce an unbroken string of 9400 Neanderthal generations. Wouldn't 9400 sequential families who lived in protected caves and shelters in such a recent period of the past have left even more evidence behind? (Consulting the table on page 113, we should expect that 5500 times 66 percent results in 3630 pieces of Neanderthal evidence.) Weren't Neanderthals a race of robust and intelligent creatures who wore clothes, built fires, made tools, and even constructed grave sites? Don't you think the caves of Europe, or other places around the globe, would yield much more than between three and four thousand fragments? Think about it.

I can see why an evolutionist would never point out that about 4 percent of the evidence has to cover about 60 percent of the time. Again, this is their ace in the hole, actually benefiting them because so little information leaves them free to imagine with impunity. Not only that, the number of discovered fossil fragments said to be between 5 to 10 million years old—when apes supposedly were starting to develop that exquisite human element—total less than ten! (And here we really mean *fragments*. For any evidence bridging chimps and "Lucy," we are talking about a single bone, or piece of bone in most cases, out of which an entire organism is reconstructed!) Now if these "superior" mutant apes existed for millions of years, why didn't they outcompete other full ape and monkey species, and leave a wealth of evidence behind?

Darwinists will shrug off the skewed nature of these numbers, but what is their reasoning? Still, problems with hominid population numbers extrapolated from available evidence are not the greatest betrayers of the monkey-to-man theory. The bigger dilemma, as with computer development, is the total lack of linear continuity from one ape-man to the next, an irritating little problem about to be illustrated next.

Reason 2: Mixed-up characteristics. *Cladistics* is evolution's sleight-of-hand attempt to show quasi-ancestry in a group of species by concentrating on one trait that could show a developmental pattern while conveniently ignoring other traits that do not fit.* This gives a handy impression, albeit a very false one, that *descent by modification* has taken place. (In birds, it would be something like sequencing the gradual increase in flying ability over time—perhaps from ostriches to hummingbirds—and calling it evolutionary while ignoring that meanwhile parenting skills show no pattern, advancing or otherwise.) In hominid fossils, though, cladograms are simply not done because the separate traits are, as it were, all over the map.

Evolutionary characteristics one might use in a hominid cladogram would include increasing brain size and extent of upright posture, as well as the presence of tools, the use of clothes, the reliance on fire, the need for permanent habitations such as caves, and the comparisons of general height and weight. But if you try to sequence any of this over time, the confusion starts immediately. For example, at this point in the game *Homo erectus* is the principle species used by Darwinists to attempt to bridge the gap between *Australopithecus* and *Homo sapiens.*† If you check the previously mentioned *Catalogue of Fossil Hominids,* you will find samples of *Homo erectus* have been found in the following locations: China, Russia, Australia, Indonesia, Kenya, South Africa, Morocco, Israel, Djibouti, Vietnam, India, and Tanzania.

---

* In *Reclaiming Science from Darwinism,* I extensively covered the concept of *cladistics* and *cladograms* in chapter 21, "For the Birds."

† As this book is going to print, geneticists are now fiercely challenging *Homo erectus* as yet another evolutionary dead end that did not lead to humans. How many of these monkey-men can you discard—with no suitable substitute—until your theory has to finally be abandoned?

Unfortunately, if you check traits in the same localities of these regions—comparing what would have to be clan to clan to clan—it is impossible to construct from hominid fossils any pattern in brain size, posture, tools, clothes, fire, shelter, height, or weight. It's as if someone took a collection of building blocks of different shapes and sizes from different manufacturers, put them all into a bag, shook them up, and then dumped them across the world map.

As another example, when a group of hominid specimens are arranged nicely by advancing brain size, the uprightness of posture is now out of sequence. Or if improving bipedal ability is the criterion, its arrangement is at the expense of cranial capacity, which now has no continuity. Amazingly enough, it is not uncommon to find tools and the use of fire associated with beings on the low end of brain size, posture, and height, and then have tools and fire be absent at fossil sites well past times when such items were thought to be common. Therefore, hominid cladistics remains an obvious impossibility. There is simply no effective way to sequence hominids at these different sites by any consistent body plan or lifestyle.

Reason 3: Geographical confusion. Just as the approach of cladistics collapses under scrutiny, so do all the attempts to document human migration. Paleontology insists, and therefore Darwinists are stuck with, having our ancestors evolve first on the African continent and then getting them all over the world without the aid of planes, trains, or automobiles. And judging from the location of Africa compared to the rest of the world, prehistoric hominids would most certainly have had to leave Africa by going north, and then spreading westward and eastward as the map below shows.

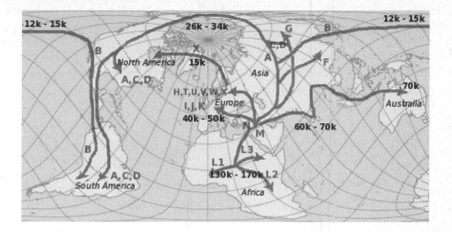

This map is similar to one included in an article called "Who Were the First Americans?" in the September 2000 issue of *Scientific American*. Most of that article dealt with the few thousand years since *Homo sapiens* was said to have arrived in North America via the land bridge over the Bering Straits between Alaska and Siberia. The article is mostly devoted to deciphering the locations, lifestyles, tools, and weapons of Native American Indians prior to any civilized influence. However, since it was probably seen as obligatory, the map also hypothesizes where Eskimo and American Indian ancestors came from—out of Africa, up to the Middle East, then to Southeast Asia, and finally to Northern Asia before they crossed into our hemisphere around 15,000 years ago.

If this is the best guess about how such ill-equipped and few primitive hominids dispersed across continents, how did they traverse high mountain ranges and arid deserts? And when they finally made it to Indonesia, for instance, how come these larger species like Java Man, called a *Homo erectus* based on the features, regressed in their ability to use tools? And how did smaller hominid species who were superior in tools and weaponry show up farther down the road? This reversibility is the vexation of supposed migratory pathways all over globe, and the expert paleoanthropologists who actually find the specimens are the first to admit it.

Louis B. Leakey, who will forever be known as the man who popularized the search for our progenitors, is undoubtedly the father of paleoanthropology. Early in his life he attempted to build some sort of imaginary progression like the one I listed early in this chapter. Darwinists, eager for proof that God is irrelevant or imaginary, grabbed on to his theories and proclaimed them as scientific fact proving that man had gradually evolved of his own accord.

However, when Leakey's own continuing research revealed rampant inconsistencies and reversibilities over time, later in life he broke ranks with the same wisdom he had created. At the end of his life he was arguing that the *Australopithecus* could not have directly given rise to *Homo erectus,* which gave rise to *Homo sapiens.* He said that though its overall size was certainly much smaller, the *Australopithecus africanus* skull was thin, high-crested, and delicate, more like a human being, while the *Homo erectus* and *Homo Neanderthalis* skulls were thick, low-domed, and stocky, more like an ape.

Therefore, Leakey could not support the theory that the road to *Homo sapiens* ever went through *Homo erectus* or *Homo neanderthalis*— seeing them both as evolutionary dead-ends belonging in their own taxon. Instead he maintained that his finds of *Australopithecus africanus* somehow vaulted directly into the human race, though there was no way to explain how a three-foot *Australopithecus africanus* morphed into the six-foot *Homo sapiens* in one 4-million-year stride. But when you have to stick to the fossil evidence, what else are you going to do?

Paleoanthropologists with Doubts

Louis Leakey's son Richard, who became a famous paleoanthropologist in his own right, made a comment about one of his own finds that had too large a brain and wrong facial features for the supposed 2.9-million-year-old stratum in which it was found. He said,

Either we toss out this skull, or we toss out our theories of early man. It simply fits no models of human beginning.

In fact, you could call it a family affair because Louis Leakey's wife, Mary, who worked both with and independent of her husband, said,

In the present state of our knowledge, I do not believe it is possible to fit the known hominid fossils into a reliable pattern.

To this you could add the words of David Pilbeam, director of Harvard's Peabody Museum and coauthor of the prestigious *Cambridge Encyclopedia of Human Evolution:*

There is no clear-cut and inexorable pathway from ape to human being.

The fossil record has been elastic enough...to accommodate almost any story. [Presumably including his own.]

But as Yale often answers Harvard, Yale Professor of Biology Keith Thomson drives the nail home by saying,

There is circularity in the approach that first assumes some sort of evolutionary relatedness and then assembles a pattern of relations from which to argue that relatedness must be true. This interplay of data and interpretation is the Achilles' heel of the second meaning [that is, human descent] of evolution.

Well said.

All these problems are further exacerbated by today's modern research and comparison techniques, such as DNA analysis. One by one, each species of "caveman" keeps being dismissed as an ancestor of *Homo sapiens*—leaving us with no ancestors even in the eyes of paleoanthropologists. It seems the only hope a Darwinist has these days is an "appeal to future evidence."

Reason 4: They don't all fit. If you believe humans evolved by natural processes, you must decide what to do with other species who do not fit your mold. For example, what do you do with two other supposed members of our generus Homo, the *Homo boisei* and the *Homo robustus?* Since they are said to be bigger than the *Australopithecus africanus* but smaller than the *Homo erectus,* shouldn't they take their rightful place in the evolutionary line? Sorry, but those problems with lack of continuity and constant reversibility have relegated *Homo boisei* and *Homo robustus* to a dead-end branch on the human evolutionary tree.

But what of *Homo sapiens* (archaic)? Do you, like me, have a junk drawer in your kitchen—the graveyard for old pens and pencils, nuts and bolts, rubber bands, batteries, a tool or two—you name it? Such was the incredible role of the designation *Homo sapiens* (archaic). Even with the general freedom paleoanthropologists have to place new hominid fossils in the slots of their convenience, there are still specimens so difficult to place that they have no home, no matter how much you fold, spindle, or mutilate them.

For some time, the term *Homo sapiens* (archaic) was the hominid evolutionary junk drawer. During the 1980s, the designation *archaic* was assigned to identify hominid species between Neanderthals and modern man that looked fully human but lived too long ago to fit the theory. How far back for an *archaic?* The designation was used to identify specimens all up and down the 4-million-year range—rare specimens that appeared fully human and therefore could not be grouped with their contemporaries. But since the classification was getting ridiculously bloated with so many unexplainable specimens, *Homo sapiens* (archaic) has been mostly—but of course not completely—abandoned.

As a specific example, paleoanthropology's most *intentionally unheralded* ex-archaic is the lower portion of a humerus (upper arm bone) found in 1965 near the town of Kanapoi in Kenya by Brian Patterson of Harvard. Affectionately known as KP 271, this bone has been dated at 4.5 million years ago. However, so human was the bone in appearance that its oddity couldn't be dismissed. Therefore, the bone was subjected to multivariate computer analysis that compared it to the upper arm of a chimp, a *Homo robustus,* and a modern human.

Seven different measurements confirmed that the Kanapoi bone most clearly resembled the human sample.

But in a classic case of preconceptual thinking, Patterson still concluded the bone must be *Australopithecus africanus* because, since the *lower* portion of an unrelated *africanus* humerus in his possession was more humanlike, the upper portion of the Kanapoi fragment must be *africanus* also. In hopes of confirmation, the bone was sent to renowned expert Henry McHenry at the University of California, and his results were that KP 271 of 4.5 million years ago was indistinguishable from modern humans.

With these findings in hand, Patterson's partner, W.W. Howells, issued the definitive statement. He said,

> We suggested that it might represent *Australopithecus* because at that time allocation to Homo would seem preposterous, although it would be the correct one without the *time element* [emphasis mine].

Did you catch that? Howells basically said the bone fragment KP 271 looks human, was stringently tested as human, and should be called human—but we will call it *australopithecus* because it didn't have the good sense to show up at the proper date. And such is what happens when you have decided beforehand that in the board game of Clue, Colonel Mustard was the perpetrator. So you massage the evidence until it fits where needed, including dropping into our junk-drawer classification of *archaic* when its convenience no longer matches its credibility.

Reason 5: Where are the transitions? I'll conclude with one final glaring problem, that of overlap of species. If you don't check any other resource, please dig up the *National Geographic* issues of November 1985 and March 1996. In the November 1985 issue, *NG* included a sweeping chart showing *Australopithecus afarensis* (4 mya) becoming *Australopithecus africanus* (3 mya) in about one million years of time. The curved line connecting them, and the changing blend of color in the lines, certainly gave the impression that the change was gradual, in finest Darwinian tradition. Then the chart shows *Australopithecus africanus* slowly becoming *Australopithecus robustus* and *Australopithecus boisei*, who then became extinct (2 mya).

But about this same time, *Australopithecus africanus* also transformed into *Homo habilis* (1.5 mya), who became *Homo erectus* (1 mya), who became *Homo sapiens* (archaic) (500 tya), who became *Homo sapiens* (Neanderthal) (250 tya), who became *Homo sapiens* (modern). Very nice, very convincing, complete with color sketches of what this progression of ape-men certainly looked like. (Read the other pages in this article that depict the ape-man's social groupings and lifestyles and you will see the unlimited power of the imagination.)

But the real eye-opener is to compare this diagram with another hominid lineage chart from the March 1996 issue of *NG*. The tremendous difference is that the second chart *does not use curved lines*. The linear bars in the newer issue certainly imply that instead of advancing gradually, these species *suddenly appeared* in some general form and, after their tenure, *suddenly disappeared* with equal abruptness.

Why this change away from Darwinistic gradualism? To stay true to the general fossil record, of course, which repeatedly gives us immutable species with no transitional forms. But then, how do you account for the transitions? "Hopeful monsters" again, a theory with no basis in fact?* And another critical difference from the 1985 chart to the 1996 chart is that the linear bars overlap, implying that as many as three of these species inhabited the Earth *at the same time*. This is difficult to explain in "survival of the fittest" terms, as it also confounds any reasonable time scale. Here is one of many infamous examples.

Consider the story of Java Man, a *Homo erectus* specimen found by Eugene Dubois. In 1891 Dubois found a skullcap (just the top of a skull) along Indonesia's Solo River that he considered neither ape nor human. A year later, in the same geologic deposit Dubois found a thighbone 50 feet away, very *Homo sapiens* in construction, that he maintained from that time forward belonged to the owner of the skullcap.

And here is the very typical riddle that has no solution. If the skullcap is indeed very old and the two bones indeed come from

---

* See *Reclaiming Science from Darwinism*, chapter 23, "Hopeful Monsters and Punctuated Equilibrium."

the same individual, it blurs the lines of demarcation between a 100 percent *Homo erectus* and a 100 percent *Homo sapiens*. If they come from different individuals, it blurs the lines of time boundaries, because radiometric dating shows them to be contemporaries.

In like manner, paleoanthropologists state *Homo erectus* generally became extinct around 300,000 years ago. "Generally" must be applied here because while that time frame nicely fits most specimens, what do you do with over 50 *Homo erectus* fossils that researchers themselves date as recently as 12,000 years ago? One of these even has an independent date of 6000 BC, putting a totally underdeveloped ape-man on the doorstep of the Sumerian, Egyptian, and Israelite cultures.

There's one additional bizarre hominid example of which evolutionists do not speak, which was written about by Jack Cuozzo in his book *Buried Alive: The Untold Story About Neanderthal Man* (Master Books, 1998). Besides having excellent diagrams and photographs, the book recounts the intense resistance Dr. Cuozzo, a highly accomplished orthodontist (and also a creationist), faced as he petitioned for permission to study Neanderthal skulls in European museums. Despite the limited access he was granted—access quickly removed when his faith became known—he was able to use sophisticated X-rays and other cranial/dental measurement tools to analyze and compare some Neanderthal skulls to those of modern man.

Certainly a practicing orthodontist is not an expert at locating, removing, and classifying hominid bones, as is a paleoanthropologist. But neither is a paleoanthropologist an expert at correct jaw placement and dental age, as is an orthodontist. Dr. Cuozzo backed up his analyses with drawings and measurements, and the results were that he found frequent improper combining of nonrelated facial bone fragments in an attempt to build a larger skull. Furthermore, he said he recognized what had to be *intentional* alteration of other dental factors, such as filing teeth and extending jaws with plastiform to give the remains a more humanlike appearance.

Why would someone fall into unintentional or even intentional deception? My guess is to support one pet evolutionary theory or another because, once again, the actual evidence never provides continuity. Expertise in one field does not automatically grant expertise in another. In fact, your ego in your status, combined with your need to prove a preconceived hypothesis, may make you even more unscientific than the average person in another field. I like commentator Lowell Ponte's observation:

> Outside their narrow field of expertise, scientists are often no wiser than the drunk at the end of the bar in your local saloon. In fact they are often more foolish than this drunk, because with the power of science, commissars often become intoxicated with the notion that knowledge and intellect in one field empowers them to speak with the authority of gods in all fields.

Returning to Dr. Cuozzo, he reports that his most startling discovery came when he was allowed to examine the Broken Hill Neanderthal skull from Zambia, now in London's British Museum of Natural History. This skull, found over 50 feet down in a lead/zinc mine and dated at 200,000 years old, had two exactly aligned holes that were consistent only with a bullet injury. The rims of the entry aperture were perfectly and precisely rounded and smooth, and the exit aperture was expanded from the inside. The preserved dual holes were not at all consistent with ancient and fragile dried bone, which would disintegrate when shot by a modern-day firearm, and the bone flanges around the holes showed no sign of healing. Forensics would only support that this supposed 200,000-year-old individual was shot with a modern bullet, but if this holds true, what a bizarre case of species overlap!

Well, I never saw those bullet holes, but let me cover a different case of hominid overlap nobody can dismiss. It's the amazing mystery of the Australian Aborigines, who, despite their looks, are every bit as much *Homo sapiens* as you and I.

If you go back to the above migration map, you will see the estimate that Aborigine culture goes back some 50,000 years. However, some researchers say 100,000 years is a better estimate. That makes them significantly older than any American Indian tribes at 15,000 years, and adds perspective to the less than 2000 years of Mayan, Aztec, and Inca cultures. And how does the map say Aborigines got to the land down under? By migrating from Southeast Asia, which ties them to Java Man up there in Indonesia.

And the problems with this? First of all, there are no other primates indigenous to Australia—not a single monkey or ape lives on that continent from which humans could evolve. That means a boat journey, right? But the Australian continent is about 1000 ocean miles from the nearest significant landmass, and 4000 miles from Southeast Asia, where the closest extinct hominid ancestors, like Java Man, have been found. For evolution, the only possible answer is an amazing maritime journey some 50,000 to 100,000 years ago by *Homo erectus* or *Homo neanderthalis*—species science would say were totally incapable of such travels. And to make such a supposition even more outlandish, there is no fossil evidence on any Pacific islands in the proximity that they were used as springboards or rest stops for Aboriginal ancestors en route.

Consider this. If the Aborigines did get to Australia by boat, they managed a journey comparable to Leif Erikson's—but about 49,000 years earlier. Then upon arrival in Australia, they instantly forgot everything they knew about navigation, travel, and construction (woodworking, canvas, ropes, and so on), and went back to the most primitive of lifestyles, such as using urine as a food preservative. Nonsense. In an evolutionary sense, there is no answer for the existence of Aborigines.

<hr />

To close this chapter, here is a summary of the five reasons why the natural evolution of monkey-to-man will always be Darwinism's weakest link in the hope to circumvent the work of God.

- *Reason 1*—The amount of hominid fossil evidence is hopelessly skewed so as to not provide evidence where it is needed most. Furthermore, the very small populations of hominids in their supposed clans do not support the possibility for random genetic change, or the long-term survivability of such vulnerable species.
- *Reason 2*—It is impossible to effectively group hominid

fossils worldwide by any consistent set of traits. From body plans to lifestyles, specific features are scattered all over the map. There is no smooth transitional arrangement of species anywhere.

• *Reason 3*—The theory of human migration out of Africa immediately collapses under examination. There is no continuity along the only available pathways, and reversibility of development is so rampant that paleoanthropologists only increasingly bemoan the unsolvable puzzles.

• *Reason 4*—The general hypothesis of human development is peppered with so many exceptions that you need a "junk drawer" for all the species in incorrect places and time periods.

• *Reason 5*—The overlap of different species living at the same time is unexplainable, and attempts to make them look sequential are flimsy at best. The existence of species like the Aborigines shows there is no gradual human development whatsoever. Yet in desperation to prove their case, Darwinists continually resort to wild speculations and creative imaginings, as well as unintentional and intentional deceptions, to try to prove monkey-to-man.

9

MORE ABOUT HUMAN EVOLUTION

New Discoveries, New Confusion

Ever since the beginning of the theory that primates could evolve naturally, the "who, what, when, where, how," and even "why," have never added up, and each new find makes it more obvious.

Let me return to the *National Geographic* August 2002 issue and its cover article, which I used to open the previous chapter. Here are some more details from the story "The First Pioneer?—A New Find Shakes the Family Tree." The specimens under study included a near complete hominid skull and many other supporting skull and bone fragments. The creature of the one nearly complete skull is termed a *Homo habilis* by the article's author, Rick Gore, based on its smaller cranial capacity, enlarged canine teeth, shorter stature, and longer arms. In the fairy tale of sequential development, this should date the fossil between 2.4 mya and 1.6 mya, in line with the other *Homo habilis* specimens found in Africa before *Homo erectus* was said to have appeared on the world stage.

Unfortunately, as I mentioned earlier, the bones were unearthed beneath a village called Dmanisi in the Caucasus region of Georgia. This violates paleoanthropology's long-standing belief that hominid migration out of Africa was not possible until *Homo erectus* evolved—with the size, strength, intelligence, and populations necessary to make the arduous journey from Africa, and then to the rest of the world. To quote the article, "It looks like the first people out of Africa came out with a pea brain," which begs the question, "How did such stupid creatures make it that far?"

The article also mentioned thousands of tool fragments at the site so you have to add, "How did such stupid creatures get smart enough to make tools?" Then the author observes—according to the migration map—that this should be the species that moved on to Asia as *Homo erectus*. Unfortunately, many *Homo erectus* finds in Asia show they apparently forgot how to use tools, so add another question: "How did creatures with bigger brains suddenly get stupid again?" Finally, the rest of the text mentions more reversals and inconsistencies, and then the exasperated scientist's quote, "They ought to put it back in the ground." Really, we need to have some sympathy for people in this line of work.

Is Any Help on the Horizon?

Have any more recent finds helped the situation? A few years back, yet another new hominid discovery was making the news. The new hominid fossil sample was again found in Africa, this time in the country of Chad, where a single skull was unearthed. The team of French and Chadian scientists were so convinced of the uniqueness of their discovery that they assigned it to a new genus other than *Australopithecus* or *Homo*, calling it *Sahelanthropus tchadensis*. The creature was also given a nickname, as many are—"Toumai," meaning "hope of life." The head of the research team, Michel Brunet, dates the fossil at 7 mya, earlier in the Pliocene epoch than any previous find.

The trouble is, the general features and dimensions of the skull are consistent with *Homo habilis*, normally dated about 2 mya. If all facts are true, this would make Toumai *superior* in development to the most celebrated hominid fossil of all—the near complete *Australopithecus afarensis* skeleton nicknamed "Lucy," shown in virtually every biology book. Since Lucy's 1973 discovery in Ethiopia by Donald Johanson, this 3.3-million-year-old, three-and-a-half-foot-tall female specimen has been considered by many to be the "genetic mother" of the human race—sort of a Darwinistic "Eve" if you will. So if Lucy is the genetic "mother" of all humans, and Toumai the genetic "son," it's a pretty good trick to have an ancestor twice as old look more like a descendent twice as young.

In commenting on Toumai, biochemist Dr. Fazale Rana aptly compares the sudden appearance of hominids with the equally perplexing Cambrian Explosion several times elsewhere in this book. Tongue in cheek, Rana refers to our family tree as not even a bush, but more of a "lawn." But if you insist that some sort of hominid "tree" of sequential development exists, be sure that on your tree...

1. None of the branches have any curves but spread out at ninety-degree angles like stair-steps.

2. Branches from different species of trees are on the same trunk.

3. Some of the branches are not connected to the trunk, but hang in thin air.

4. At least three branches of mixed-up sizes lie right on top of each other.

5. Other branches go back and forth many times in diameter, from fat to skinny to fat again, as they go outward.

6. Some branches are way too skinny to support the weight at the end.

7. Lastly, you have a separate tree trunk on the side to "pigeonhole" branches more puzzling than those in the first six conditions.

Please reread these seven observations, for this is really the heart of my argument. I'm making a powerful statement here by saying there is no way you can sequence the hominid fossil evidence used to support the monkey-to-man theory.

And you know what? Though they would never admit it, the most prominent names in paleoanthropology agree with me in principle. I've already cited many experts who bemoan the lack of hominid continuity, but I've saved the best for last. There is no more revered or active research site on human evolution than the Max Planck Institute for Evolutionary Anthropology in Leipzig, Germany. One of its leading scientists, Svante Paabo, is currently working to sequence the entire genome for the Neanderthal people, much as was done for chemistry of human inheritance a few years back.

The latter project was difficult enough—trying to identify the roughly 3 billion nitrogenous base pairs that make up our DNA. However, finding enough usable Neanderthal DNA was a daunting task in its own right. For instance, in 60 Neanderthal bone samples Paabo could extract usable DNA from only two, and the contamination of foreign DNA from fungi, bacteria, and even previous human handlers was a constant problem. But if the project is ever completed, you can bet the similarity between Neanderthal and human DNA will be much closer than the 1.23 percent variation currently reported by the Institute as the difference between chimpanzee and human DNA.

But here's the rub. About ten years earlier Paabo completed a study of Neanderthal and human mitochondrial DNA only. In 1996 he reported what is now generally accepted:

> Neanderthals lie on a separate branch of the human family
> tree, and are not our direct ancestors.

Doesn't that raise a huge red flag? It's amazing for me to hear scientists say that the creature considered closest to us did not give rise to us, and then not feel obligated to tell us who—or what—did. To me it's like 1) believing that firearms most definitely evolved (without any intelligent assistance, of course); 2) saying that research indicates the automatic pistol is not related in origin to the automatic rifle; 3) having no alternative explanation for the origin of the automatic pistol from any other more primitive weapon forms; 4) still believing that firearm evolution happened through blind luck; and 5) encouraging others to accept something that has no scientific or historical basis. Yes, human evolution is that badly represented by most Darwinists I know.

What Do Fossils Really Tell Us?

Let me briefly mention a hominid fossil find generating much attention as I type these words. In the *National Geographic*'s November 2006 issue, yet another "monkey man" (actually a female) graces the cover.* The hominid article is titled "Origin of Childhood" and is about another *Australopithecus afarensis,* dubbed "Dikika" after the hill where it was found next to the Awash River in Ethiopia—a scant six miles away from the site of Lucy's discovery. The uniqueness of this find was that it contained a complete skull and torso, along with nearly a whole leg and some fingers, which is remarkable considering how soon bones unattached by cartilage easily get scattered over time. And the reason the find is causing such a stir is because the skull is obviously a baby girl's, approximately three years old according to its baby teeth.

But before we call evolution true, just know that if Dikika is authentic, it's still just a youthful sample of Lucy and another male (skull only) *Australopithecus afarensis* found in the same area. This means there is no new information any more unique than what a human baby would provide on a human adult. And there is no rationale to try to rewrite human evolutionary history, which will always be in complete collapse anyway.

However, the Dikika baby *did* lead evolutionary expert Dean Falk to make an impressive observation. He basically said the ultracute baby might have accelerated human speech development by eliciting the language of "motherese" from its caretakers. Later in the article, author Christopher Sloan observed that Dikika's bigger brain had to be a caloric "gas hog," which required her kind to need more protein. Then Sloan hypothesized that this need for extra protein forced the abandonment of an exclusive vegetarian diet. This in turn required abandoning the trees, which led to standing upright, which led to hunting for meat, which required the invention of tools, which led

---

* I am not intentionally picking on this publication. It's just that *NG*'s bias causes them to do a major layout on nearly every hominid fossil discovery. And with their great journalistic style they always add extensive details—the specificity of which always makes the flaws of evolution stand out starkly. (Their zeal to underwrite Darwinism can further be seen in the exact same issue in another article titled "A Fin is a Limb is a Wing" on how fortuitous fish accidents eventually became better accidents in amphibians, reptiles, birds, and mammals. It's as if *NG* is saying, "Yes, Virginia, Santa Claus is an accident, and so are you."

to more protein in the diet, which led to bigger brains, which led to more inventions, which led to bigger brains...and as the author said, "The rest is history."

But this is just fairy-tale history to my mind, and Falk, Sloan, and anyone else who buys this description should read about Ernst Mayr's views later in this book (chapter 15). These conclusions are nothing more than highly speculative narratives, and narratives that are ridiculously Lamarckian at that.*

Don't get me wrong, Dikika is a cool discovery. But it would also be *very* cool to find that legendary brand-new 1967 Corvette with less than 1000 miles on it. You know, the one hidden in the grandmother's shed by the grandson, who then left for the army but, sadly, was killed in Vietnam. But it still wouldn't give you any new information about Corvettes.

More Problem Fossils

Let me say I do accept these hominid fossils according to their approximate body features and even the millions of years of age assigned them. But again, this is only the beginning of the problems, not the end.† Moreover, my acceptance comes with a big proviso because outright mistakes and intentional frauds exist among these 5500 samples we have.

Do a little research on the Nebraska Man fiasco of 1922. In this story, a single tooth gave rise to a whole new genus of ancient hominids called *Hesperopithecus*. The *Illustrated London News* offered full-body drawings, picturing these remarkable ape-men hunting in a Stone-Age backdrop. The excitement of "missing links" in North America reigned for several months—until the tooth was properly identified as that of a wild pig.

Or how about, much more recently, the "Feathers for T-Rex?" article in *National Geographic*'s November 1999 issue? (Though this is not a tale of a supposed hominid fossil, the story is very instructive—and cautionary.) Here Chris Sloan, the same author who wrote

---

* Read about Jean-Baptiste Lamarck in chapter 10.

† See *Reclaiming Science from Darwinism*, chapter 14, "How Old Is the Earth?"

the Dikika article, announced to the world that a feathered relative of the dinosaur therapod family had been found, China's *Archaeoraptor liaoningensis*. (*Therapod* is the dinosaur body style of walking on big hind legs, freeing the front limbs for other tasks—perhaps as in flight for a developing chicken.) Sloan further proclaimed, "We can now say that birds are therapods just as confidently as we say that humans are mammals." And to prove it, artist Michael Skrepnick drew us a picture of a fuzzy-feathered baby T-Rex under mama's watchful eye. Cute.

Unfortunately, the specimen turned out to be a composite of ancient *and* modern bones found in an excavation pit long used by local chicken farmers for the disposal of dead bird bodies. Needless to say, the article became an instant embarrassment. To *National Geographic*'s credit, it did print a correction of sorts four months later in its March 2000 issue, but in my view it was no more than a weak admission of rushing to judgment. The *NG* still felt the find *could* have been fully authenticated with a little more research—though it never was. This cloak-and-dagger story at the highest professional level had many twists and turns, but the summary of Storrs L. Olson, Bird Curator for the Smithsonian Institution, can probably be trusted: "*National Geographic* has reached an all-time low for engaging in sensationalistic, unsubstantiated, tabloid journalism."

Hominid Hoax

Today's venerated hominid evidence may even contain another outright hoax like the 1912 Piltdown Man, a deception that stood for over 40 years. The Piltdown Man, scientifically named *Eoanthropus dawsoni*, was a hominid discovery once held in highest esteem. Unfortunately, it turned out to be a modern human skull intentionally fitted with a modified orangutan jaw and placed in an English quarry where admission was sold to hunt for fossils. The trickster was never identified.

Are there other errors like this among those 5000-plus hominid specimens? I'd place money on it. But we shall never know, because these fossils are tightly controlled in the many separate locations where they are housed. Attempts are not made to get them together for comparison, because linear comparisons are futile. And permission to examine them on site by independent researchers is a near impossibility, especially if they suspect you are some sort of "designer in sheep's clothing"—in which case you would automatically be disqualified.

A Trail Going the Wrong Way

As has been stated previously, trying to follow any continuous trail of hominid development is similarly exhausting and fruitless as trying to trace your home computer step-by-step back to the MITS Altair 8800. The bottom-line truth is that the fossil record, hominid or otherwise, does not support either Darwin's phyletic gradualism or Neo-Darwinism's punctuated equilibrium, the only two games in town. Despite the excitement, each new find leads evolution yet further away from any cogent "self-made" explanation. So why is the belief that monkeys turned into man not abandoned?

You must also view with a critical eye even the most professional sources if they have an obvious ax to grind against any opposing theories, like Intelligent Design. Using one final *National Geographic* example, check out their April 2003 issue. The cover story—once again a Darwinistic message right up front—is titled "The Rise of Mammals." This highly imaginative piece, in the finest *NG* tradition, offers only one true fossil and three reconstructions from fragments. But it does include 22 different drawings, impeccably citing the names of the contributing artists in the notable absence of contributing paleontologists.

Why does such an otherwise fine publication make mistake after mistake? Once again, the fault is in assuming from the get-go that fossils support any type of natural transitional advancement from apes to humans, when they do just the opposite.

And there are more "imaginative" examples than this. Right now I'm staring at a short article by Associated Press writer Matt Crenson. It covers a chimpanzee/human genetic study done by the Broad Institute of MIT and Harvard that analyzed approximately 800 times more DNA codes than earlier efforts. The article's title is "DNA Study Uncovers Sexual Link of Chimps and Man—Then a Divorce."

Let me just give you the short version of the article. By comparing many corresponding sections of their genetic codes, the researchers conclude that chimp and human progenitors first diverged from a common ancestor (never identified) about 10 million years ago and evolved independently for a brief period. But then about 6 million years ago, the two cohabitated for a short time just before both their individual ancestral lines went extinct. However, the sexual union produced a hybrid chimp/human that later branched yet again to produce today's chimps and humans. If this article wasn't identified as a product of MIT and Harvard, I'd guess it came from a supermarket tabloid under the title of "Chimps and Humans Divorce, Remarry and Have Children, Parents Go Extinct, Children Become New Chimps and Humans."

I'm sure this research is based on the most sophisticated techniques done under the most stringent controls. I'm also completely confident it's a real study with real findings. Why? Because as the newscasters often say about bizarre stories on TV, "You can't make this stuff up." What's more, it's commendable that after comparing several analogous segments of chimp and human genes (instead of analyzing both genomes in general), the team had the integrity to report their findings according to their experimental design.

However, do these researchers really think this is how humans evolved down through history to give them their great-great-grandfathers? Or did J.S. Jones and S. Rouhani, writing in the magazine *Nature*, say it perfectly with these words:

> The human fossil record is no exception to the general rule that the main lesson to be learned from paleontology is that evolution always takes place somewhere else.

In the end, there is only one answer to the hominid fossil record that makes sense at all. It's the same answer that clarifies every perplexity encountered with Darwinism. The "Giver of Information" began His work around 13.7 billion years ago, and has obviously remained active even in these last 5 million years introducing new hominid changes.

Allowing a Designer solves the riddle of the fine-tuned big bang, puts closure to the perfect settling of our galaxy, solar system, and planet, dots the "i" and crosses the "t" in complexity of chemicals, allows for the first metabolic cell, introduces new species during punctuation and maintains them during equilibrium, monitors the success of the impressive mammals—especially the ones walking upright—and, as the crowning achievement, places an eternal spirit in a biological pair in a pristine garden.

Along with that, an omnipotent God removes all the barriers imposed by mathematical probabilities. If my opening analogy still holds, each new unit, be it computer or hominid, is introduced by the intentional and intelligent action of its designer/Designer. I'm positive accepting an omnipotent God as the answer is a difficult big single step. But how much more infinitely difficult are the number of impossible smaller steps in the staircase of natural evolution?

Out of the Mouths of Babes...

I was once asked to speak to a bunch of second- to fourth-grade students about the differences between God's version of creation and man's version of evolution. First I tried to explain to all these fresh and eager seven-to-nine-year-old faces how some people think that monkeys slowly turned into us over time by first becoming "cavemen." (Luckily, I had those insurance commercials to use as examples—the ones where Neanderthals have a hard time getting service in a restaurant though they are wearing ties.)

I had barely broached the subject when the kids stopped me and asked almost in one voice, "What happened to the cavemen? Why aren't they still around? The monkeys are still here—why did the cavemen have to go away if they were better than monkeys?" You have to admire the simplicity of their thinking. But you know what? From the youth to the elderly, everyone eventually asks this same type of question: "Why did prehistoric hominids all go extinct before we arrived, while less-fit monkeys and apes survived?"

Extend, if you will, the children's thinking here. Have you ever heard it suggested that, upon his arrival (however that came about), modern man decided to wage war on his more primitive ancestors and wipe them out? There's no evidence, documentation, or record of that anywhere. So why aren't the TV-ad cavemen still around?

Did extinction perhaps finally happen by natural means? Then, as I've suggested before, hominids were amazingly lucky in their tenuous lives to hang by a thread for millions of years until modern humans arrived. But did they then look at the potential competition and just throw in the towel? Once more, it's a puzzle with no suitable evolutionary answer.

10

VESTIGIAL STRUCTURES
AND BEHAVIORS

Another Dead-End Argument

The previous chapter basically said that because there is no continuity in the hominid fossil record, there can be no coherent scientific theory of hominid evolution. However, there is one other quasi-scientific approach repeatedly used to try to directly connect us to those mysterious "monkey men."

———

Here is a sight to which people of all ages can relate. Your indoor family dog, which lives primarily a safe life is about to bed down for the night in his favorite basket with the soft cushion. But as he steps into the basket, he suddenly starts doing circles as if chasing his tail. Then just as suddenly, the revolutions stop, and with one last satisfying stretch, he curls up in quiet repose.

Strange as it may seem, an activity such as your dog's bedtime ritual is often used as an argument favoring natural evolution. The basis of the argument is rooted the title of this chapter—"Vestigial Behaviors and Structures." Here's a dictionary definition of *vestigial.*

A mark, trace, or visible evidence of a condition or practice which is no longer present or has lost its use.

You see, even if the dog looks like a little white powder puff with its rhinestone collar and painted toenails, and even if it's so afraid that it trembles every time you touch it, Darwinists say it has still descended by modification from an aggressive and savage wild canine species. (In this case, the process producing the frizzy dog is not natural selection, but artificial selection, where people instead of nature have selected the traits most preferred.) Therefore, before bedding down, this powder puff is still programmed as a wild dog to 1) run in circles to flatten the vegetation for the comfort of a softer bed, and 2) while circling, check for rocks and thorns, or worse, anthills and snake holes.

Returning to the definition of vestigial, Darwinists say this visible practice of circling, once very necessary but now certainly no longer needed, is still programmed in the animal's genes. Therefore, this is proof that the dog originated from wild ancestry by a combination of natural and artificial processes. Furthermore, since this highly bred dog was produced—or created, if you must—by humans through artificial selection in a few hundred years, then nature can certainly create life and finally mammals given millions and millions of years.

Looking at Humans

Now on to mammal humans. Darwinists say our bodies *and* our behaviors are a veritable treasure trove of vestiges left over from prehistoric times. One of the best known of these is body hair on *Homo sapiens.* Again, you see, we have descended from monkeys and chimps. But over the span of a very few million years, we have invented several ways to protect ourselves from heat loss. We have learned to make clothes for warmth, find shelter under lean-tos or in caves, and harness fire. The obvious result is that we are now adept at conserving body heat—and total body hair, not being needed, is going away. Call it similar to unused muscles we all know will atrophy if not exercised.

And there's more proof. Goose bumps have also been cited as evidence of our lost need for hair. Back when we were giving up swinging in trees to walk upright on the flatlands, we still needed to make our hair stand on end to fluff up our body covering for insulation. Or when we were scared or under attack, we needed to make ourselves look larger than life by our hair follicles erecting our fur, much as a cat's back fur rises up when it is startled. Well, insulation and security are no longer the problems they once were, but our skin still crawls in response.

So to see hominid body hair from a Darwinist perspective, imagine human history in rewind. As time goes backward, the amount of hair on our ancestors would slowly increase until we have fully donned monkey pelts. Conversely, if you could fast-forward another half-million years or so, current patterns of baldness would likely render both males and females completely hairless head to toe.

For many Darwinists vestiges constitute a very powerful point. In fact, the explanations for the spinning dog as a vestigial behavior, and receding hair as a vestigial structure, may seem unassailable.

And the notion pops up everywhere. In the popular South Beach Diet books, author Arthur Agatston, M.D., says back when we were hunters-gatherers, we were forced to eat the very healthy food items that today's diets now lack. For example, as cavemen the bulk of our diet had to be high-fiber roughage like coarse vegetables, seeded fruits, and grains, and if we did get meat, it was lean wild game, not cholesterol-laden corn-fed beef.

Furthermore, with respect to fats, salts, and sweets, we became genetically programmed not only to crave these rare dietary inclusions, but to overindulge so as to *store* them against the threat of scarcity. And now, unfortunately, the craving still exists for the fats, salts, and sweets with which snacks and fast food now so obligingly overload us. (Dr. Agatston promotes a name for what he views as our genetic predisposition to still eat like we were swinging from trees. He calls it "The Thrifty Gene Theory.")

At first glance all this makes a lot of sense, especially if you add the following vestigial structures and behaviors that have always generated great discussion.

Vestigial Structures

- rudimentary pelvic bones and leg spurs in some whales and snakes that perhaps were once fully functional legs

- underdeveloped wings on ostriches and other flightless birds

- rudimentary eyes and lack of skin pigments on blind cave salamanders that live in total darkness

- bright colors and strong scents to attract insects on flowers of herbs, shrubs, and trees that no longer need such because they have become self-pollinating

- tails on various crustaceans (except on lobsters or crayfish, which obviously need them) that now serve no purpose and must be tucked under the carapace

- on an occasional human fetus, fine hair called *lanugo* first covering the entire body, but usually disappearing about the fifth or sixth month of gestation

- nipples on mammalian males

- smaller organs that often get infected because of modern-day limited use and therefore must be removed, such as appendixes, tonsils, gall bladders, and so on

- muscles that, though rotating ears for detection on most predators and prey, are also functional on some humans and most seals though not useful

- human intestinal length (a little over 20 feet), which is longer than necessary, but perhaps was essential when prehistoric diets contained so much roughage and little extractable nutrition

- a human coccyx, or tailbone, possibly representing the prehensile tail once needed by monkeys for grasping and climbing

- sexual scent attraction in humans, not essential as the pheromones for mating are in other animals such as mammals and insects

- human wisdom teeth which often need removal due to lack of service, perhaps not a factor when used in prehistoric times to crack seeds, chew rawhide, and grind roughage

Vestigial Behaviors

- play behavior in young domestic pets (for example, puppies playing tug-of-war as if tearing prey apart in pack situations, kittens playing "stalk and pounce," baby bunnies playing "dash and dodge," and young lambs playing "head butt"), perhaps once necessary skills to practice for an adult life in the wild

- domestic dogs living inside fences still using urine to mark their territory, possibly once essential to protect feeding and breeding territory in the wild

- domestic cats burying their waste, though there are no real enemies or prey from which it is necessary to hide their presence

- groups of modern humans in social situations still establishing pecking orders similar to fowls (for example, students in middle school) and often exhibiting behaviors of pack mentality typical of wolves and primates

- the modern human tendency toward grooming practices, perhaps similar to primates like chimps who comb each other's fur for burrs, parasites, and so on (a possible connection to today's women, who seem to take inordinate pleasure sitting in the beauty parlor chair having their hair "done," and today's men, many of whom like a good old-fashioned back scratch?)

- sporting contest of ground acquisition (football) and business practices (corporate takeovers), being reflective of tribal raids by prehistoric males to enlarge territory and obtain spoils

- perhaps echoing Darwin's theory of sexual selection, modern humans acting just like animals when they engage in courting rituals at school dances and singles bars, where women display their most attractive plumage and males their virility and prowess

- modern human females being generally more adept at making or supplying clothes, food, and other domestic needs once essential in prehistoric settings, and modern men being highly motivated to work with tools and hunt and fish, as if for sustenance

- modern human females tending to trade physical responsiveness in order to get emotional responsiveness from males, and males tending to trade the emotional to get the physical

Evaluating Vestiges

Concerning the last six bullets above, on human vestigial behaviors, volumes upon volumes have been written in the fields of social psychology and human sexuality. As a lifelong educator who constantly deals with "the vagaries of the human maturation process" (educationalese for having to deal with hormone-enraged students), I am intrigued by some parallels between the way we behave and the proposed behaviors of monkey-men.

To begin, there could be no formal marriage vows in prehistoric times, right? But perhaps there were mechanisms already in place to foster a "family" arrangement. For example, an australopithicine female like "Lucy," relatively unable to protect herself and provide for her offspring, would likely permit regular sexual advances from a male in hopes of allegiance. On the other hand, an australopithicine male, both able to protect and provide for himself, would still share regular time and resources with a female in return for sexual responsiveness. This would form a type of *pair bond,* which by association would also enhance the survivability of the female's children—and therefore the species in general.

I also understand that today the arrangement of females "trading sex for love" and males "trading love for sex" is still very much alive. For example, on prom night, for which they both prepared their finest courtship plumage, it's always the high school girl who says, "But do you love me?" And at that point, the high school boy would even chew aluminum foil if she asked him to in order to get the one thing he desires.

But the question is, have these behaviors been a direct evolutionary transference, and have all such vestiges been produced under the watchful eye of nobody—nothing but a random sorting process? Then if random, do these traits disqualify the involvement of God? First, though, some more examples of vestiges—other possible echoes of our hairy past.

Wouldn't you say a prehistoric female better at domestic abilities and devotion toward young was more likely to have her offspring survive than another female who wasn't? Makes sense. And if the prehistoric mother's daughters would tend to be as capable as she—which you would expect—this would strengthen the gene pool down through time. Therefore, some say evolution is the reason that women of today are more geared to matters of the home than are men—who are still busy driving their Flintstonesque pickups in search of new fishing and hunting spots.

Or how about a female who was more selective and exclusive about the breeding partner she chose than another female? Logic says she would experience more male fidelity and less rivalry, allowing her more individual success in raising children—which, by the way, would allow her entire clan more collective success down through time. In contrast, if a prehistoric male scattered his genes among as many females as possible, his activities were more favorable to enlarge his clan, also helping ensure the survival of the gene pool. Some Darwinists say this led to the general trend of fidelity in today's females and promiscuity in today's males.

Then add that the male *Australopithicus* had to outcompete other males for female attention, causing modern men to often fight for dominance of their local "harem" (as is also easily seen in today's big-game herds, like elk). But this fighting seldom leads to death, and is actually to the overall benefit of the clan/herd/society if the most virile male gets all the females he wants and is producing the majority of offspring.

The final outcome? Many Darwinists say remnants of this selection process *naturally* exist today, in that modern human females tend to be less competitive and more concerned about domestic stability, while modern human males are more competitive and less concerned about home life than careers, status, or possessions. And more than that, these differences actually enhance the survivability of our species over time. Finally, when you add the "wild" structures and behaviors mentioned in animals above, some see this whole concept as an evolutionary slam dunk.

Looking More Closely

Before you think there is nothing left to explain, consider these ideas. First of all, some of these structural vestiges do not support the above definition of "lost" use. For example, if you examine a human coccyx which supposedly once bore a tail, you will find it plays a vital role in balance for our upright stance. That is because it has important anchor points where tendons attach muscles, and evolution could not "further reduce" its size one bit without disastrous effects on our ability to move. Also, it is true we can live without wisdom teeth, tonsils, a gall bladder, and an appendix, but when they are healthy, they serve at least a supportive purpose.

More difficult to explain is the gradual disappearance of parts that actually would have been advantageous, sometimes extremely so, which is absolutely contrary to the theory of natural evolution. Paleobiologists are unified in saying snakes didn't grow legs and become lizards, but prehistoric lizards lost legs to become snakes. So did natural selection choose crawling on the belly over running on legs?

And of course, some ancient ostrich types didn't start out as nonflyers with no wings at all in the past and now have grown pitiful wings in the present that will eventually allow them to fly in the future. No, the present inadequate wings would have to be vestiges of formerly functional wings that are going away—not coming on. Therefore, some prehistoric bird had to begin giving up the tremendous advantage of flight as his wings shrank in size to finally render him a walking ostrich, which then developed running speed and stamina.

But does not natural selection favor improvements, not impediments? Not only that, these supposed transitional lizard and bird ancestors with shrinking legs and disappearing wings left absolutely no fossilized remains. The game of "subtraction" just doesn't automatically become "addition" that makes new and improved species.

Another justified observation is that the list of supposedly vestigial structures and behaviors has shrunk dramatically since the concept became understood. My two lists above took much investigation in order to get just more than a handful, and some of them are an admitted stretch. This is because science is continually finding important functions for what seemed trivial at first glance. The nuisance of nose hair? A nice "brush" for removing microscopic particles headed for the lungs. Fingernails—because we lost the claws typical of most mammals? I once had a Darwinistic student actually tell me fingernails *were* useless vestiges of former claws. So I asked him to trim his down to the absolute nub and keep them that way for a couple of weeks to see what life was like. He later admitted how often he was unable to pick up small objects, like loose change, so common in our lifestyle. (As a pitcher on our baseball team, I assume he also missed scratching himself in front of all those onlookers.)

Also, consider here that paleobiologists are unified in believing the vast majority of species ever to inhabit the planet have already become extinct—easily above 95 percent of all past life-forms, maybe as high as 99 percent. Perhaps the list of vestigial structures should be *growing* immensely larger instead of shrinking, as the fossil hunters provide us with more and more lost species that died bearing signs of their handicapping deprivations.

DNA Problems for Darwinian Views

Here is the biggest problem with using vestigial structures to support Darwinism, and it's a stab that truly goes to the heart of all the mechanisms touted in natural selection. Disappearing structures and behaviors assume that environmental factors have the ability to alter genetic codes. This has been found to be absolute balderdash. In promoting vestiges, Darwinists actually resurrect the theories of French biologist Jean-Baptiste de Lamarck, whose explanations from 1809 have since been found to be laughable. Lamarck said, among other things, that giraffes got long necks by stretching them to reach for leaves on tall trees, and then somehow these longer-necked giraffes passed this trait on to their offspring. (But go easy on Lamarck. He made these speculations way before anyone knew anything about the laws of inheritance and the DNA molecule.)

Though the Darwinists can't seem to see it, they use the same reasoning in the case of whales and snakes losing legs, ostriches losing wings, cave salamanders going blind and, of course, humans losing hair. Using that last example as typical of the entire thought pattern, Darwinists assume that when cavemen started wearing animal furs, standing close to fires, and living in shelters, the extra warmth somehow changed their DNA patterns to produce less hair. And just as with the giraffes, the lessened need for hair was then passed on genetically to their offspring—who somehow altered their DNA to produce even less hair in the next generation.

Applying this to something like whales losing their legs makes the theory appear even more ridiculous. On the way to leg disappearance, the proper Darwinian reasoning is that the seas were once filled with whale progenitors having DNA coding for all sorts of different leg lengths.* Now with all these leg lengths to choose from, nature selected in favor of those that had shorter femurs that were less of a handicap in the water, especially ones that had a weird flipperlike mutation. I guess the rest either went back on land or went extinct because they couldn't compete.

Then another round of mutations happened that left some whales with femurs now subcutaneous, where they would produce no water drag at all. Meanwhile, evolving flippers also mutated into full-sized flukes. The proto-whales with shorter legs and partial flippers, who used to have an advantage, are now in turn selected for extinction. And voilà—all the competitors in the sea have disappeared, and we have whales! This is the Darwinian method of descent if environment can't directly alter genes—which it can't.

The first piece of unreality here is that nature has to use this process to produce not just one whale species, but approximately 70 of today's various whales, dolphins, and porpoises. That means unless seawater changes genes, a burgeoning and assorted number of these large prehistoric mammals once had to cram the oceans with their biomass until several waves of change finally "selected" the 70 nature wanted for survival. The second piece of unreality is that all this change had to

---

* This view of the oceans once having multilegged life is perfectly in line with evolutionary thinking because water mammals have to come from land mammals first, and all land mammals have legs of various lengths. The only alternative is to have whales evolving directly from fish—a connection that even most kids know doesn't exist.

happen in just a few small ticks of the evolutionary time clock, whales being one of the very last arrivals before hominids themselves. And the final and ongoing unreality is, there exists no supporting evidence from paleontology for all the intermediate species that certainly should have lived and died.

Therefore, when you encounter any such arguments for vestigial structures, or any type of evolutionary argument where natural change is assumed, you will catch a whiff of Lamarckianism. And you will recognize the rank odor as soon as the person implies—or sometimes even states directly—that by living close to the water, starting to run more than fly, living in a dark cave, or wearing animal skins...a species changed over time. As with the Dikika baby from chapter 9, whose brain was said to grow in size from being on a protein-rich diet, you'll have better luck trying to prove hopeful monsters.

Try this one on for size. I have often asked my science classes, if you begin to cut the tails off laboratory mice—and also start whacking off the tails of their mice babies for a few generations—will their tails disappear, or at least start to get shorter? Every student, except perhaps the woefully nonanalytical ones, always rightfully says, "Of course not." They can easily understand the explanation that the environmental factor of a slicing knife cannot directly change the genes of adults or subsequent offspring. But—if you believe the presence of vestigial structures supports natural evolution, then you must also say, "Yes. The mouse tails will get shorter."

Good Design Is Good Design

In his succinct book *Hallmarks of Design*, author Stuart Burgess posited as an overriding assertion that similarities in features—wherever they are found—are never signs of random processes. For example, when a set of twins walks by, who would think their looks are coincidental? (I've often been told there is no way a Poppe baby could be left on a doorstep. They all bear such similarities that they would immediately be returned to the parents.)

From artwork to automobiles to family members to everything—including vestiges—visible parallels are always the signs of a successful designer. It is easy to see why this is so. If an initial object in a series operates with precision and then more sophistication follows, it is wholly expected that certain optimal features be reused. From needlepoint to nuclear reactors, "Good design is good design is good design." And why do optimal features get reused? Because they maximize certain natural laws, principles, or equations already in place that govern the development of any object in this genre.

For example, only when engineers and architects fully understand formulas governing their specialty can they go out and practice their craft. And within the limitations of these laws, principles, and equations, each craftsman leaves an indelible personal style on each product. And with the "carryover" effect you would expect to find certain stylistic features that once played a more integral role, but were still left at the designer's whim and are now more vestigial.

Nascent Structures—A Problem

Despite the strength of the above arguments, they are still just one side of the coin. Not only do you have to explain away the problems with vestigial structures, you also have to come up with a whole new theory for its flipside—*nascent structures*. *Nascent* is generally the opposite of vestigial, meaning "beginning to develop, on the advent, or recently having come into existence." In other words, unless natural evolution has ceased as a mechanism, it should still be generating new organs and useful body parts as we speak—read, that is.

Do we see any animals today growing useless appendages that may someday turn into something? Well then, how did it work in the past? Okay, take that prehensile (grasping) monkey tail that somehow disappeared from the end of our coccyx. How did that highly complex sequence of several tail vertebrae and accompanying musculature first *appear* on something like spider monkeys, primates with nimble hands but on the primitive end of complexity?

The most-proffered ancestors for spider monkeys are a blend of lemurs (with long but non-prehensile tails) and raccoons (with great manual dexterity but no usable tails). Sadly, lemurs exist, alive or as fossils, only on the island of Madagascar off the east coast of Africa, and monkeys with prehensile tails exist only in South America—which is west of Africa with an ocean in between. And double sadly, raccoons are raccoons, not primates. But unless "prehensile-ness" appeared fully formed on spider monkeys by accident, wouldn't you have to blend in some unrelated animals, like certain shrews that can also grasp with their tails? And if any such tail blending did take place, can we please have at least a couple of fossil intermediates within that nasty time crunch? Finally, could I have my prehensile tail back? Just think of the many things I could do with an extra "hand." However, going back to vestigial structures, nature deprived first apes, then chimps, hominids, and finally me of something very useful.

Believers in a Designer often point to all the structures necessary for vision in the mammalian eye as the pinnacle of an irreducibly complex organ. And well it is. Yet natural evolutionists dismiss our eyes as organs that sprang from a long series of more primitive vision organs—developing through time in fish, amphibians, reptiles, and birds. However, wouldn't each eye improvement, however small, have to be nascent at some point? Shouldn't we find, worldwide, examples of dangling eye improvements in one species or another that will someday spread to the entire population? It just isn't happening.

However, let's try to accept for a moment that we "see" only because all those others saw first. But how do you explain creatures like bats and woodpeckers? Both exhibit structures that also would have to be nascent at some point, yet there are no parallels for their specialties anywhere in the animal world to provide a developmental template.

Bat fossils are well known in paleontology, and many detailed and excellent specimens exist. It is also agreed upon that bats suddenly appeared worldwide in the fossil record about 50 mya—fully formed. If you investigate echolocation in today's bats, you will find it has, biologically, sophistication equivalent to today's radar. Problem is, the excellent detail in the earliest bat fossils shows that the echolocation apparatus was there from the start. So if bats evolved from rodents like mice, which is a choice forced due to their similarities, what nascent mechanism suddenly provided a mouse with radar? (True, I'm ignoring bats' wings. But one impossibility at a time.)

Wait—dolphins have a similar sonar system. Was it transferred from dolphins to bats? No—chronologically, bats came first. Was it transferred from bats to dolphins? No—certainly dolphins could not have bats as ancestors. Did both echolocation systems develop independently by similar miraculous accidents? How fantastic a set of dual mutations that would be! Somewhere there needs to be a yes. But where?

How about the apparatus that has no real parallels of any type anywhere, found in those feathered jackhammers, the woodpeckers? The red-bellied woodpecker's hammering ability actually has at least three subsystems, all typically operating in concert as follows:

- The skull has reinforced layers of bone, once described as being as hard as concrete. It will not break apart under blows that would shatter an ordinary bird's skull. Also, between the beak and the skull is a separating layer of spongy shock-absorbing tissue unique to the woodpecker family. Finally, the brain is tightly packed in the skull with a minimum of cerebrospinal fluid, preventing otherwise certain brain concussions. (Woodpeckers are the quintessential crash-test dummies.)

- The neck contains specialized muscles that provide a blow strong enough to chip into wood. These muscles also allow the rapid head movements and a straight and true blow to hit the precise cracks being widened.

- The most amazing tongue is attached to ultrathin hyoid bones driven by brachiomandibularis muscles that fold at rest like accordions. Impossible as it may seem, these muscles actually run back from beneath the tongue, under the head, around the back of the skull, up over the top, and finally attach at the pit of the nostrils. This arrangement allows the tongue to extend three times the length of the bill, and the back-pointing barbs at its tip can now impale and withdraw a juicy beetle grub.

- Two more features also deserve mention. I would add the woodpecker's *zygodactyl* feet, with two toes pointed forward and two toes pointed back. That unique arrangement makes it a cinch for the bird to hop around the rough bark of a tree trunk. And what a nice touch to add a few tightly packed feather bristles over the woodpecker's nostrils to prevent the inhalation of sawdust. Good ideas—I wonder who thought of them?

Call it *specified complexity, irreducible complexity,* or create your own terms. With the woodpecker you have components in an apparatus that are as interdependent from within as they are unique from without. Was it one huge nascent development, or did the three subsystems arrive piecemeal? If piecemeal, which one of the above three systems arrived first and had no function while waiting for the other two? In fact, can even two of the systems have a purpose if you are still waiting for the third? Can you even allow the woodpecker all three subsystems, but take away his nose guards and leave him stuck with perching toes, like his only possible ancestors had? If you play the game of "vestigial structures" you also have to deal yourself in for a hand of "nascent structures" to explain the origin of these systems. But the deck is hopelessly stacked.

From Circuitry to Cases—
An Analogy from Computer Design

A close friend who is a computer whiz supplied me with an example that explains vestiges well. He said every computer maker's next-in-line product reuses a great many previous design features, from the circuitry to the case, and in short order he can quickly recognize the manufacturer's external or internal signature without a label. Also, my friend will tell you that circuitry in all computers has no choice but to abide by such laws, principles, and equations as Ohm's Law ($V = I \times R$; that is, Voltage equals Current times Resistance). Therefore, the gauge of your wires must match the electric load they carry whether you like it or not.

Most applicable to vestiges, my computer-whiz friend asked me to consider how many keys or buttons on the computer keyboard I actually use. I took a look and found command and symbol keystrokes I couldn't explain. (How many of you can name the functions of the F1 to F12 keys? And did you know you can activate these functions with other commands?) To drive the point home, my friend asked me to show him what command I used to print a document. Then he showed me four additional ways to activate the "print" command. (I guess someone could say that 80 percent of the available print commands are unnecessary vestiges, but in this case nobody seems to be saying that the machines are not worth buying until computer makers remove the extra commands.)

Vestigial Human Behaviors

Vestigial human behaviors, perhaps the most intriguing of all in the descent by modification arguments, need to be approached from a slightly different perspective. Using behaviors to prove evolution is, on the whole, unique to the debate on human ancestry. However, if natural evolution is right and we truly are, as author Desmond Morris called us, "naked apes," then we would be just another creature in a sequence of both increasing physical *and* behavioral complexity. Just as we are biologically at the end of the line, with genes just barely 1 percent ahead of chimps, so should the sum total of our behaviors be presently 1 percent ahead of chimps.

Envision a continuum of developmental sequence from 1 to 100, in which bacteria are #1, chimps are #99, and humans are #100. And of course, evolution will soon replace us with organism #101—both genetically and behaviorally a step ahead of us. But here's the rub. Though perhaps we *Homo sapiens* have just a 1 percent edge physically, 99 percent of our *behaviors* are unique compared to anything living or extinct, real or imagined. View it as more like counting from #1 to #99 for the rest of the animals, even including Neanderthal man, and then jumping straight to humans at #1,000,000. Why is this so? It all begins with the spiritual factor I've mentioned previously.

Ask any number of strangers you meet if they believe they have a soul. Ask these people if the only thing they inherit for a lifetime of effort is a burial plot of ground. Or if they are cremated, ask them if all they earn is an urn. If statistics are correct, approximately four out of five will say there is life after death—something that remains that cannot be defined by biology. So if you believe humans are a combination of both biological and spiritual factors—the biological being the "instinctual" portion and the spiritual providing the "choice" parameter—why would the biological tendencies need to disappear? Since most systems of thought believe the spiritual piece was added later on, I say the designing author was smart to leave certain basic biological desires intact to see whether we would follow the urges of our bodies or the gentle entreaties of our souls.

For example, as males we can still act like we live under the pre-historic system of dog eat dog and be driven by possessions, status, and a mentality to take what we want when we want. This is "nature's way," and nobody would criticize it in any other animal. Females, on the other hand, can treat men as no more than sperm donors and sugar daddies, and be so obsessed with their plumage that they have nothing to wear in a closet full of clothes. And yet as humans we can practice the alternative, such as that quaint trait called the Golden Rule, which in essence challenges both males and females to think of others before ourselves. (Now there's a nifty nascent behavior that appeared in some form in every civilization ever discovered. Wonder who thought of it?)

It is true that both negative stereotypes of men and women certainly inhabit our world, and yet we seem to hold people responsible for their actions. In fact, if people step too far over the line, we correctly reject their "right" to behave this way, and even apply sanctioned punish-ments because of their choices. If you think about it, if our whole world of crime and punishment is justified, then our legal system is highly nonevolutionary. Or if our negative behaviors are properly excused as evolutionary echoes, then our legal system is highly unfair. (The concepts of "rights" and "wrongs" will be a central theme in chapter 13.)

Do you know why I'm sure some form of legality is valid, and we cannot relegate our errant behaviors to an evolutionary view that can have no law but personal survival? Because we either admire or envy those who rise above urges we ourselves cannot master—something no other animal is capable of doing. When you consider the presence of human vestigial behaviors, if we can rise above them, then the concept of choice is validated.

———•◦•◦•———

To close this chapter, the short lists of vestigial structures and behaviors in no way proves that natural processes did all the work to separate us from a chimp or a Neanderthal Man. Furthermore, when you add nascent structures and behaviors, you literally can't tell if we're coming or going. But as the presence of these traits is still inadequate to define us as non-humans, the list of non-animal traits we exhibit puts us light-years beyond any Darwinistic explanation. In coming chapters you'll learn more of the uniqueness of being human for which science is at a loss to explain.

And let's start by examining what you and I are doing right now—communicating through symbols.

11
HUMAN LANGUAGE

Just More Sophisticated Grunts and Whistles?

Einstein—yes, back to him once more. Albert Einstein. Born in Germany in 1879 to Jewish parents. Considered an underachieving and unteachable student in public schools. Published his famous papers on the theory of relativity in 1905. Criticized for challenging conventional Newtonian physics in the 1910s, and exonerated in the 1920s as his work was continually validated. Emigrated to the U.S. to escape Nazism in the late 1930s. Lent his voice to those urging President Franklin Roosevelt to develop the atomic bomb in the early 1940s. Declined the offered post–World War II presidency of Israel in late 1940s. Died in 1955.

If you ask anyone in any walk of life, you will find Einstein is undoubtedly the most recognized name associated with scientific brilliance. Can you even think of a close second? Though people probably envision him among test tubes and bubbling glassware, as a theoretical physicist his subject was math and his tools were paper and pencil, chalk and chalkboard.

If you study Einstein's life and writings, you will find he extended his intellect into several other fields. Therefore, quotes by him abound on a variety of subjects, as you have seen throughout this book. (Do you have a favorite Einstein quote? As an educator my choice is, "Education is what remains after one has forgotten what one has learned in school.")

This next quote is one of those less well-known. Einstein once said,

> The most incomprehensible thing about the world is that it is comprehensible.

At first examination, perhaps you, like me, view this quote as a comment on the marvelous and supernatural order exhibited by the cosmos—an appropriate statement from a man who fully believed in God. (As I said back in chapter 3, never let anyone tell you Einstein believed otherwise.) But like most things Einstein produced, there is more here than meets the eye—a deeper meaning when he speaks of the "comprehensible universe."

———

I'm betting you never knew Einstein also spent much time investigating the origin of human speech. He, like many other scientists, wondered how human beings were able to communicate as effectively and profoundly as they do. And it is no wonder that the development of oral communication was also a subject addressed by Charles Darwin. In *The Descent of Man,* Darwin made it obvious he believed language developed from primates along the same path of evolutionary gradualism that had previously produced the species themselves. Consider this quote from *Descent of Man:*

> I cannot doubt that language owes its origin to the imitation and modification of various natural sounds, the voices of other animals, and man's own instinctive cries.

If you read all of *Descent,* you will see Darwin believed that our language through symbols most likely began like this:

1. Some evolving apelike animal narrowly escapes death in the attack of something like a giant cave bear.

2. Returning to his small clan of relatives, he mimics with gestures and growls the attack of the bear to another adult, through a game of "prehistoric charades."

3. To better animate the story, he makes a one-syllable grunting noise that sounds suspiciously like our word *bear* (try it, it's fun), and repeats it until the listener connects the concept with the sound (much like Patty Duke did with "water" when she portrayed Helen Keller in the movie *The Miracle Worker*).

4. Now that this particular grunt means *bear,* it is incorporated into the previous collection of grunts, squeaks, whistles, and mumbles that are already recognized by the clan as meaning food, water, fire, and so on.

5. As more of these grunts, squeaks, whistles, and mumbles are repeatedly shared, other sounds for more abstract concepts like danger, hunger, pain, and so on, are also generated, driving language on its way.

6. Then as many more hominid generations pass, and many more concepts are translated into accepted words, the many different languages form in their isolated pockets around the world.

7. Now all that's left is to translate sounds into scratchings in the dirt or ciphers on cave walls, and written words and numbers became a reality, permitting the establishment of civilizations.

To many people this sounds like another excellently packaged evolutionary explanation that requires no designer, intelligent or otherwise. But did Einstein concur? On the contrary, Einstein agreed with a multitalented contemporary theorist and friend named Charles Peirce (pronounced "purse"; 1839–1914) who explained that our ability to communicate originated not from without, but from within. Peirce said conversation is possible only because we link to the external world through *innate* conceptual capacities unique to *Homo sapiens*. In other words, both Einstein and Peirce agreed that the ability of humans to speak at their level had no true parallels to any other form of communication in the animal world.

Dolphins

But before we go more into the theories Peirce advanced, let's examine the animal believed to be, after us, the world's champion communicator—the bottlenose dolphin, *Tursiops truncatus*. Professor Louis Herman of the University of Hawaii has done in-depth research into dolphin sensory capabilities, and he and other researchers claim dolphins have a "language" of over 30 different sounds, which mean 30 different concepts to other dolphins.

Furthermore, these sounds are accompanied by at least as many body movements that have additional meanings, and all of these convey more than simple biological urges like food and mating. Professor Herman says dolphin communication involves such technicalities as "behavioral mimicry," "memory retrieval," "object categorization," "discriminatory matching," "pointing gestures," "fixed gazing," and even "synchronous creative behaviors" with other dolphins. That list makes it sound as if they had legs, they would almost be human.

So would Charles Peirce express amazement at a mature dolphin's lexical prowess? Not even compared to a human two year-old he wouldn't. You see, what all the rest of the animal world lacks in communication is the use of Peirce's specialty, *semiotics,* or the theory of signs. As a bigger handicap than a lack of opposable thumbs, animals are confined to communicating in the here and now and can generate no signs or symbols that represent anything more than the need at hand.

In contrast, Peirce amassed more than 76 different sign typologies that humans use in their communications—all 76 of which have multiple nuances that are out of the reach of even dolphins—and he grouped these 76 under the categories of *icons, indices,* and *symbols.* For example, my two year-old daughter, Emma, equates the sound "blankie" to more than just a piece of cloth as such. Her blanket is a special icon that represents abstracts like peace, stability, and assurance—concepts developed from her past that are projected into her future—even though in itself that dwindling scrap of fabric contains no such power. And how much more do humans use such symbolism when our brains have reached full development? Think about it. And while you're at it, perhaps be amazed that unlike the dolphin, you *can* think about it!

One other point. I've been to Sea World and have seen Shamu, the Great Killer Whale perform. What a smart whale! But then again, if memory serves me correctly, every time Shamu does a trick, someone slips him a fish. (When they recently closed the show because Shamu attacked his handler and aggressively dragged him around the pool, was that a Freudian slip of repressed anger over years of substandard working conditions?) And despite the feelings we humans attach to such accomplishments, the orca's tricks are still the result of good old-fashioned stimulus/response. Call it just another version of the ringing bell and Pavlov's salivating dog, except the spray of water exceeds the dropping of drool. To be sure, as an infant, our Emma was a bag full of simple responses to the simple stimuli in her life. But before she was even a year old, she also was employing a growing list of Peirce's 76 signs. Anyone who has spent much time with a child knows exactly what I'm talking about.

Primates and Language

No discourse on language development would be complete without addressing all the attempts to see what primates can be taught. Most everyone has heard of the spate of experiments with primates and language in the 1960s, '70s, and '80s. Names of famous chimps and apes like Koko, Lana, and Washoe became more famous than the names of their handlers (Patterson, Premack, and Gardner respectively). These studies ran their course in due time, when the achievement limits of their hairy subjects had obviously been reached.

Here are the cumulative results after decades of work. It is now known that no primate ever used a sign independent of its immediate situation—the immediate situation being the stimulus that elicited the response. For example, no primate ever gave the sign for *banana* when not hungry. Furthermore, no ape ever extended the concept of time into past or future constructs (mentioned yesterday's banana or tomorrow's banana), or ever formed a sign into a simple question ("Where is a banana?"). And when it came to spoken vocabulary, the primate limit is a chimpanzee said to have learned four garbled utterances of *mama, papa, cup,* and *up*—but not *banana.*

It might be well here to look at the Herculean efforts people have undertaken to show just how "human" primates can become. (And I'll eat a whole bunch of bananas if most of these researchers aren't Darwinists trying to prove a point.) The four words *mama, papa, cup,* and *up* were the total vocabulary of the famous "Vicki the Chimp."

Vicki was no "9 to 5, Monday through Friday" research project. Catherine and Keith Hayes acquired Vicki when she was three days old and raised her as their own daughter—bottle-feeding her, changing her diapers, having her in a highchair at the table during meals, tucking her into bed each night, and so on. Unfortunately, Vicki died unexpectedly at six years of age, perhaps due to the shortened life span of any wild animal in captivity. However, this effort was hardly an experiment cut short before its objective was reached. This is because a six year-old chimp is a full-grown animal at the stage of a young adult human, and Mr. and Mrs. Hayes knew Vicki's vocabulary limit had been reached quite quickly. So this 1950s experiment has not been repeated since—not by the Hayes family nor anyone else I know of in the literature.

In the end, researchers were unable to extend primate communication beyond its common modalities, and if that were innately possible (as Peirce said it wasn't), it should have certainly been accomplished given all the concentrated effort. In fact, none of the projects that attempted to teach apes, orangutans, or chimps to speak or "sign" took these animals one step beyond the capabilities they already possessed—capabilities to communicate immediate needs and basic instincts typical of other chordates like fish, amphibians, reptiles, birds, and other mammals.

In comparison, how much do you think a human subject would have learned with an equal amount of time and attention, or even by indirect exposure? Better yet, how far ahead of "Vicki the Chimp" will be my "Emma the Dooda" in language and communication development by the time she's six? Since Emma could say *mama, papa, cup, up, banana, blanket,* and a whole host of other words well before she was two years old, I'm sure the differences will be mind-boggling. Trying to link primate communication to "evolving" human communication produces no link at all.

Information—The Key

Enter Philadelphia native and MIT Professor Emeritus Noam Chomsky, everyone's definitive twentieth-century scholar on linguistic development. Though not a man of professed faith like Einstein and Peirce, Chomsky still maintained that lower levels of communication never gave rise to today's higher levels of conversation any more than breathing gave rise to walking. He also steadfastly maintained that human language capacities were the result of special design properties entirely lacking in other species, to the point of being accused of being a "closet creationist" in his younger years.

As the bottom line, Chomsky said the ability to speak through symbolic words was an "all or nothing" affair, and that humans were equipped with a unique "deep structure" in order to produce the discourses that we routinely do. Now, I find this "all or nothing" position quite curious because Chomsky, being an evolutionist, never bothered to offer an explanatory mechanism for the origin of this *deep structure.* However, Chomsky's *deep structure* term still holds the key to why human language has to have an origin beyond the explanation of evolutionary science.

I'm convinced very few people realize the one main difference between how humans and all other animals communicate. Take for example the marvelous directional dance a honeybee scout does when it has found a new source of food. Returning to the hive, the bee does a circular "waggle/wiggle" dance that conveys the directional angle between the food and the sun, and the number of turns in the dance indicates the distance from the hive. Then, after the dance is over, worker bees fly off to investigate.

But the difference is—and this perhaps is the key point of this chapter—the bee has only one language, and bees of the same species worldwide possess it at birth. As for me, though, I could tell you this story in English, in the broken German I learned in the military or, if I would take the time to learn them, in any one of the 6800 different world languages estimated to exist by SIL International (Summer Institute of Linguistics). What's more, just like the lowly honeybee, so it is with the "highly advanced" chimpanzees and dolphins. All other animals, except us, are born with the genetic capacity to make only one set of communicational gestures and sounds, and this one set is perceivable by any other of their species. Or more succinctly, every dolphin born is automatically able to speak "dolphin," and every dolphin born is automatically able to understand "dolphin," even if both communicating dolphins are born on opposite sides of the planet.

In amazing contrast, humans are born with the genetic ability to process and evaluate *information* (a key word in upcoming chapters) regardless of the medium sending it, and in fact can be trained in an infinite number of transmission forms. More succinctly, the messages in human communications are multivariate and *independent* of the methods of transmission, while in all other life forms the messages and the methods are singularly *dependent,* and one and the same.

For this reason, two people can look at a big dog and have widely different responses, which a language barrier may prevent them from sharing until they learn common symbols—while two cats will look at the big dog and have the same autonomic response that either could interpret. The key here—and what will forever separate humans from cats, dogs, bees, dolphins, chimps, or whatever—is *the nature of information* and our unparalleled ability to process it. (I'm saving "The Ultimate Objection—The Nature of Information" for chapter 14.)

This is what Einstein, Peirce, and even Chomsky were referring to as our basic language difference. A single set of sounds and gestures is innate to each type of animal, and the ability to process information *regardless* of the sounds and gestures sending it is innate only to humans. I'm sure these are the two entirely unique forms of the same deep-structure concept to which Chomsky referred, and both forms surely must be encoded differently in our DNA. That means we have yet another critical difference in genetic sequence that separates us from the chimpanzees from which Darwinists say we evolved—vastly improved genetic information whose increased complexity once again must be generated by no method known to science. (Again, more in chapter 14.)

Prehistoric Language Development

Addressing the possible communication modes of prehistoric humans—were ancient hominids limited in their "hard wiring" just like even the smartest of animals? Were they able to communicate only through sounds and gestures about immediate needs? Or were they more like us—able to comprehend abstracts, use symbolism not only for present but for past or future constructs, and evaluate or even generate new information? Or was Darwin correct in saying there was a gradual developmental sequence?

In other words, as we underwent the imagined transition from *Australopithecus afarensis* to *Australopithecus africanus* to *Homo erectus* to *Homo neanderthalis,* did we keep adding developmental communication pieces until Cro-Magnon Man almost had it perfected—and civilized man added the fine touches? The trouble is, our ancient furry friends left little behind as far as concrete documentation. We can only guess from bones, tools, and dwellings the extent to which they could verbalize and interpret. However, we do have one piece of evidence to assess—cave drawings.

Actually, for the sake of comparison we are a bit limited as to what we can use as ancient artwork from creatures not language-capable—or not yet, so a Darwinist would say. No Egyptian hieroglyphics, of course. These were civilized people well versed in abstract symbolism. But no Eskimo totem poles, Navaho runes, or Anasazi rock carvings either because though they may go back well over 10,000 years—or 50,000 to 100,000 years in the case of Australian Aborigines—paleoanthropologists consider these people *Homo sapiens* and as language-capable as are we. Instead, we need to go to examples from European Neanderthals.

Probably the most useful would be the Chauvet-Pont-d'Arc cave drawings of some 30,000 years ago. Located in Southern France, this labyrinth of caves contain as many as 400 separate drawings depicting as many as 13 different species—some of which, like the rhinoceros and giant cave bear, were obviously extinct in this area well before civilized times.

Since there is no other type of artwork undeniably going beyond Neanderthal times (though a few try to sell some), the question becomes whether these pictures are more closely related to the expressiveness in the many chimp faces of 30,000,000 years ago or to a Sumerian businessman's account ledger of 6,000 years ago. And the problem here is the same as in the fossil record—gaps, gaps, gaps. The truth is, no reasonable evidence exists that ancient hominids gradually developed the use of symbolic representation between 30 million and 30,000 years ago. If we acknowledge the first supposed surge forward from a chimp toward a human—said to be the altogether pongid-like *Aegyptopithecus* of 25,000,000 years ago—we still must jump ahead 24,970,000 years, with nothing in between, from what science still calls an ape to a creature in a cave making 400 drawings.

And here's the bigger problem. The pictures of horses were *pictures* of horses—not words, or numbers, or symbols for horses. They could well have been drawn close to the day the horse was seen, perhaps the very day, meaning they were not the nostalgic reminisces of an aged hunter recalling the virile days of his youth. As to Chomsky's two choices for innate language capability, this would imply that Neanderthals had only the animal form of communication, which groups them with bees, dolphins, and the rest. The only difference is that they could respond to immediate stimuli not only with sounds and gestures, but also with manual dexterity and opposable thumbs. (You could also wonder why these 400 drawings contained no figures of humans. Did they all have some kind of autism and were they unable to interact with their own kind?)

In my view, such cave drawings are still light-years away from the Sumerian who just wrote down the figures for yesterday's transactions that he will need to share with his partner during tomorrow's business. And we aren't done. We still have to find a random way to launch the Neanderthal language far forward into one based on Chomsky's deep structure—our Sumerian again, with the totally advanced DNA codes that put him on the same communicative footing as us.

Finally, consider the numbers crunch more closely. From the

Aegyptopithecus to the *Neanderthalis* to us, we do not make any real communication progress during 99.9 percent of that stretch. And then we suddenly lunge forward to the Sumerian businessman in the last 0.1 percent of time.

Finally, I have already indicated that the struggle for survival in early hominid clans must have been fierce. Though the dinosaurs have been gone for about 60,000,000 years before any hominids came on the scene, many dangerous predators were still about to those coming out of trees to live in caves. You could also add the threats of poor diet, makeshift shelters, sparse medical care, and small clan numbers that would allow a mighty slim chance for rebound from a group disaster. Also, geologic timelines of all paleoanthropologists show that at times as many as three different hominid species overlapped at the same time period, and therefore coexisted. This not only puts them in potential competition, but it also adds a wrinkle in the game of "who begot whom?"

Common sense (which isn't all that common on this subject) asks, "If the innate capacity to launch forward in language and symbolism existed before the first documented civilizations of 6000 years ago, why didn't the dictates of 'survival of the fittest' put them to valuable use much earlier to stave off extinction?" No, just like the unexplainable Cambrian Explosion of long ago, humans fully conversant in spoken and written words and numbers suddenly exploded on the scene about 6000 years ago. (Isn't that what people of biblical faith who study the book of Genesis have been saying for centuries?)

Here we have yet another either-or dilemma. It's just a choice of two, really. Either Darwin was right, and human language developed slowly from animal sounds—or Einstein, Peirce, and Chomsky were right by saying there are no parallels to the natural world in how we communicate. As a species we just suddenly learned how to fully talk, cipher, read, and write. That's a lot to ponder.

———◦•◦•◦———

Let's end this chapter where it began—with Einstein's quote about the "comprehensible universe." Here's what I think he really meant by that line. Who better than Einstein to have a feel for the complexity in levels of science from the smallest atoms to the largest galaxies? And because he realized both the tremendous complexity and precision in every aspect of our universe, he was amazed that our minds were pre-programmed with discernment power at least equal to any of these mysteries. In other words, I would rephrase the quote like this.

> Einstein found our mental capacity to *analyze* the science of our universe to be even more incredible than the science of the universe itself.

Furthermore, this deep-structure programming was accompanied by the necessary sophisticated language capabilities and manual dexterities to communicate to others our most complicated hypotheses as well as our deepest wonderments—not only through sounds but through printed letters and numbers. Einstein realized this capability could *never* be a product of natural evolution, which in his mind left one alternative—the God to whom he so often referred. And when was the last time Albert Einstein was proven wrong?

Try this. Stand with both arms outstretched and imagine that the distance between your fingertips equals what science says is the age of the Earth: 4.6 billion years. Using that distance as a scale, then the appearance of this new type of intelligent symbol-user called *Homo sapiens* came at the sliver of a shaving of a piece of your fingernail—.0000014 of all available time. How could we have made this huge leap in such a short amount of available time? And if strict Darwinism is the total failure it has been repeatedly proven to be, then how *did* civilized communicating humans get here? If natural selection is an impotent answer, what *are* the truthful details? Try the next chapter for an answer.

So What Do You Think of This Book *Now?*

I believe our ability to communicate first through speech and later written language has to be the rapid influence of an outside intelligence rather than the slow product of a mindless, blind evolutionary process. In this chapter, though, I said very little about the extreme complexities of human language capabilities as we now observe them. But just think about this book. Thousands upon thousands of words, each representing a concept of some type, each linked with other words, had to be assembled into a harmonious whole.

Further, I am no remarkable talent as a writer. Though I bring certain knowledge and experience to this book, I'm an educator by profession, not an author. In other words, millions upon millions of human beings have the ability to do what I've done here. Just think of the way we can bring order to such complexity. Amazing, isn't it?

Just to fill you in, this volume involved further complications. Specifically, I never started out to write a book. (Who was it that said, "The trouble with people who say they have 'half a mind to write a book' is that they go ahead and do so"?) Many chapters started out as short optional reading essays to give to my public school biology students whose faith was tweaked by all the Darwinistic philosophies infused in their science textbooks and replete in public education. These essays contained *scientific* information that, I believed, would clearly show any student who read them that natural evolution was a completely bankrupt theory—one having no right to continue to monopolize the science found in research, in publication, and especially in education.

These essays I wrote for my students continued to grow in number as I attempted to cover every reasonable challenge to natural evolution. However, my continued writing became more book-length, and through the help of some respected scientists, the vision of the great professionals at Harvest House Publishers, and the literal grace of God, I assembled a portion of these essays into *Reclaiming Science from Darwinism*, which was released in September 2006. Because there was too much material for one book, you now find the balance of the essays in *Exposing Darwinism's Weakest Link*.

The whole process of book development, writing, editing, production, design, and publication requires an unimaginable number of discrete human capabilities not shared by other primates. I ask again, just where in the supposed progression from monkey to man did these changes appear? And how?

12

Adam and Eve

Fact or Fiction?

After all the scientific discourse on fossil evidence, vestiges, and communication in the previous chapters, permit me what will feel like a change of gears—to concepts more philosophic. However, the science will not be absent. In fact, it will become more obvious and prominent as you read on.

Let's go back to what so many think is a tale in the grandest tradition of fiction. It's a story line that the fantasy world of Hollywood can truly admire. Adam and Eve. An innocent young couple very much in love. A highly influential, kindly, and wise benefactor to oversee them. A dastardly and deceptive villain bent on destroying all that is good. Paradise gained...and then lost. Blessings and curses. And of course, a gratuitous scene or two with fig leaves. It has all the necessary elements for heartrending fiction as well as a powerful and realistic message. But it can't be true, can it? It's just too perfect, right?

Now, if you are one of those truly rare individuals who believe humans do not have a soul, no need to read on. (In fact, it's amazing you got this far!) If you believe that after death you receive the requisite hole in the ground, are covered over with dirt, and slowly become humus, then go to other reading material. That is because the crux of the Adam and Eve story is not just the arrival of another advanced biological life-form. These two *Homo sapiens* that Genesis says were driven from the Garden about 6000 years ago (in what science would say was toward the end of the Holocene epoch of the Paleozoic period of the Cenozoic era) were the first life-forms to be termed a *neshama*.

Scholars who study the original language in the ancient teachings of the Torah (Jewish law) and the Pentateuch (first five books of the Old Testament) often have clarity of meaning that is lost when studying English translations. Consider Genesis 2:7:

> God formed man of dust from the ground, and breathed into his nostrils the breath of life; and man became a living being.

Here the word *soul* (or in some versions, *spirit* or *being*) is translated from the Hebrew word *nefesh* to properly mean having a "biological" body that made the organism an oxygen-requiring metabolizer. To extend that concept further, from a bacterial clump to a bonobo chimp, any other life-forms previously made were also *nefesh,* which possessed the general spirit of life—a portion of the collective harmony in nature's grand recycling symphony.

But Adam and Eve did more than just join the panorama of organisms created thus far, for God made it clear earlier in Genesis 1:27 man was going to be in His "image"—in His likeness—which most certainly was not referring to an oxygen-breathing being with two arms and two legs. No, the Hebrew term here to correctly capture the true essence of Adam and Eve is *neshama*, which means "human spirit being." Whether you believe the Eden tale or not, this is a pivotal point in the Genesis account. Here God takes two organisms with corporeal *nefesh* bodies not unlike their closest biological relatives and imparts to them that eternal *neshama*—"spark"—that "essence," if you will, that defines who they are well beyond the explanation of science.

Of course many Darwinists say this is just supposition—another of the many legends typical of all cultures that gets passed down and embellished from generation to generation until fact is lost in fairy tale. These same doubters also say that the accuracy of the story had to survive too much chance for contamination, especially since Hebrew scribes contend all of Genesis was written down by Moses well over a thousand years after the events.

Because of this, skeptics say that by the time the stories eventually reached Moses and he finally recorded the tales of Noah and Abraham and such, who knows how much his ancestors had altered the tales? And Darwinists would also say that, after Moses, how do you know other writers did not build more folklore around the remaining bits of truth, so that after several hundred years of additions and alterations, you ended up with a big book of fairy tales? As one of my former students said of the Bible while holding up a dictionary, "Here's a big book. People can write big books."

Finding a Replacement

Do you want to discard the Genesis account like so many others do? Well, what becomes your replacement story? Remember, by reading up to here you've tacitly agreed that you have a *neshama*—this "spark" that continues after your biological existence. So if you reject Genesis and you have an interest in the "origins" debate, don't you need a substitute story for the arrival of the first soul? Furthermore, doesn't your replacement story have to describe a bellwether event like in Genesis? The advent of the *neshama* into the world would be a big deal.* I suppose an alternative possibility is that the soul could also have evolved, but how do you describe a soul under construction over time? And under construction by what processes? No, the soul is another either-or proposition, and you have to decide whether you have one or you don't.

If you admit you have some eternal essence, but want to avoid the Genesis account, what other origin "legends" are available, and how suitable are they? Stories framed in terms of nature abound among

---

* The New Age movement—a westernized form of Hindu reincarnation—offers no coherent explanation for "soul travel" through time. Also, how come all New Agers used to be people such as princesses and warlords in their former lives? Don't we need a few librarians and short-order cooks?

cultures like the American Indians, Inuit (Eskimos), or Aborigines. Figures on a totem pole near Anchorage, Alaska, tell this story:

> The Sun God commissioned the raven to watch over the wheat, corn, and fish. Then when all was ready, the Sun God sent the eagle hatchling who grew to become the first spirit man, and woman was born of the wind under his wings.

Need a story with more details? How about this one from ancient Babylon about 3000 years ago?

> From an eternal and divine swamp, pairs of gods emerged when earth signaled her readiness. Children of these swamp gods became demigods who ruled the sky, land, and water. The new young demigods did not want to share their glory and started killing their divine parents. Marduk, son of the earth god Ea waged war with Tiamat, one of the original swamp gods. Due to the power of Tiamat's origin, Marduk was not able to defeat her—until he finally was able to snare her in a net. Then he crushed her skull with a club, and cut her in half. He suspended one part of her body in the sky above to become the heavens, and placed the other half in the ground to become the fertile soil, and fashioned from the resulting bloodied mud the first humans that were a combination of the spiritual and the temporal worlds.

Like Eden, it's an interesting tale with plenty of details, but it doesn't come close to providing me with resolution on the human spirit issue. I guess there still are other options. I seem to recall a picture from Greek mythology showing a turtle on whose back the Earth rode as he traveled among the stars. Are any of these stories intellectually satisfying, however? Then perhaps the answer to the *neshama* really does reside in the Genesis story, which is embraced by the three main religious faiths encompassing over half of the world's believers—Islam, Judaism, and Christianity.

As for other major religions, they offer no bona fide creation story. While addressing the influences of the human soul is central to Buddhism, learning about its origin is not. Buddhists have no central God or gods as such, and rather than deal with the origin of the spirit and its final destination, the focus is on each person's present life. Meditation on self-denial, truth, and beauty is the key. Existence before one's life is obscure and of little bearing, and if one has lived a life of true worth, the afterlife will take care of itself. In short, Buddhism has no answer for the origin of the soul.

In contrast, Hinduism does have its own spiritual gods and demigods, and the former state and future destination of the human soul are keys in the concepts of karma and reincarnation. But the idea of the ongoing transmigration of the human soul is predicated on *renewal* but never on *new*. Even the ultimate origin of Hindu gods—and the suspiciously human attributes they possess—are not secure within its doctrine. Hinduism may explain the "beta" through "psi" of spiritual life, but explanations for the "alpha" and "omega" are absent.

The Facts of Genesis

We are—even if only by default—back to Adam and Eve. If you reject the beliefs of Judaism, Islam, and Christianity and call the story of Adam fiction, what is your substitute "soul" story?

Facts. Have you ever examined the first few chapters of Genesis for the *facts* of the events beginning in Paradise? These verses tell the best known and most widely accepted story of the ultimate origin of the physical world and the humans who inhabit it. The Garden of Eden existed between four rivers, two of which, the Tigris and the Euphrates, still exist today. That would locate the Garden somewhere in central Iraq.

At the end of creation, Eden had to be a stable place. God had already completed all scientific aspects of the world—physics on Day One, chemistry on Day Two, geology and botany on Day Three, astronomy on Day Four, and zoology on Day Five and Day Six. Then at the culmination of Day Six came the Earth-shattering pronouncement, "Let us make man in our image." So Adam was formed out of the dust of the ground, and when God breathed through his nostrils the breath of life, Adam became the *nefesh* as well as the *neshama*. Adam was then provided with a *neshama* mate fashioned from one of his ribs, and they were both placed in Paradise to be eternally sustained by eating from the "Tree of Life."

It makes perfect sense that in their initial state, Adam and Eve were completely innocent and unaware of evil. But they did have one command—not to touch the "Tree of the Knowledge of Good and Evil" lest they die. Then enter the villainous serpent, the disobedience, the curses, and the expulsion.

At this point, one critical concept cries for an explanation. Anyone even remotely familiar with the Adam and Eve story knows the pair was said to be ageless before "the fall." Most people also know that when the serpent told them they would "not surely die" if they touched the forbidden tree, Satan was employing one of his favorite deceptions— using a little bit of truth to sell a big lie. Sure, Adam and Eve did not fall over dead upon touching the tree, but their disobedience led to expulsion and the aging process—as immortality was now forfeited. When the angel with the flaming sword blocked their way back into Paradise and the Tree of Life, Adam and Eve started to experience the same aging process we do. And if that's true, only then can we begin to count time in the human terms that give us a little over 6000 years since the end of the Eden story.

But once again, how long was our couple in Paradise *before* they were disobedient? If time has no human meaning until after the fall, then what's to prohibit our couple living on as old an Earth as you like until then, which could easily make Bible time compatible with geologic time? (If you think this is giving in to evolutionary thinking, remember, even a 4.6-billion-year-old Earth has absolutely no chance of validating Darwinism.)

Validated by Science

My intent in all my writings is to stick with scientific reasoning as opposed to wild conjecture, and rational thinking as opposed to emotional responses. So where has putting all my biases aside and sticking to the trail of fact led me? *I believe the story in the Garden to be 100 percent true.* If you examine the order of the creation as outlined in Genesis, it generally follows what science purports, and violates no principles of nature. The first event, "Let there be light," and the big bang seem an interchangeable description of the same event. Then the "separation of the waters" parallels nicely with the cooling and settling of the planet, especially if you read the other lesser-known creation story in Psalm 104. After that, both accounts say you get light before autotrophs (photosynthetic plants that make food), autotrophs before heterotrophs (consumers that must eat food), sea life before legged life, and finally mammals—before the mammal called "man" appears at the very end. And if Adam and Eve began in the Garden, when creation's duration could not be measured by any human standards, you have all the time necessary for many of Earth's geological, prehistoric events to take place before our couple gets expelled and begins the civilized world, where everybody has a limited life span.

Valid Curses

With both faith and fossils being compatible with biology, geology, and philosophy, other facts from the Old Testament fit nicely with history and sociology—such as the curses in the third chapter of Genesis. There, God tells Adam that because of his disobedience he will now have to work hard for a living. Remember from my description back in chapter 3 how everything in the Garden once freely gave him its abundance? Well, the party's over. Adam will now have to toil and sweat, fighting both literal and figurative thorns and thistles all his life. Then in final irony, he must surrender his body right back to the very elements from which he was fashioned, and against which he struggled in futility all his life. Doesn't the course of a human life tend to sound rather like this?

> Cursed is the ground because of you; in toil you will eat of it all the days of your life. Both thorns and thistles it shall grow for you; and you will eat the plants of the field; by the sweat of your face you will eat bread, till you return to the ground, because from it you were taken; for you are dust, and to dust you shall return (Genesis 3:17-19).

Don't those verses describe how it feels during some of those excruciating days on the job? You work, work, work—toil, toil, toil—and keep getting further behind. And after all that effort, something like the following takes place: 1) you are still "in the red," 2) someone else gets promoted, 3) you are "put out to pasture" as soon as you are no longer useful, or 4) someone else inherits what is left and your name is forgotten.

Then, God says that Eve, and her subsequent daughters, will now be under the domination of their husbands: "Your desire will be for your husband, and he shall rule over you" (Genesis 3:16). This may seem strange to us in the twenty-first century. However, ask a grandmother, or better yet a great-grandmother, about the social life of married women in her generation. Before birth control, baby formula, and disposable diapers, women could never get very far from those inevitable offspring.

Or if you still aren't sure whether males have tended to dominate, simply go to any mainstream culture found since the dawn of civilization and check the mores. The rule has been, and still continues to be, that men pursue their significance in the prowess conferred by their avocations, and women find their fulfillment within a stable domestic setting.

More Compatibility

Beyond the direct male–female curses, there is a lengthy list of additional prescient factors from the first few chapters in Genesis that are highly compatible with the state of things today—scientific and otherwise. Try these on for size.

- The Hardy-Weinberg law of genetic inheritance states that the proportions of dominant and recessive genes in populations remain remarkably stable. This means allele frequencies in a certain gene pool do not change as time passes or as the population fluctuates. Or in the most succinct language, creatures reproduce "after their kind" (Genesis 1:11).

  Unfortunately for Darwinists, the Hardy-Weinberg Law is a piece of scientific bedrock that is perfectly compatible with Genesis but absolutely contrary to natural evolution. (Charles Darwin's term *descent by modification* means that gene frequencies must change in complexity, and by large-scale advancements as opposed to regressions. This has never been observed in nature or laboratories.)

The phrase "after their kind" is significant. God used it *ten times* in the first chapter of Genesis alone—almost as if He expected Darwinists to be like the kid with fingers in both ears making babbling noises to drown out the sound of truth.

• From one chemical perspective, our impressive bodies and brains are not unique at all. They are still just composites of 99 percent simple carbon, hydrogen, nitrogen, and oxygen atoms you find all over the universe, with a few major and minor nutrients thrown in. "The LORD God formed man of dust from the ground" (Genesis 2:7). And of course when the body dies, decomposition ensues, and all elements become part of the next cycle of continuing life.

• Though not the biggest, fastest, strongest, or the most fearsome, man is given dominion over all animal life, and animals will fear him with an unreasonable fear: "The fear of you and the terror of you will be on every beast of the earth and on every bird of the sky…into your hand they are given" (Genesis 9:2). Ergo, that huge bull elk I'm stalking during archery season, the one that could easily maul me into stew meat, runs like a rabbit as soon as he catches my slightest scent.

• Here is one you should check out. Rib bones are the only bones that will readily regenerate if they are removed. "The LORD God fashioned into a woman the rib which He had taken from the man" (Genesis 2:22).

Reconstructive and plastic surgeons routinely extract and transplant rib bone mass during their surgeries on accident victims or enhancement patients. If they are careful to "peel" back and leave in place the rib's covering, or periosteum, rib bone regeneration is assured in almost every case, due in part to a rich blood flow supplying the intercostal muscles.

• The pronouncement that the males and females of our species were meant to form a permanent and monogamous pair bond is a unique method of procreation separate from all other sexually reproducing animals: "A man shall leave his father and his mother, and be joined to his wife; and they shall become one flesh" (Genesis 2:24).

If the parentage of any other animal can be traced at all, you would have to sort out the confusion of polygyny (a male with more than one female mate) and polyandry (a female with more than one male mate). In the few instances in nature where exclusive paring does take place (geese, bears, and so on), it is only seasonal at mating and rearing time, after which they go their way until the next breeding cycle. And I think you can safely say that type of pair attachment is merely biological and certainly not psychological.

• For His deception of Eve and then Adam, the serpent is cursed to this fate: "On your belly you will go, and dust you will eat all the days of your life" (Genesis 3:14). Now evolution says that snakes evolved from lizards that lost the legs of their other squamate relatives. The proof? Why, the vestigial leg bones just under the skin of many snake species, of course!

But going back to the chapter 10 discussion, why would "survival of the fittest" ever work over time to deprive an animal of superior mobility? Can you just imagine the lizard that gave birth to an offspring with less effective or missing legs that now must outcompete its ancestry? (Besides, there's that hogwash of "hopeful monster" again.) Personally, I find the biblical explanation of the long-lost leg bones of snakes to be superior to the Darwinian version, in that the Genesis account has a reasonable chance to be true.

• Consider that the near-instantaneous appearance of the

very first civilization was around the area where Adam and Eve were expelled from the Garden: "Cain went out from the presence of the LORD and settled in the land of Nod, east of Eden…and he built a city" (Genesis 4:16-17). The oldest civilization known by its ancient records—one that had societal rules, a written language, and a numbering system—is the Sumerian culture of the well-named region called the Fertile Crescent. Archaeologists say the Sumer people go back as far as 6500 years, which would put them in a biblical time frame near Cain, one of Adam's grown children.

Before we leave Paradise, there is one final point from the Garden— purely scientific—that puts Darwinists in a difficult situation. It is the issue of painful childbirth. This is the first curse put on Eve, just before the one about "your husband will rule over you." It says, "I will greatly multiply your pain in childbirth, in pain you will bring forth children" (Genesis 3:16). What could possibly be the evolutionary origin of this purely human phenomenon—the excruciating pain of giving birth? (If you didn't know, all other orders of mammals, from monotremes to monkeys, experience *painless* childbirth under normal conditions. In fact, this is even true of the egg-laying species.)

Why, therefore, would the most advanced species on Earth ever get struck with such a sudden reversal? If anything, it makes more sense that *Homo sapiens* should have the absolutely easiest birthing process. But since that's not the case, what type of evolutionary process would suddenly, or gradually, add intense pain to a peaceful biological procedure for the next species in line—pain heretofore unheard of over millions and millions of years? The most common Darwinistic explanation I hear is a doozy. It goes something like this: "Environmental forces caused the expansion of our brains and craniums, whose growth outstripped the expansion of the more slowly evolving female pelvis, making it more difficult for the larger baby's head to pass through the birth canal." But there is that Lamarckian odor again—the implication that environment can alter genetic codes. (And it's an odor I plan to neutralize in chapter 14, "Information Theory.")

Try It Yourself!

I once had a Darwinist student who engaged me in an ongoing debate over the "painful/painless" birthing issue. When I shared with him the Genesis account of Eve's curse, he first responded by saying that *any* pain anyone thinks they are experiencing is not real but a manifestation of an undisciplined mind. Then later he declared that a woman's pain in childbirth was also psychosomatic and could be controlled through proper concentration.

Somehow I doubted his analysis, so I e-mailed his observation to several female friends who have delivered children. Consider these responses: "Tell him to stretch his lower lip over his forehead and pretend it doesn't hurt." "Let me slam his hand with a hammer and have him keep a straight face." "Ask him what he thinks it would feel like to pee a bowling ball." And my favorite: "Imagine the Rock of Gibraltar as your kidney stone."

No doubt about it—childbirth definitely stimulates nerve endings that shoot powerful electrical pain messages up the spinal cord and to the brain, and they are so intense they can't be ignored. And this is as perfectly normal in humans as it is abnormal in other mammals. Yet while a human female's pain is momentarily so intense, we all know that under normal circumstances it leads to no permanent damage, and the suffering is immediately forgotten once it's replaced by the joy of a new child (see John 16:21). It almost seems that the experience of human birth is the moral to a story that is part of a much bigger whole.

Here are a couple of examples that really drive home the painful birthing issue. A rancher friend of mine named Joel manages a cattle operation in northern Colorado and has seen thousands and thousands of calves delivered. He says that if there are no complications, it is such an incredibly easy process that some of the heifers don't even bother to lie down. Also, I was once able to watch one of our Chesapeake Bay retrievers become a first-time mom as she gave birth to seven pups. I was amazed at the ease of the entire process, through which "Lacey" made not a single sound—certainly not one that paralleled all the maternity ward noises I heard during the six official "visits" when my own children were born. No, all animals but the "human animal" breeze right through the normal birth process.

How about a reasonable alternative to all this evolutionary side-stepping and tap-dancing? How about something more firm than all the Darwinistic guesswork that often begins with "Well, what about…?" I say again that the Garden, the immortal couple in God's image, God's one rule, the forbidden tree, the serpent, the deception, the disobedience, the curse, the expulsion are all real, right down to the last detail. (Remember, if you reject this, what's *your* explanation for the soul's origin?) And if it is all real, how huge the implications are for the validity of events surrounding other people in the Bible (like Adam and Eve's murderous son, Cain) and for the truth of overall Scripture!

Resolving the issue of the origin of the human soul takes a touch of faith somewhere along the way. And other than the Genesis account, sensible options from all of the world's religions are nonexistent. Furthermore, when you read the Genesis account with an open mind, don't people in it sure act like people? When I read all these accounts, I see real reflections of the real mistakes I make daily, as well as ways to triumph over them. To me, that goes a long way toward legitimacy.

To close, the Genesis account says that at the end of each day in the creation mosaic, God stood back, surveyed His handiwork, and assessed that day's efforts as "good." And so they were. The physics of Day One, the chemistry of Day Two, the geology and botany of Day Three, the astronomy of Day Four, and the zoology of Day Five and Day Six all seem to work quite efficiently here on good old Earth. Also, the nonliving phenomena of our planet sure seem harmonious with the living *nefesh*—those creatures without an eternal spirit that nonetheless have the general breath of life.

However, when the *neshama* finally walked the Earth—creatures with that eternal spark who beget additional spiritual offspring, that's a whole other story. In that case, God pronounced the day's outcome "*very* good."

13

IF SCIENCE IS ALL, WHENCE VALUES?

"Random" Can't Account for Right and Wrong

Darwinism, in many ways, is constantly exposing a critical weakness, in that it denies the absolutes that surely exist. I say good and evil are definite realities. And yet, "random" cannot account for them, which leaves evolutionary science at a loss to explain our special existence separate from animals.

By *absolutes,* I mean there are firm rules and values that don't change when times change or people change. If you disagree with me and say there are *no* absolutes, I say you cannot successfully argue your position. Most likely, confirmed Darwinists and I would be at odds in this debate. That is because if we are products of the mindless mechanisms of evolution, how can any one person dictate guidelines to another? (Ever hear the phrase, "Who died and left you in charge?") The conflict Darwinists have with bedrock values is immediate and unavoidable.

The first obstacle for anyone who wants to maintain there are no absolutes is that this person must evaluate and justify each and every violation of a proposed rule, law, or guideline. Take murder, for example. I would say the prohibition against taking another's life is the foremost standard among civilized people—one found anywhere a culture establishes any behavioral guidelines that apply to all its members.

However, those who believe rules are relative immediately point to contradictions. For example, in American society we have something called justifiable homicide, which basically seems to say, "Okay. You killed the guy. But he was basically a jerk so you can take a walk." And even though God through Moses said, "Thou shalt not kill," in the Ten Commandments, He later had Moses command the use of capital punishment, "You shall not show pity: life for life, eye for eye, tooth for tooth, hand for hand, foot for foot" (Deuteronomy 19:21). Ostensibly, the point here is murdering a murderer is not murder if it is sanctioned by duly authorized law. And it can get even more complicated.

Relativism

But here is the greater problem in saying there are no absolutes such as an ironclad rule against murder. I believe anyone trying to summarily excuse murder from a blanket prohibition is saying there is nothing inherently wrong about the act itself, and that there is the possibility of justification for any instance of killing. This view is commonly called either *situation ethics* or *moral relativism,* both terms meaning something akin to, "No action is either right or wrong until you analyze it in its backdrop."

Sorry. Murder is just plain wrong—no matter what. Yet can you categorize murder compared to other actions over which we have a choice? Thinking back to the previous chapter on Adam and Eve, I'll reiterate that what makes this story seem so genuine and applicable is because I'm convinced the facts are 100 percent true. In the choice they had, they failed no more and no less than we all do. (Wait. I said Adam and Eve "failed." But how can there be failure to choose correctly if there are no rights or wrongs?)

Now let's take a look at events in Adam and Eve's life after they are expelled from Paradise. How about Adam and Eve's two boys? I would say their eldest son, Cain, commits the first recorded act of true evil in the premeditated murder of his younger brother Abel.

Once again, if the Garden of Eden story is accurate, why then would this follow-up story be a fable—a story with a motive acted out daily all around the Earth? Such a cold-blooded killing truly must be called evil, or else how can anything be called evil? Unfortunately for Darwinists, they have a difficult time interpreting such an act. (This might also include people who buy into situation ethics, moral relativism, secular progressivism, human existentialism, and so on—those who from my experiences make the most ardent believers in evolution.)

You see, killing is not only expected in natural selection, it is the essential way the "fit" survive in the competitive food webs that comprise a randomly developed planet. The trouble is, the details in Cain taking Abel's life in no way show a reenactment of a predator-prey situation. Cain receives no tangible benefit from killing Abel—neither food, nor mate, nor secured territory. In fact, the consequences that might stop many animals from aggression, such as obviously being undermatched, were ignored, in that God warned Cain that retribution was at hand if he proceeded (Genesis 4:7). Furthermore, there was nothing "relative" here. There is absolutely no indication that Abel's attitude had any complicity in Cain's feelings. No, Abel's actions were "right," Cain's were "wrong," and it turned into cold-blooded, premeditated, and totally evil murder.

We should all realize that, in the absence of rules and absolutes, it's biological anarchy and survival of the fittest. You have to admit, it's the Darwinistic way. And some humans are presently living in just such "dog eat dog" conditions as you read this—not just in those desperate foreign countries, but even in certain sections of our larger American cities.

Absolutes and Choice

If you hold to absolutes, it allows immense possibilities for evil. Is not this a proof for the non-involvement of a God? Perhaps it's best to hold to random origin of human beings and, following the implications as we've seen, eliminate such problematic categories as good and evil.

Here's a different suggestion. God could have made us robotic (as indeed do the utterly instinctual results of Darwinism), but perhaps He wanted to see if, given the choice of good versus evil, we would stay our hand out of respect to Him and submit to His authority in appreciation for the rather impressive backdrop He made for us.

Yes, He could have made us totally indifferent. Then like all the rest of the biological *nefesh* we would only have to feel pain and maybe occasionally even loss, yet we would never have to spiral into the depths of heartache or bitterness known only to the spiritual *neshama*. In such a state we could also experience contentment and maybe occasionally even companionship, yet we could never rise to the pinnacles of joy and love. So, no ability to fully mourn our pain when we've been deeply hurt, and then no sense of the power of love to raise us from those depths? No true feelings of any kind? How incredibly drab the world would be!

No, I believe the correct summation of choice is this. When the birds sing that God made, He no doubt finds it enjoyable. However, due to instincts and programming, the birds have no choice. But then He gave *Homo sapiens* the option of that expression. This means we could sing strictly for our own enjoyment, or choose to sing for His—which, by the way, would bring Him much more pleasure. But unfortunately, according to the facts surrounding the first known case of evil, this freedom to choose includes God's allowance to even kill our brother if we think satisfying our pride is more important than following any set of absolute laws.

In this chapter, yet again we are running up against crucial either-or propositions. First, for human beings either there are absolutes in this world derived from good and evil, or there aren't. As for me, I say these absolutes most certainly exist, and are greater than any one person's desire to dismiss them. Second, either there are specific practices under both good and evil, or all life is chance and there are no such thing as "proper" behaviors in an altogether instinctual world. Or else, *compassion* is definitely a good act and *murder* is definitely an evil act.

As for me, I say a variety of good and evil acts exist, and had their origin from the concept of choice given to the world's first couple made in the image of God. This option to decide is what we all would have requested, and choice is the dividing factor that suddenly puts humans on a spiritual plane totally separating us from either the bacterium or the chimp, which remain on a biological plane only. Third, either the specific tale of the origin of good and evil (and the general tale of the creation of the universe as well) is told with unerring accuracy in the early chapters of Genesis, or it's just another societal legend and perhaps even an outright fabrication.

Now I surmise many readers will accept the first truth about the existence of absolutes without much debate. Perhaps the second truth about the existence of good and evil will set well also, though most people do not like to contemplate the existence of the implied negative consequences. But I want to emphasize the veracity of the third truth because so many see the Adam and Eve story, and usually the whole Bible, as a thick book of interesting tales that may or may not be taken seriously.

If you still doubt the truth in these stories after all I have said, I insist you investigate. Go to any objective source and discover the miracle of how the Bible managed to survive and come together though its individual books were written thousands of centuries and thousands of miles apart. Also investigate the amazing agreement from so many ancient manuscripts from so many dispersed locations, and how the Dead Sea Scrolls verified so beautifully what was already in existence. I'd even encourage you to approach historical biblical facts with the highest amount of skepticism you like, because like all the rest, you will find they usually lead to faith. And if that first man and woman truly did pluck the forbidden fruit, what powerful implications for the rest of the stories within!*

Values Transcending Time and Culture

Science is ignorant of values.

JACQUES MONOD

In 1965 Jacques Monod won the Nobel Prize in medicine for his work in evolutionary molecular biology. He's right, you know. Science *has to be* ignorant of values. How could it be anything else? There can

---

* An excellent resource that deals with these topics is *Searching for the Original Bible* by Randall Price (Harvest House Publishers, 2007).

be no values, even morals, inherent in what science measures because pure science only concerns itself with theories based on hard data. As far as judgment calls, science must be coldly indifferent to subjective interpretations and mere guesswork. Some say science should be free from having to either confirm or deny what is proper moral behavior in humans.

In my experience, this supposed chasm between science and values has been enough to send some scientists firmly into the religion called atheism, and it sure seems true in Monod's case. Consider this short excerpt from his 1970 book-length essay called *Chance and Necessity:*

> Chance alone is at the source of all novelty, all creation in the biosphere. Pure chance, only chance, absolute but blind liberty is at the root of the prodigious edifice that is evolution.

Well, maybe some see this as a safe route. What I mean is, while the fight over what constitutes proper values is so emotionally charged, perhaps following science with its rational approach subjects one to fewer "roller coaster style" peaks and valleys.

However, I'd be the last person to say that following science leads one to atheism. Nor did the man who said the following believe such a thing.

> Science without religion is lame, religion without science is blind.

Recognize the quote? Albert Einstein again! And I'd like to use the rest of this chapter to show that, as Einstein felt, the existence of values, obviously born mostly of religion, definitely underwrite the existence of God Almighty.

Values and Religion

All five chapters in part two of this book were devoted to science and math, and how God's hand is so obvious everywhere as He prepared the world for the arrival of civilized humans. So when you shift from science to philosophy do you have to leave God behind? Well, the previous chapter on Adam and Eve showed the concept of God was not only a good fit, but the only scientifically reasonable alternative to explain our origins. In fact, the only scientific arguments that didn't make sense were those attempts in chapters 8 through 11 to explain human evolution, vestigial structures and behaviors, and human language *without* God. So let's further investigate the presence of values through the eyes of divine necessity.

To begin, I'm sure we agree that the study of statistics and probabilities, especially at the collegiate level, is a rigorous mathematical tool especially valuable to science. (Ask my son Kenny, currently sweating through the statistics battery as part of his economics degree.) After all, stats are driven by exactitude and detail, with bias and emotion having no role. Statistics even include built-in stringent calculations of error to determine the level of confidence one can have in results. So what happens when stats are applied to values and morals? Will the scientific component disappear or hold fast?

First, there is a probability of "one" that an organized culture will have some form of religion. It seems that people throughout all of time, and in every location, must seek the source of power and meaning that is superior to and responsible for, but not contained in, their physical-biological world. As a way to amplify this thought, if you go to any poor village in any less developed country, it may not have a health clinic, it may not have a store, it may not have a town hall, it may not even have a school—but it will have a place of worship. And through this place of worship comes the values that govern this society—values (and consequences) that supersede an individual's desire to violate them.

If you examine the standards within different sets of societal rules, you will find an amazingly high rate of statistical consistency for something otherwise so widely separated by space and time—indicating an order of law higher than ourselves. And the correlation among these sets of rules would certainly not be the result of superstitious fear, but of necessity, for without these basics there would be the disastrous unraveling of even the most primitive societal fabric. Disagree? Think of how many historical examples we have where cultures like the highly advanced Greeks and Romans died not from enemies without, but from stagnation and degradation within?

A well-known example of societal rules—the Ten Commandments—was given to the Israelite nation in about 1450 BC on Mount Horeb at the southern tip of the Sinai Peninsula east of Egypt and the Gulf of Suez. Take a look at my one-word rendition of the evils the Ten Commandments sought to prevent, and then compare them their philosophical opposites that the same commandments were designed to promote.

Prohibitions in the Ten Commandments	Promotions in the Ten Commandments
1. Irreverence	1. Ability to be humble
2. Materialism	2. Not being controlled by possessions
3. Profanity	3. Speech tempered with restraint
4. Selfishness	4. Willingness to put self second
5. Disrespect	5. Respectful of elders, like parents
6. Murder	6. Valuing life's sanctity
7. Infidelity	7. Loyalty to one's spouse
8. Theft	8. Honoring the property of others
9. Lying	9. Honesty and truthfulness
10. Envy	10. Contentment

So how would these ten stack up to other lists of values or morals? How about comparing them to the Noble Eightfold Path of Buddhism? Or the 42 Declarations of Purity from Egyptian Ma'at Law? What about the code called the Chivalric Order of the medieval knights? Or the Ten Pearls of Wisdom of the Free Cherokee? (Why not even consult the 12 Ideals of the Boy Scouts of America?)

If you do, here's what will happen. You will find an amazing level of agreement among all these sources as to what values, morals, and rules constitute proper human behavior. (For you statisticians, if you did a comparison test to determine "type one error" that there is no correlation among these lists, and set your level of rejection of the null hypothesis at the .05 level, I can guarantee you there is less than 1 chance in 20 that the agreement in these lists is mere coincidence!) Or you can look at it one more way. If you were devising your *own* code of human behavior from scratch, what would you include? More specifically, which of the ten above would you feel comfortable *excluding?*

Are Values Compatible with Darwinism?

Here is the central point of this chapter. Inviolate standards for human behavior exist, and these absolute values and morals supersede any individual's right to violate them anytime or anywhere.* The presence of good and evil alone proves the existence of some force greater than flesh and blood that evolution cannot hope to explain. It also sets us aside from all other animals that at best have only instinctual parallels to true human abstracts, for example, *predation* as opposed to *killing* and *parental care of offspring* as opposed to *loving your children.* In fact, some human abstracts have no animal parallels at all, for example, *aspirations* and *bitterness.* And since the Genesis account of the origin of this greater force is accurate, reasonable, and without competition, the traditional God of Adam to Abraham claimed by the Arabs, Jews, and Christians is at the heart of it all.

With the details to follow, you may get a better grasp of the significance of human uniqueness with regard to abstracts. One very interesting book in this category is by author David Stove with the self-explanatory title *Darwinian Fairytales* (Encounter Books, 1995). In *Fairytales,* Stove does a thorough job debunking many of evolution's more technical tenets, such as selfish genes, hereditary errors, nongenetic memes, extended phenotypes, and so on.

But Stove shows his greatest alacrity to Darwinian error by discussing the many biologically unfavorable human traits that are nonetheless alive and well in our species. These traits, with both good and evil connotations, have no business being around when they should have been "rigidly destroyed" long, long ago by natural selection. Stove says you can flop open any dictionary, and from the A's to the Z's, from *altruism* to *zealotry,* the uniqueness of humans will come flooding

---

* Consider the thoughts of columnist and ex-atheist Mike S. Adams who says the existence of values is best proven not so much in our "actions" which are inconsistent, but in our "reactions" which are highly predictable. What Adams means is people may disregard commandments such as "Thou shalt not lie" and tell lies to satisfy some biological need, but everyone feels violated in a totally nonbiological way when lied to.

forth with characteristics that in the fight for *physical* survival can only be a setback.

So using Stove's reasoning, take another peek at the "ten prohibitions" listed above and ask yourself two questions. "Are the prohibited things advantageous to the survival of our species?" (Not hardly.) Then, "Are they rampant among us?" (You bet.) Furthermore, also look at the "ten promotions" and ask yourself two questions. "Are these advantageous to the survival of each individual?" (You bet!) Then, "Are they easy to maintain?" (Not hardly.) Clear enough that if natural selection has produced our species, it suddenly went haywire in us, wouldn't you say?

"Do Unto Others Before They Do Unto You"

You know, Richard Dawkins has quite a dilemma in his quest to make evolution appealing. I previously identified him as the last of the remaining prominent Darwinistic voices of the twentieth century. Highly educated and acclaimed Oxford University professor. Accomplished zoologist. Prolific and humorous writer. Has lots of admirers. Even enjoys a great-looking photo on his various book jackets.

But the dilemma is, his most popular book would hardly fill each of us with a hope for similar success, academic or otherwise. Called *The Selfish Gene*, it explains why the Golden Rule should be replaced by the version you see in the heading above. As Dawkins's book title clearly states, it's not the individual species that are engaged in "survival of the fittest," but the genes themselves that are in a "to the death" struggle to outpropagate each other. Therefore, the goal of each gene, in what he calls "universal ruthlessness," is to wrap itself in, and continue to fine-tune, an organism most fit to do battle. That's what I call cutthroat!

And Dawkins implies that since the human gene is the most successful, ours are the most selfish, and our selfishness can readily be seen in how we pursue our careers, families, marriages, relationships, and so on. With selfishness as his underlying theme, Dawkins then must repeatedly use doublespeak to explain how a variety of our seemingly altruistic behaviors are actually related to selfishness. For example, in chapter 12, called "Nice Guys Finish First," Dawkins explains a four-square game called "Prisoner's Dilemma," basically saying that people are constantly forced to help others as the only way to best help themselves. (Now that's comforting.)

The book also ends uniquely. In the last chapter, "The Long Reach of the Gene," Dawkins closes with another backward explanation as to why life on the planet could still be so diverse after millions of years if each organism's genes are bent on its neighbor's destruction. According to Dawkins, it seems that all genes have developed a cooperative system to selfishly exploit the weaknesses of the others. Call it similar to a parasite that only repeatedly harms its host rather than kills it. What this creates is a bizarre interdependent network of self-sustaining bloodsuckers where nobody can completely get the upper hand, even we humans.

Perhaps Dawkins would say this is why the most advanced gene in the pool—ours—lives in greatest fear of the least complex gene—the virus. At any rate, I do wonder how Dawkins's genes might be exploiting the genes of others through the writing and selling of his books.

Primates and Percentages

I am truly amazed at how frequently Darwinists compare humans to primates as if this constitutes proof of natural evolution. So do Darwinists think concepts like values can be dismissed just because of our physical similarities to a chimp? To expand on this idea of physical similarities, I wonder how many of you have seen the scientific exhibit called "Body World 2," by Gunther von Hagens? I caught the display at the Denver Museum last summer, and in a word, it is outstanding. Using more than 20 actual human bodies preserved by the process of "plastination," you can observe the mechanisms for movement, digestion, circulation, and nerve function almost as if they were happening before your eyes. You can also observe the effects of disease and injury when problems arise with our marvelous but vulnerable bodies. As

I left the exhibit, I kept thinking, *I wonder how a Darwinist would explain such absolute precision?**

I imagine every Darwinist walking out of Body World 2 or some similar display on the human physique would be secretly saying something like, *Oh well, the chimpanzee from which we evolved is still 98.4 percent just as impressive. And the spider monkey is maybe 97 percent as cool—and the lemur is 96 percent—and other mammals 90 percent— birds 85 percent—reptiles 80 percent—amphibians 70 percent—fish 60 percent—bacteria 1 percent. Nope, don't fret. You're safe. The "God" thing is an adult form of Santa Claus you have cleverly outgrown.*

First of all, no such nice gradual regression exists in comparing DNA codes from complex to simple life. Despite the obvious differences, a simple bacterium is a metabolizer in much the same fashion as we (digestion, respiration, waste removal, and so on), accomplishes cell division much the same way as we (interphase, prophase, metaphase, anaphase, and telophase), must generate the same cellular organelles as we (mitochondria, ribosomes, vacuoles, and so on), and produces new DNA with the same procedure as we (separation, transcription, translation). So in many ways, there is no doubt that all life is built on a similar genetic platform.

Uniqueness by Design?

Beyond that, I wonder how a Darwinist would respond to the following list? For about the last ten years that I taught tenth-grade biology, to open the unit on the human body I have always had my students journal on the topic of "What Behaviors Do Humans Exhibit that Have No True Parallels in the Animal World?" Every year I got repeats, but here is a consensus list that I saved for several years—I guess for just a time as this.

---

* This was the same question I kept asking myself as I read Geoffrey Simmons's fine book *What Darwin Didn't Know* (Harvest House Publishers, 2004). Dr. Simmons is an M.D. with 40 years of experience, and his book expertly points out how much science has learned about human physiology since Darwin's book *The Origin of Species* was published in 1852. (Can you grasp how far medicine has come in 150 years?) By detailing every ultimately fine-tuned human structure from biochemical building blocks to cellular components to organ systems, I'd say Simmons proves his opening paragraph—that based on just what science has learned about our bodies since 1852, today Darwin would be unlikely to even get his work published.

Humans Are Unique Because...

1. We weave clothes for ourselves out of plant fibers, and raise other animals specifically for their skins.

2. We have overcome the fear of fire and electricity, and use them for warmth, cooking, and communication.

3. We have domesticated plants, and we cultivate, harvest, preserve, interbreed, and engineer them for our uses.

4. We do the same with animals as with plants, and also train them to work for us.

5. We confine and keep other animals as pets to bring us company and enjoyment.

6. We are concerned, even obsessed, with our appearance as a means of self-expression, and try a variety of artificial enhancements.

7. We have developed the art of healing, and have distinct potions, procedures, and locations to aid our health.

8. We suffer from stress that is often unwarranted and self-induced, and we even take our own lives because of it.

9. We have developed methods of birth control, and find ways to enhance sex only for the sake of pleasure.

10. We have mastered metallurgy, and mine and smelt ore from the ground to make tools and machines.

11. We have invented the wheel, and use it for transportation, communication, and recreation.

12. We communicate with abstract letters and numbers, and keep a historical record that conveys facts and even feelings over long distances and periods of time.

13. We have mastered flight, though it is completely unnatural to us, and now rely on it to a great extent.

14. We feel purpose for our lives, and set goals and have aspirations for ourselves, our children, and even our descendants we will never meet.

15. We have developed religious systems in every culture ever studied in an attempt to answer who or what is bigger than ourselves.

16. We develop a personal code of morals we believe is right for ourselves, and believe our code is superior to those of others.

17. We violate our own personal code, and then turn to denial, rationalization, or guilt as a means to compensate.

18. We bury our dead in sorrow with some type of ceremony that gives us closure as well as hope.

19. We engage in sport and competition for entertainment, and the outcome has a big bearing on our self-concept.

20. We have agreed on which common objects to call "money," and are willing to trade these, agreeing they represent goods and services.

21. We use a variety of mind-altering substances for entertainment, mood changes, or escape.

22. We desire possessions whose size and sophistication go far beyond a functional need, and then envy those who have surpassed us.

23. We send our young off to specific locations to be educated, relying on complete strangers to teach vital skills.

24. We are the only animals whose females are on the menstrual cycle, and where painful birth is the norm rather than the exception.

25. We wage war over ideologies, and often kill members of our own species because we cannot come to agreement on abstract concepts.

26. We commit aggressive acts like stealing in a premeditated fashion for revenge, triviality, or excess.

27. We use self-mutilation and other types of permanent body markings as a means of self-expression.

28. We have a deep need to enjoy and even create original

pieces of art, music, literature as a way to express our inner being.

29. We eat for pleasure way beyond sustenance, and make dining more of an entertainment than a nourishment event.

30. We have invented intricate waste removal systems and devices to dispose of our excrement and refuse.

31. We do knowing damage to our environment, and persist in such behaviors even when cognizant that they lead to long-term destruction.

32. Our personal hygiene goes far beyond what is necessary for health, and it includes a variety of cleansers, scents, and lotions, as well as devices to apply these.

33. We engage in homosexual and lesbian behaviors, and through them set up pseudo-breeding pairs to imitate those that actually do sustain the species.

34. We create differences in local cultures that can be identified by unique rules, customs, activities, and holidays.

35. We communicate in over 6000 different languages though we are all one species.

36. We look up at the stars, and wonder...

For my students, a list that came from their thoughts always seemed to carry nonevolutionary implications without a single comment on my part. To me it totally reinforces the "Darwinism's weakest link" title of this book. In my view, if we are just an evolutionary extension of primates—even prehistoric hominids—how did we jump so far in development and sophistication in a hairsbreadth of time?

Despite the 98-plus percent genetic similarity between chimps and ourselves, the observable differences (such as the 36 compiled by my students above) are overwhelming. So Darwinists have just two choices in defending natural evolution—elevate primates to as near human status as possible...or lower us to theirs.

No Ground to Stand On

As I close this chapter, I would like to present to you a person I know. This man believes that monogamy is stifling a very natural urge to mate with as many females as possible, an urge obviously inherited from our primate ancestors. He also believes the general prohibition of adultery has been generated by a narrow-minded and stodgy society that has no right to decide other people's personal behavior standards. Such a view certainly puts him in a statistical minority in our population, since I know of no other who promotes polygamy as openly as he does.

But at the same time, this man is completely repulsed by any instances of child abuse. I can tell he is well acquainted with the scars such abuse leaves on children, and this is the likely reason he favors swift prosecution and stiff prison sentences for convicted violators. On this issue, I would now put him in with the statistical majority who see child abuse as a particularly heinous evil. So it seems my acquaintance freely violates one absolute and steadfastly adheres to another. So would you find him 50 percent wrong and 50 percent right?

For the sake of argument, let's suppose someone believes a little bit of controlled sleeping around is not all that evil if it doesn't become habitual, but this same person still cannot stomach child abuse. Then is this person 25 percent wrong and 75 percent right? How about another person who believes adultery will ultimately cause divorce and then child abuse, and if we would devote our energies to marital fidelity, we wouldn't have to worry much about child abuse. Is he 75 percent wrong and 25 percent right? Or how about a man whose intentional infidelity causes divorce after divorce, and also believes leaving marks on his son with a belt teaches the proper lesson? Is he 100 percent wrong? And one more. Consider a male who maintains a long-term married relationship, but one who also secretly practices the deliberate exploitation of young boys on the side. Is he 50 percent right and 50 percent wrong—a complete reverse from my acquaintance friend?

Is this confusing to you? It certainly is to me! I guess that's why in a civilized society there is rule of law, and duly appointed arbiters who are assigned the difficult task of deciding how wrong the wrong was.

But here's the major point. If we are all a product of random scientific forces, it makes no difference. There's no 25 percent, 50 percent, 75 percent, or 100 percent—no percentages at all. If Jacques

Monod was right—science has no relationship with values—and if ardent evolutionary apologists like Michael Ruse and David Hume were right—God is not, and science is all there is—how can there be any values at all? For instance, if you believe ax-murdering is proper, how can anyone who is just as big a statistically random accident as you declare his or her position superior?

Besides, I'm sure *you* can look at his life and find something amiss. What's your opinion? How about adultery, compared to yelling at your wife? Child abuse, compared to being a bit too gruff with your kids because you had a rough day? Plunder, or borrowing with no intent to return? Murder, or a rude shove? If these are all only random events in an unspecified world without a God, then there can be no values, no morals, no rules, no absolutes, no controls—no nothing. There also cannot be any accountability, and no system such as sowing actions and reaping results.

No—societies and common sense show the truth lies in the alternative. Values exist, and their existence proves there is a Giver of values. In fact the correct explanation is this. Science always assumes an outcome has *causation*. Likewise, morality (whether right or wrong) assumes causation. Finally, since evolution is a dismal failure, causation of the universe assumes God. Then when you tie it all together,

$$\text{Science} \approx \text{Causation} \approx \text{Morality} \approx \text{Causation} \approx \text{God}$$

A quick note about evolutionary apologist Richard Dawkins, who rejects the concepts of commandments and guidelines—and therefore, in my opinion, evil. He makes an interesting revelation with this comment.

> My own feeling is that a human society based simply on the gene's law of universal ruthless selfishness would be a very nasty society in which to live...Be warned that if you wish, as I do, to build a society in which individuals cooperate generously and unselfishly toward a common good, you can expect little help from biological nature.

When Dawkins says "simply" in the first sentence, it implies there is a higher level other than gene selfishness to which we can connect. And when he says, "you can expect little help from the biological nature," that also implies there is another, higher nature to which we can aspire.

The revelation? All his life Dawkins has been saying there *is* no force other than simple biology—there *is* no other nature to appeal to than physical selfishness. But do the above words mean that, deep inside, Dawkins believes we have a nonbiological option that chimps and everything less complex do not have? It would seem so.

--- • • • ---

Permit me one parting look at evil. On September 11, 2001, in an unprecedented display of solidarity, people worldwide arose and unequivocally called the same thing evil. On 9/11 we all indignantly said a universal value had been violated and a rule had been broken.

The weird deal is, if you are a Darwinist from any culture, you have to call this event just a collection of aluminum and jet fuel molecules colliding with a collection of metal and masonry molecules—whose impact randomly disassociates and denatures a collection of organic molecules (in some cases, the human tissue of children) that just happened to be present in the two separate collections of inorganic molecules.

However, the trouble with this explanation is that even the most hardened Darwinists were spiritually and morally moved by this event, while all other animal life-forms not directly affected by the explosions surely were unmoved. This proves beyond argument that an *evil* took place that day. Furthermore, it most surely happened among the *neshama,* because the *nefesh* were not created to comprehend it.

14

The Ultimate Objection

The Nature of Information

Before we get to the heart of the matter, could I interest you in a "get rich quick" scheme? If you can pull off any of the following, you will have a fortune that Bill Gates would admire. All you have to do is design a mechanism that neutralizes gravity, perfect and patent cold fusion in a fruit jar, or identify the human aging gene and find a way to reverse the process. On the other hand, these may be lofty or even unreachable goals. So maybe you might pursue a discovery that was once, like changing lead into gold, considered a matter of time. Just produce a naturally black rose. You first will claim a long-standing seven-figure cash bounty offered by horticulturists, and then floral enthusiasts from the creative to the odd to the morbid will beat a path to your greenhouse.*

Some people argue that the many scientific impossibilities of Darwinism only tend to leave you with "God" more or less by grudging default. I disagree with the "grudging default" argument, and I challenge it by posing three questions.

---

* Do you wonder why this paragraph is here? Keep reading.

---

1. Can the reality of "God," in whatever form you interpret Him, be argued more from the standpoint of necessity?

2. Can the possibility of a self-made universe be irrevocably rendered untenable, unthinkable, and therefore unacceptable?

3. Can the reality of the requisite Being of designing power and constancy be traced to its origin, and so forcibly identified that it becomes a matter of law?

This chapter on information will pursue "yes" for all three questions.

Introducing Information Theory

As I said earlier, I am convinced the most powerful argument for the presence of God originates in the realm of information. Either intended information is part of our reality and has been introduced by an "Informer," or random and unintelligible has somehow given rise to the "appearance" of detailed precision. If the presence of the Informer is provable beyond reasonable doubt, then we have that Superior Being by necessity and not by *nolo contendere*. And in this case, the proof that removes reasonable doubt—leaving you with only *unreasonable* doubt—comes from an established wing of science, the field of *information theory*, or IT.

Scientists working in the field of information theory are a unique assortment in that they never seem to align themselves with either science or religion. Their bipartite quest is to understand the origin, quality, and transmission factors influencing data no matter the source. Like many specialized scientific branches, IT has its own tailored vocabulary. It also has its own pet theorems and phrases such as, "An information sphere in a high dimensional 'before state' will reach a low dimensional 'after state' once it has traveled its chosen its pathway." That's a mouthful! Perhaps this quote is more decipherable if you read it as IT's general governance, "Information transmission must be paid with dissipation." If this is still not clear, read on.

An efficient way to understand information theory is to use the approach of statistical analysis that employs the *null hypothesis*. The null hypothesis states that despite your suspicions of a possible link (however strong those suspicions are), there is as yet no established concomitant relationship between two suspected variables until you have statistical proof. For example, you may fully believe that the DNA molecule is far too complex to have an accidental origin, and therefore a Giver of such information must surely exist. But to prove your suspicions about DNA, you first must collect valid and reliable data, and then statistically establish a connection between your two variables within acceptable levels of error. Only then can you reject the null hypothesis with confidence.

As my source for data on information, I would simply like to use the italicized first paragraph of this chapter mentioning Bill Gates and the black rose. In case you weren't counting, it contained 143 words (not counting the title) made from a total of 792 letters, spaces, and punctuation marks. Now imagine, if you will, all these letters and spaces mixed up and loaded into a "letter shooter" which begins to randomly fire them at a page machine gun–style one character at a time in sequential left-to-right rows. After all 792 total characters have been fired, you have another paragraph of writing to compare to the original.

Now, you have to admit that one possible outcome is to receive the *same first page* back again, right? And if that happens, according to IT, no information has been lost. But wouldn't you say a perfectly reproduced paragraph is unlikely? I would. But how unlikely? Well, since there are over 10^{1134} different ways to reassemble the characters in that single page of information, and the commonly estimated number of atoms in the entire universe is 10^{80}, I'd say *virtually unlikely* would be a whopping understatement. To put this value into perspective, if that one in 10^{1134} probability of paragraph duplication is equal to a quantity of atoms, and if there are indeed 10^{80} atoms that make up our entire universe, you have enough atoms to make an additional 13-plus universes the size of ours! Therefore, are you willing to say the odds of getting that page back may be virtually impossible, but still not just plain *impossible?* Read on.

Dissipation

In this random transmission of all available characters from the letter gun, I say there will be such a great loss of information that the new paragraph is now completely unintelligible. But can we at least agree that the quality of information should show at least some degradation? This is because IT says that letter transmission such as this is a form of "dissipation," and the price for dissipation is the loss of information.

Let me give you a common example. Remember one of those clever cartoons or printed lists of funny sayings that has passed from office to office and hand to hand until it reached yours? You know the one. It's where you get a good laugh and then say, "Hey, let me make a copy of that." So you run it through your photocopier, and it picks up yet another dot, smudge, or smear from the glass window of your machine. In this case, IT says the "price" of transmission from photocopier to photocopier is the dissipation of informational quality of your page of humor. And you know which ones have been on the "laugh circuit" for quite awhile because they are getting blurred. Teachers especially understand this potential problem. We always try to save the master of a document like a test or assignment we intend to photocopy again, and not copy a copy of a copy so we can preserve as much clarity as possible.

To explain it in IT language,

> After following the path traveled, the binamics in the humorous page's "before state" is more ordered than in the "after state," and information has been paid by dissipation. Also, in any resulting copy there can be no improvement from any chosen "sequence marker" on the page as it translates through the "sequence logo," unless there is intelligent intervention.

To clarify all this, I'm sure you realize that in the end you could render your page completely unintelligible if you run it through enough photocopiers. Plain enough, I hope.

Going back to my example of reconstituting paragraph one, I'm sure the dissipation effect would be much more quickly apparent than in the photocopier scenario. In fact, as I said earlier, I expect that the dissipation would be totally complete after our letter gun has fired its alphabetical ammunition the very first time. But again, if there are

10^{1134} possible outcomes, is it possible to find anywhere on any of those resulting random paragraph lines the appearance of improvement? Most certainly.

More than that, the appearance of what looks to be improved information must be *expected* because as letters and spaces appear in strings, you are sure to find new words. For example, the word "design" appears in that first paragraph, but not the word "side." Well, let's suppose the gun fires out these four letters from the word "design" in this order, "s—i—d—e." This would obviously give you a new word, but is this truly new *information?* IT says "no" because now you have irrevocably lost those four letters in "side" necessary to form the key word in "design," and the part of the text requiring "design" may be severely damaged or lose its meaning altogether. (For that effect, read the third line in the first paragraph omitting the word "design," and get a feel for the loss of information.) Again, "Information transmission must be paid with dissipation."

But that's just a start. This might seem amazing, but in paragraph one (based on the availability of the letter "b") the quantity and selection of letters exist to make the word *antidisestablishmentarianism* a whopping nine times! But after you extract a total of 252 letters to make those nine words, which removes 32 percent of its letters, will any of the remaining text be readable at all? No, because once again, in a major way this time, "Information transmission must be paid with dissipation." So is there any random way to genuinely improve information with just the letters at hand? Read on.

Smuggling in Information

First, I could also build a case that not just new cognitive words like *side* or *antidisestablishmentarianism* are possible, but random could also produce "affective" improvements as well—affective as in new feelings. For example, there are more than enough letters from the first paragraph randomly fired from the letter gun to reorganize into a Japanese haiku poem, that special poetic form comprised of three lines and 17 syllables in the precise 5-7-5 pattern. Consider my original.

Ode from Dog to Keeper
Fresh food in my dish.
Soft cushions and soothing strokes.
You must be a god.

In actuality, the poem above not only *could* appear, but it *must* appear in at least one of those over 10^{1134} possibilities of page one. (*Must appear.* I hope you caught that.) This is because all letters, spaces, and punctuation marks in the poem, including the necessary repeated letters, are available in the first paragraph. What's more, there are even sufficient letters left over to generate the second haiku poem that appears below on the same page, giving you more affective improvement on yet another possible outcome in those 10^{1134} page combinations.

Ode from Cat to Keeper
Fresh food in my dish.
Soft cushions and soothing strokes.
I must be a god.

It might be interesting to compare the paragraph's after state to the before state once letters necessary for the poetry have been removed. Therefore, let me extract the 108 characters required to make *both* poems. Starting with the removal of six "f"s (from the words *"fresh/ fresh" "food/food" and "soft/soft"*), four "r"s, and so on, here is what is left of the first paragraph.

Beore we get to the heat of the ater, culd I intret you n a "get ric quc" cheme? If yu can pull any of he follwing of, yo will ave a fotune that ill Gats wuld admr. All yo ave to do i desin a mechani that nutralze gravity, perfct and patent cld fusion in a frut jar, r identi the huma agin gene an find a wa to revere the proces. n the other hnd, these my be loty or even unreacable goal. o aybe yu might pursu a discovey that wa nce, lie canging lead into gol, cnsired a mtter o time. Just prduce a aturally blak rose. Yo fir will clim a lng-tanding seven igure ash bunty ofered by oricultust, and then flral enhuiat fro the creatve to the od to the mrbid will eat a pah to yur greenose.

Well, there you have it. Two poems needing 108 letters extracted from one short paragraph, and I will readily admit the text is still generally recognizable. Eureka! We have generated much new cognitive and even affective information, and the dissipation by which it was paid was not that great a loss. At this point the natural evolutionists feel justified that new information can come from random sources, and that as long as you have enough celestial activity over enough time, energy will organize into inorganic matter, inorganic matter will organize into organic matter, organic matter will organize into cells, and cells will eventually organize into people. So Darwinists say "thank you very much" and stand up to file out of the stadium, even though there is way too much time left on the game clock.

If you buy the above explanation as a random event, you have conveniently ignored my use of the Darwinist's favorite ploy in their explanations—the constant infusion of smuggled intelligence. In order to leave the first paragraph passage as readable as possible, I intentionally and very carefully extracted letters from the most auspicious locations. For example, a "d" out of the word "odd" still left a rather readable "od." Also, any silent consonant, like the "g" in "design" can be extracted, causing minimal impact when you read the word "desin."

Another deliberate decision on my part cannot be overlooked. I myself as a semi-intelligent being, and not a hoard of chimpanzees banging on a computer, can take full credit for the generation of the information in the paragraph and both poems. I know that's obvious, but with Darwinists, the obvious is what often escapes them most.

The Result of Blind Luck

Now to extract intelligence, can you imagine what would happen if I *randomly* plucked the 108 letters of the poems out of the first paragraph in blindfolded fashion? Here's how luck picks 792 characters.

> *Gvxuel do loc yh epo grdmv nh tsv ahhfit, hgtum c sefynitr iol wa g "nml haro sglob" yfdaow? So cof vrf enwa owt jw llt hdeinfonk hnc, nyt bgum fras c gmteusa pvee inem ulbos ulfnd ddsiyi. Nue ybt cole oo ha eu rutpph n eoreatiyc rvar sawnictroim lsaeeme, eeyaunu ylb rgfsdg aabs seydun ih t*

eaecv usk, ed rlaggsfo ber ndnej rusts torh nap tioc o gle ci sihadtc hie tmttuao. Tu ale osdoe airp, aaato efo be eatta rd hsow voireaurfea fnyrn. Tt tcafs nie lehrs edtcne f ntgiunhae erdo hyl buth, sood ehmaiuqt snie ztie usey, aroollawdl l niorfa ng etnh. Dngh risrlts t tahntuifi tohmr aiut. Nef siaid otst reoen a elme-ateoamti dnase iarrto hhel nibuls cicetea et eaelmuilroioett, eoe auny tyihaf tgcideehhkc hntr ane ntyotocg oe lae aef ol rge ltotfe rnoa rpee i daha tl toui efrgetyiai.

Quite a mess, eh? The only intelligent choices still in effect are that a specific number of 792 letters have been used, and the spaces and punctuation have been left in their original locations. Also, the "chirality" of the characters, meaning their rotation and reflection, has been intentionally manipulated so you don't have to read letters that are sideways, upside down, or backward.*

So when you get a fully realistic look at what random produces, is anything left that is readable? Obviously, such a paragraph constitutes just one outcome in those 10^{1134} possibilities, but when randomness is operative, there is no doubt other paragraphs will look much more like the italicized latter than the former.

These results align well with IT that presupposes informational patterns arise from intelligence and are therefore detectable and testable, while luck can only produce unusable trash. In other words, test as many people as you want, and see what they detect in the above paragraph of gobbledygook. "Nothing" is the answer.

Yet the impressive results of luck are exactly what evolutionists assume when they say random forces did tasks like placing nine perfectly sized planets around a sun perfectly sized for life on a perfectly suited third planet, or assembling the correct string of 100 amino acids in a protein before DNA was present. Using phrases like *The Blind Watchmaker, Climbing Mount Improbable,* and *Unweaving the Rainbow* (titles of Richard Dawkins's other books besides *The God Delusion*) Darwinists assume that not only does "Mother Nature" get lucky, but though totally unskilled, still knows exactly what she's trying

---

* See *Reclaiming Science from Darwinism,* chapter 8, "Cellular Recipe," to see what a huge hurdle to evolution chemical chirality actually is.

to assemble. And they believe in such as Dawkins's book titles even though they also admit evolution can have no preset goals.

But someone might jump up and say, "Now wait a minute. Random still *can* produce information, and you just showed how. The words 'do' and 'so' and 'ha' and 'be' appear in that new jumbled italicized paragraph, as do 'nap' and 'ale.' And if your name is 'Ed Cole,' take note. Your last name is found on line three, and your first name on line four!" So is the appearance of all these new words the work of intelligence? Or how about the most complex word I found in the mixed-up paragraph—"rusts"—which is the second to the last word on the fourth line. Can all these small words—even the five-letter one—be considered bits of new information on the way to becoming bigger bits of "newer" information, and do we only have to shuffle the letters sufficiently until the desired results are obtained?

That's bogus reasoning because if we shuffle these letters again, what would keep those previous words around to wait for improvements to the developing text? Furthermore, since Darwinists often claim evolution reverses itself to a previous spot (finch beaks, for example), how can we possibly hope our newly developing text is going back to the original paragraph? Or, since Darwinists must admit evolution has found the same spot more than once (wings on five totally unrelated animal types—insects, pterosaurs, birds, fish, and mammal bats), how could we get the same new paragraph five times?

Study these thoughts carefully, because this is exactly what Darwinists believe who place great faith in pre-cellular biochemistry that randomly organizes and self-advances. And since Darwinists must wait patiently for the desired end results, they also fully believe that useless molecules, however complex, still lie waiting until larger useful molecules (useful to what and made from where?) come along.

No, let's be very clear here what happened to that first paragraph when it was shuffled. Without any operative intelligence to assist in transmission, there was a complete loss of former information. Also, intelligence had absolutely no role in what little new "information" did appear. So the results are as IT always says—the dissipation process paid the bill in full. I would say the null hypothesis is on the way out, and there has to be a Designer.

How Far Can "Luck" Be Stretched?

Before the full weight of the information ax is laid to the trunk of Darwin's tree, it is useful to know what forms information can take, and how far "luck" can be stretched. When the word "rusts" first appeared on its own above, those five letters of information were obviously not a complex occurrence, and it was not an event that would turn any heads. However, when I intentionally typed the word *rusts* just now, you can say that this very "non-complex" word was at least specified by me.

Now, comparing the forces that make a tornado to those producing a five-letter word, a tornado is quite a complex display of physics. And yet tornados are completely *non-specified* in that they are not the intentions of the storms that produce them. The point? It is obvious that "random" can generate *specific* (finding the word "rusts" in a jumble of letters), and that "random" can certainly be *complex* (finding a tornado in a windstorm), all without a shred of intellect. However, the pivotal question is, "Can *specific* and *complex* ever travel together without having to pay the bill for dissipation?" Or more simply, "Can luck generate *specified complexity?*"

William Dembski, in his book *No Free Lunch,* uses rigorous math and logic to prove in undeniable fashion that the answer is a resounding "No!" For example, Dr. Dembski's "No Free Lunch" theorems in his book explain that there is a rather quick limit to what luck can accomplish, and the odds of generating *complex specified information,* or CSI, quickly surpass even the most stringent of remote probabilities.

Based on Dr. Dembski's work, a logical ensuing question would be, "When it comes to probabilities, what exactly constitutes remote?" Going back to our 10^{1134} odds of reproducing paragraph one, calling those odds "remote" is a gigantic understatement. Yet the addition of another single exponential zero now takes us to the "11,340th power," which explodes an already unfathomable number into a realm that human vocabulary cannot describe—and there are still an unlimited number of exponential zeros one can add in the generation of *theoretical* probabilities. Dizzying!

However, what constitutes *practical,* or *believable,* probabilities? Dr. Dembski again provides an answer by describing when "remote" odds become "impossible" odds. He proposes a *universal probability bound*—a boundary beyond which any other probability contained in the universe is not just highly, extremely, and outrageously unlikely, but *zero.* *

Take the common estimate of the number of atoms in the entire universe, 10^{80}, and multiply this by the smallest division of time that any one of these atoms can undergo any type of change that could be an evolutionary advance of some kind—derived from the commonly held Planck constant—10^{45} changes per second. Then multiply that by the common estimate of the age of the universe, which translates into 10^{25} seconds. The combined math looks like this:

$$10^{80} \times 10^{45} \times 10^{25} = 10^{150}$$

What it means is if you take the smallest particle reacting in the smallest amount of time with the maximum of time available, that will give you one possible event out of an absolute limit of 10^{150} events. Or for the short version, you have accounted for *every possible particle, any possible change, in all of possible time.* What odds could be greater? Therefore, any probability beyond 1 out of 10^{150} chances has to be assigned a chance of "zero." And remember, since our odds of our "letter gun" giving us back our first paragraph are one in 10^{1134} attempts, you do not have anywhere near enough particles and time in all the universe to *ever* allow the occurrence of that short paragraph to ever come back to you.

Furthermore, the odds of generating even an average-sized body protein out of its amino-acid components—at 10^{325}—far surpasses Dr. Dembski's boundary. His own summation perfectly supports the key point of *Darwinism's Weakest Link:*

> Implicit in the universal probability bound such as 10^{-150} is that the universe is too small a place to generate specified complexity by sheer exhaustion of possibilities.

From that there can be no dissension.

---

* Dr. Dembski's boundary formula is thoroughly explained in *Reclaiming Science from Darwinism* in chapter 7, "A Sword with One Edge."

Genetic Improvement—A Possibility?

Now, what better place to scientifically investigate the origin of information than to examine what drives most of the research in the life sciences—the master molecule called deoxyribonucleic acid, DNA. If you cannot use totally natural means to account for the workings of the chemical template that is behind all of life, then the "yes" of God and the truth of the *Exposing Darwinism's Weakest Link* title has been answered.

The aforementioned guidelines in information theory for information transmission are perfectly applicable to genetic sequencing. In fact, DNA studies are the darling of IT research, because how can the exact sequencing of three billion nitrogenous base pairs in humans—the A to T and C to G sequences—not be information of the highest order, considering it produces the vast complexity of our bodies?

Also, if you resolve the issue of information with respect to DNA, and whether intelligence produced it, you have in fact resolved the creation issue for anything living on our planet. That is because the proteins coded by DNA ultimately become responsible for (in this order) cells, tissues, organs, organ systems, and whole organisms in all plant, animal, and microscopic kingdoms. Then these DNA-induced individual organisms go on to build populations that comprise food webs in communities that become ecosystems making up the biomes of our planet. Call it absolute perfection at the largest and smallest features of both the living and non-living worlds. And beyond the strictly scientific, DNA must also be at the heart of the instinctual, emotional, and intellectual behaviors from protozoa to people. It is truly a blueprint for a series of machines far beyond the complexity of anything Detroit could ever imagine.

Francis Crick, joint discoverer of the structure of DNA, realized this significance. However, rather than deal with the issue of God's presence on the Earth, he deferred the problem to unknown aliens. Crick's "panspermia" theory says the first DNA molecules were delivered through intergalactic "express mail" by some species beyond our ability to identify. Then once the DNA was released here, natural evolution took over by generating increasing genetic complexity of its own accord—that is, steady improvements in DNA producing *macroevolution,* which transmuted simpler species into more complex ones.

Remarkable Faith

Think back on everything we've covered in parts two and three of this book. Darwinists have reduced all of that to mere chance: galaxies and solar systems, electromagnetic spectrums, water and other inorganic and organic molecules, cell organelles and cells, and human organs and organ systems—considering them not all that complex, and certainly not specified by any superior intelligence. They also believe all this complex specified information falls under the 10^{150} ceiling of the universal probability boundary. I say the amount of faith they have in their beliefs is truly amazing. It surpasses that of most of the religious people I know.

But unfortunately for Darwinists, the only proffered examples of such evolutionary changes are always types of *microevolution* or simple variations, not macroevolution or major speciations. Yet Darwinists still hang on to simple variations as if they are proof of macroevolution—as if they are a "single still frame" of an ongoing 4.6-billion-year-old video of gradual change that certainly must have happened. And of course they favor the term *microevolution* to allow the supposition that a small natural adaptation is part of the bigger natural evolutionary process.

But to show there is no connection with the supposed and the actual, let's allow information theory to expose "variations," "adaptations," and "microevolution"—or whatever you want to call them—for what they are: merely *gene sorts* and horizontal transfers of DNA's coded information *already in existence*.

Using What's There

To explain a *gene sort* as a horizontal or lateral genetic move, as opposed to a supposed fortuitous mutation that is a vertical or upward move, first imagine Darwinists looking at a poster of different dog breeds. They must salivate at these "obvious" examples of vertical change as wild dog species became everything from toy poodles to Great Danes, chihuahuas to St. Bernards. (Having raised chickens, I can also guarantee you that poultry genes exhibit great variety as breeders generate chickens with features from naked necks to "poofy hairdos.")

But we must constantly keep in mind that all dogs are *Canis familiaris* and all chickens are *Gallus domesticus*—single species of domesticated dogs and chickens that, despite the window dressing, are still able to freely interbreed. Therefore, these genetic concoctions are not a testament to the power of mutations, for a mutation producing a new species has not taken place. Instead, the credit goes to the tremendous *preprogrammed* versatility of alleles in canine and fowl, as well as in cat, horse, tropical fish, corn—and roses, if you haven't lost sight of the paragraph that opened this chapter.

In all these examples of *artificial selection,* there is nothing more happening here than breeders sorting among preexisting genes in their breeding stock. Now it's true that these extravagant traits are often recessive genes that tend to remain hidden, but by careful selection they can be allowed to dominate the gene pool in a way that nature has not. In this fashion, it is certainly possible to produce an entire nation of left-handed people—as long as you choose all the breeding pairs, that is—because artificial selection produces *no new genetic information.*

These examples of what breeders can do constitute no proof of newly appearing species any more than the gene sorts in nature. For example, when "Darwin's finches" on the Galápagos Islands undergo beak variations with changing climate conditions, these beak changes are predictable, and most importantly, *reversible* when prior weather conditions are restored. But this certainly doesn't mean finch DNA mutated once again and miraculously ended where it started.

As another example, I predict the deceptive saga of the English peppered moth will soon disappear from public school biology textbooks. If you don't know the fairy tale, this is the moth that "evolved" from light to dark (*industrial melanism*) to survive in the now soot-blackened tree trunks of industrial England in the nineteenth century. To expose this fraudulent application to macroevolution, these ancient studies of 200 years ago were made invalid by faulty and sloppy research methods. It is now known that for photographic purposes these nocturnal moths were pinned on tree trunks in the bright of day where and when they seldom land, and this was followed by the inference that they were collected in this "natural" habitat.

But even with these deceptions aside, nobody doubts the "dark phase" moths were *already present* in the predominant "light phase" moth population prior to the soot blackening of the English countryside. The original graphs bear this out. Even if moth color is indeed linked to shade of foliage—something never proven by laboratory research—who would doubt that the peppered moth population would shift back to a predominance of white moths if the foliage lightened? So, as with finch beaks and peppered moths, *no new genetic information.*

Sticking with Gene Codes

But the Darwinist's favorite examples of microevolution are the celebrated drug resistant bacteria and pesticide resistant mosquitoes— two shaky microevolutionary struts that some believe are sufficient to uphold the heavy weight of never-observed macroevolution. Here we have shifting chemically resistant strains of microorganisms and insects, and what they are doing is playing "peek-a-boo" not with mutations but only with the gene codes available.

For example, imagine applying an extermination treatment "A" to a pest population known to be generally effective. You find the results are satisfactory when almost all pests are wiped out. But consider that the pest population also contains a few individuals with an unusual but heretofore unneeded genetic combination making them resistant to treatment "A." Obviously they survive. (In populations as large as mosquitoes, or especially bacteria, there is every reason to think such a few "black sheep" exist.) Now our hardy survivors suddenly have the advantage of no competition, and they repopulate with a strain of "A" resistant pests that are often called a *mutated scourge.*

But if you apply another effective treatment, "B," which knocks out all but those few "B" resistant individuals, you likely have "sorted" your way back into an "A"-susceptible population. So maybe you continue the game of cat and mouse by introducing a "C" treatment, and bacterial/mosquito populations shift once more. If you doubt this process, ask a pediatrician who must decide which antibiotic to prescribe for children who catch all those "bugs" going around school. He will also say it is especially difficult to find an effective treatment for those kids who do not finish the prescribed medications, leaving many levels of resistance in variations of the same species.

Another way to verify this as a gene sort is to realize that if the path of evolution is truly a blind journey—for how can it be anything else if there's no guiding intelligence—how come these species are able to "mutate back" to the identical genetic codes they once had? Furthermore, just like in all the artificial selection work with fruit flies has never produced one new and improved fly, neither have all the antibacterial soap or various insecticides ever created new "superbugs" possessing advanced genes that completely prevent their control—though the "doomsayers" continue to predict such.

The end result is this once again—*no new genetic information.* So if you still insist on calling all of the above mutations and not gene sorts, then when two brown-eyed parents from a long line of brown-eyed ancestors produce a blue-eyed child, you must declare these parents have miraculously produced a wild mutation, a wild mutation that has occurred in so many other babies. The truth? The informational gene for blue eyes has been with us since the human genome was created, while the gene for, say, purple eyes does not exist.

Going back to my dog and cat poems, producing a biological variation is analogous to selecting letters already present in a paragraph and reorganizing them to produce a poem. The poem may contain a certain new look, even a new look never before seen, *but it is always at the expense of the original information,* which has now been severely degraded. So it is with a dog bred to have a more luxurious coat, or a chicken with extremely long tail feathers. To selectively bring forth these hidden genetic oddities, the survival effect of more visible and useful genes are compromised, if only even slightly. Therefore, the animal's gain is at the expense of a greater loss elsewhere, and information has been paid yet again by dissipation.

If you work with animals enough, you see this truth. In my biology classes, for years I have had the students incubate chicken eggs. They love for me to order the exotic breeds, such as the fancy feathered types, but the students quickly learn these always have a lower hatch rate.

And after birth, these highly specialized chicks have a greater mortality rate as they are less able to defend themselves or compete for food. These are not exactly advantages to survival, are they?

Specialized dog breeds face a similar dilemma. Try to imagine dachshunds (like my sister's little sausage dog named Bailey) making it in the wild. The currency they used to purchase their stubby legs and elongated bodies is survivability. Also, any bird hunter has heard about overbred dogs that may make fancy displays in a dog show, but couldn't find a downed bird unless they stepped on it.

Corn plants make another excellent example. The challenge among botanists is that after you produce bigger ears, more kernels, and a sweeter taste, how do you protect the plant from resulting higher disease susceptibility, greater nutritional needs, and increased temperature sensitivity? And as all breeders know, the farther you get from optimum gene expressions, the more problems you experience in reproductive ability, including that nasty little trait called *sterility*—a slight impediment in the game of survival. Of course a breeder wants to get a better product to market, but improvements with commercial value are not improvements as nature measures them.

The bottom line is, you simply cannot use variations as proof that unseen macroevolution took place, and not once, but millions of times over. This is because IT also says in so many words, "You must balance the genetic books." Just as one population of mosquitoes is affected by one pesticide today and by another tomorrow, so are exotic breeds of plants and animals also cases of *no new genetic information*. And with breeding, the sum of the matter is that the greater the variations become, whether through artificial or natural selection, the greater the degradation of the information from the original species. And no amount of embezzling from another genetic account can negate this.

Conservation of Information

Another major point about information has been saved for this section, though it has already been reinforced throughout the chapter. The concept is the *conservation of information*, and it puts a powerful exclamation point on what random can and cannot accomplish. This belief could be stated as, *Information appraisable only by modern humans is a separate entity with a preservation quality all its own.*

Stop and ponder that statement. It's huge. The concept has been highlighted by Sir Peter Medawar, who received the Nobel Prize in medicine in 1960 and was also knighted by the British Crown for his pioneering work in immunological transference and organ and tissue transplantation.

After lifelong work in this field, Medawar realized the ultimate barriers to what such medical work can accomplish. As we all know, recipients of foreign tissue, organs, or proteins (such as in vaccinations or transfusions) can face a multiple of problems with compatibility and rejection. As Medawar found out then, and as the rest of us now know, the best you can hope is for transplant patients to return to a "near" healthy state, knowing that certain complications will almost surely arise that must be addressed by medication, diet, or exercise. Conversely, in no way does a successful transplant—even something as a brand-new "right out of the box" artificial heart—make a patient's state *superior* to the state of his own organ functioning properly.

After a lifetime of trying to reduce the negative effects of transference, Medawar wrote a book with a title that would bring a shudder to people who place great faith in natural evolution. Published in 1984, the book is called *The Limits of Science,* and in it Medawar discards what every Darwinist obviously believes, that complexity can advance of its own accord. Perhaps Medawar's most poignant quote in the book is this one:

> No process of logical reasoning—no mere act of mind or computer-programmable operation—can enlarge the information content of the axioms and premises or observation statements from which it proceeds.

What I believe Sir Peter is saying here is that the bedrock statements in any body of information can perhaps be continually unraveled, but never be extended—even with the aid of computer power.

Medawar's quote obviously extends barriers to creating new information beyond more than in the biological sciences. Furthermore, his book makes it clear how this concept called the conservation of information applies to business, literature, and music—even computers. (Including computers is especially prophetic because Medawar made this observation during the fledgling years of the computer age. Over 20 years later, with computers so dizzyingly powerful, they still can produce no information beyond what their intelligent programmers programmed them to do.)

Medawar goes on to explain that conservation of information is deserving of *law* status (a mighty designation in science) because it holds true for all time and circumstances, and he says all we can do with the science already in existence is to study it, and maybe add what he termed "empirical furniture."

Limiting Luck

It should be obvious that Sir Peter Medawar would agree that the law of conservation of information imposes limits on luck. How could a roll of the dice do what a person with a computer cannot? (Or how can nature produce a mitochondrian when the best scientists with the best lab equipment cannot?) The law also says that in a random sort, the very best you can hope for in information transmission (such as an organ transplant) is to break even and be prepared for a loss of quality.

Going back yet again to the first paragraph of this chapter, if you load the 792 letters, spaces, and punctuations into our letter gun and fire them onto a page, your most stringent expectation is to get the original page back, which would happen only one time out of every 10^{1134} tries. But as a student once told me, "Hey, one chance in a gazillion still means *one* chance, right?" No, not really, because in some cases the law of conservation of information absolutely prohibits certain outcomes, and I can prove it.

First of all, our probability in question outstrips the universal probability boundary of 10^{150} in ways that are impossible to capture with words. Yet there are other examples that serve as more digestible explanations. It has already been shown that a short extracted poem has to be at the expense of the rest of the text. But unlike letters and words, if you believe you can carefully extract certain chosen amino acids for a short protein from a long protein and still have a long protein the body can use, consult your local molecular biologist.

But here's the impossibility. What is the chance that our letter gun fires out the word *box?* That probability is not "almost certainly zero," but *zero*—because the letter "x" did not appear on the first page at all when I front-loaded the original information. Similarly, though the following text needs no "x," is it possible to extract letters from page one and randomly produce this Dr. Seuss tongue twister from his book *Fox in Socks?*

> *Luke Luck likes lakes.*
> *Luke's duck likes lakes.*
> *Luke Luck licks lakes.*
> *Luke's duck licks lakes.*

No. You simply cannot get through even the first line above because there are only three "k"s in the first paragraph and you need sixteen for the rhyme.

And now you've found the prohibition of the black rose. The genetic code combinations for the black color *do not exist* in any breedable rose species. Not even as a recessive hidden gene, such as the yellows and whites that have been brought forward by breeders. Therefore, no amount of selection, artificial or natural, can produce the information for "black" in roses, any more than the first paragraph could produce the word box or the Dr. Seuss poem.

What Would Be Needed?

What it would take to produce a black rose is more than a gene sort or a horizontal gene movement. It would take totally new genetic information for black color, which would be that vertical jump the Darwinists believe happened many times over in ancient history, but has never been seen. And from what source? Well, don't count on today's genetic technology any time soon. Present research is currently limited to identifying certain codes, such as disease genes with hopes of deactivating them, and splicing other existing codes on genes already present, such as bioluminescence, to try and create a hybrid. But anyone can see that these experiments are just working with genetic information *already present.*

Conceptually, this is not much different than first locating a well-hidden radio in a Chevy, a radio that is very hard to remove without damaging it, but still successfully extracting it and then transferring it to a Ford that does not have one. In other words, nobody had to invent the radio in order for the Ford to have one. Even something as bizarre and (semi) funny as the joke about crossing a turkey with a centipede to get multiple drumsticks at Thanksgiving is *still* working with preexisting gene codes.

But let me be perfectly clear here. Do not ever doubt that I am very excited about the cutting-edge genetic work done by today's scientists. Gene selection and engineering have been giving joy to many would be parents, unlocking answers to many debilitating diseases, and bringing many products to the market that have improved the quality of life. And yet when the world takes notice in January 2007 because the first cloned woman gives birth to her own healthy baby, all are simply working with genetic information in everyday eggs and sperms present from the beginning of human history, harvested from people producing them the natural way.

These are difficult concepts sometimes, but to illustrate, I borrow an idea from the previously discussed concept of wave mechanics to describe the fallacy of true genetic improvement this way. Anyone can tune in a variety of AM stations on the 530 to 1600 KHz frequencies. True, some stations will be stronger and weaker than others, and some you may not even hear unless you move much closer to the transmission tower, but these are all horizontal searches. But try to receive an FM station on the AM band. You simply cannot receive an FM station until you vertically transfer to a higher frequency band. And you cannot truly improve genetic sequences without the intelligent altering of DNA.

So in the case of producing the black rose, what it would take is to identify all genes and alleles that affect flower color, add entirely new base-pair sequences that cause black color in a single pollinated rose ovum (if such a sequence indeed even exists), and hope that the changes don't adversely alter or destroy other required genetic information in the growing plant. This is how you know such creations are currently out of the reach of our science. If such were possible, we would sure be putting it to more applications than changing flower colors.

Of course, the other option is to wait for nature to produce a black rose. So there you are waiting for that theoretical "good" mutation via the harshness of radiation, lightning, or heat that evolution says produced biochemistry in the first place, and then later accomplished additional impressive feats like putting pelvic girdles and leg bones on fish. I'm sure tortuous lab experiments have been done on roses, and like genetic engineering attempts on the poor fruit flies, *no new genetic information* has ever been generated.

Studying the effects of human aging genes is another area of research that Darwinists often use in relation to "creating" new genetic information. For me, it is comical when people try to build a case that human microevolution is observable in present time. Invariably they will cite how an American in colonial days lived an average of 47 years, but now can count on up to 76 years in the twenty-first century. You may also hear how the average American, once 5-foot-6, is now up to 5-foot-10, and how the NBA once had only one seven-foot player (Wilt Chamberlain) but now seven-footers are common in high school.

Perhaps you will even hear we are getting smarter with all our technological advances. Of course this means to the wishful Darwinist that in a million years or so, *Homo sapiens* will have been replaced by a new species *(Homo maximus?)* that normally lives over 100 years, is at least a foot taller, and has an enlarged cranium to contain the brain of a superintellect.

Unfortunately, no reputable scientist who studies human trends believes these statistics represent evolution in action. Even the casual observer properly attributes them to maximizing the genes we already have through better health practices, more disease control, and a less dangerous environment. Natural evolutionists cannot use changes in today's humans to account for advances in yesterday's hominids.

But even if geneticists legitimately engineer a way to enhance longevity far beyond its present constraints, is there any doubt that limits will apply, and that a whole new set of biological problems associated with extreme aging (and no doubt social ones) will be introduced? There is no way around it. If you approach macroevolution scientifically by trying to explain how random forces produced new genetic information (instead of philosophically by dreaming up one wild theory after another), you are hoping that by digging out one medium-sized pile of dirt you can end up with two medium-sized holes.

A New Law?

William Dembski, the coiner of the term *complex specified information* for a reliable indicator of the work of intelligence, goes Peter Medawar one better by suggesting that the law of conservation of information should be added to the universal and inviolate laws of physics. The first, second, and third laws of thermodynamics deal initially with the conservation of matter and energy, and then define the nature and relationship of matter and energy by entropy and enthalpy. Dr. Dembski says a fourth law is needed to account for information because, as its own entity, information is neither substancelike (matter) nor powerlike (energy), but wordlike (code). He explains that information produced by intelligence can be reliably detected and measured, something done constantly by archeologists and cryptographists who search for signs of intelligence and know it when they see it.

Dr. Dembski suggests a fourth law of thermodynamics to explain the limits not only on the transference of present information, but the emergence of new information. On the transference of information, the fourth law could simply be worded according to what every computer operator knows, "Output can never exceed input." To restate, a source Set X that gives rise to a smaller Subset Y has resulted in a net loss, and to union Set X and Subset Y is to still have only Set X, producing no new information. For a teacher's example, to translate a 97 percent grade on a test to just an "A" in a grade book is a loss of numeric data. However, if the number is written down, also recording the letter is superfluous if you know the grade scale.

Dembski's examples of how his own proposed law applies include observations like

• Two copies of Hamlet contain no more information than one.

- A dog contemplating his master is less complex than a master contemplating his dog.

- Player pianos will always be inferior to piano players.

From a biological perspective I would add,

- A snake with two heads does not get better nutrition than a snake with one.

- A cow with five legs does not run faster than a cow with four.

- A man with six fingers cannot play the piano better than one with five.

Dembski goes on to use statistical analysis that shows evolutionary algorithms based on pure chance can in no wise outperform blind luck and improve information. Just like his book title, *No Free Lunch*, implies, advancing complexity must be purchased by intelligence, because all random can do is dissipate.

A subsequent issue for this fourth law, the conservation of information, is the origin of information itself. If in transmission the best you can hope for is to break even, but expect a loss of quality, then it follows that initial information in any closed system has been front loaded in its entirety, for nothing new can emerge.

This follows perfectly with the first law of thermodynamics, which says creation was a one-time event; the second law of thermodynamics, which says since the creation, all ordered activity is heading to disordered inactivity; and the third law of thermodynamics, which says all activity will cease at a temperature of -273° C. that as yet has not been reached. (In short, sum up thermodynamics this way: 1) Since all was made, you can't win, you can only break even. 2) You can only break even at -273° degrees C. 3) The temperature of -273° degrees C. cannot be reached.)

Your computer is a perfect example of all three laws relative to the one time front-loading of original information. First, if you have enough clues to follow, you can trace back to the specific date and time when the programming was placed on your hard drive. Then, once out of the box and plugged in, your computer can obviously do no better than operate its current applications, which it will cease to do when wear or lack of power makes it inoperative, or you cool it down to -273° C. But even when your computer is at optimum working order, if you have the knowledge to run an advanced program you still cannot do so without a programming upgrade.

Therefore, if the physics, chemistry, and math behind your computer have been in existence since the work of your machine's designer, and the eventual existence of your machine's designer and all that applied technology were intended "in the beginning" by the Master Designer, then this Designer must have created the information long ago. This means that the intelligence capability given to you, through your DNA that you can see, and through your spirit that you can't (this form of complex specified information, CSI, if you will) has a "forever" quality. Consider that—information has a "forever" quality.

A Match with Scripture

In all this science, permit me a scriptural aside. The first law of thermodynamics that says creation was a one-time event is a perfect match with Genesis 1:3 (and surrounding verses) which says, "Let there be light." The second law of thermodynamics, which says since the creation was finished, all order is heading to disorder, is a perfect match with Romans 8:20 (and surrounding verses), which says, "The creation was subjected to futility." The third law of thermodynamics, which says we can only guess what happened before the big bang and after -273° C. has been reached is a perfect match with Romans 11:33-34: "Oh, the depths of the riches both of the wisdom and knowledge of God! How unsearchable are His judgments and unfathomable His ways. For who has known the mind of the Lord, or who became His counselor?"

That leaves the proposed fourth law of thermodynamics. This one says that information has an initial creation, and from there can only dissipate when it is transmitted without an intelligent agent. This is a perfect match with one of my favorite sections of Proverbs, which personifies "wisdom." In this section, Solomon says that from the very beginning of creation, and then all the way through, wisdom—read *information*—was with God. So let me cite Proverbs 8:22-31, inserting the word *information* beside every use of the word *wisdom* and its pronouns. It reads like this.

> The LORD possessed me [wisdom, or information] at the beginning of His way, before His works of old. From everlasting I [information] was established, from the beginning, from the earliest times of the earth. When there were no depths I [information] was brought forth, when there were no springs abounding with water. Before the mountains were settled, before the hills I [information] was brought forth; while He had not yet made the earth and the fields, nor the first dust of the world. When He established the heavens, I [information] was there, When He inscribed a circle on the face of the deep, when He made firm the skies above, when the springs of the deep became fixed, when He set for the sea its boundary so that the water should not transgress His command, when He marked out the foundations of the earth; then I [information] was beside Him, as a master workman; and I [information] was daily His delight, rejoicing always before Him, rejoicing in the world, His earth, and having my [information's] delight in the sons of men.

Again, a perfect fit, I'd say. You can now add all the "information" from part two of this book: the perfect ordering of biotic and abiotic factors to create perfect food webs; the perfect math such as general computation, circles being governed by pi, and the divine proportion governing the rest of the universe by phi; the perfect chemistry like water molecules and DNA; the perfect physics like the organization of celestial objects and electromagnetic waves; and the perfect amount of time to develop them all.

Then you can add God's occasional removal and subsequent addition of new genetic information throughout time bringing about new species as described in Psalm 104:29. "You hide Your face, they are dismayed; You take away their spirit, they expire and return to their dust. You send forth Your Spiri, they are created; and You renew the face of the ground." Perfect.

This then sets the stage for the reality of Adam and Eve and their descendents, whose stories explain the origin of language, good and evil, and values as hominid evolution and vestiges never could. Finally, if all this information has guided our history from the beginning, and if Scripture continues to provide scientific and philosophic answers at every turn, then these closing verses from Revelation 22:18-19 are more than a warning. They are a scientific statement of fact about the eternal quality of God's information and our inability to change it just because we disagree. They also verify that the notion of our accidental existence is Darwinism's weakest link to the highest order.

> I testify to everyone who hears the words of prophecy in this book: if anyone adds to them, God will add to him the plagues which are written in this book; and if anyone takes away from the words of the book of this prophecy, God will take away his part from the tree of life and from the holy city, which are written in this book.

So now we have reached the crux of the matter. If, in all this discourse, you still maintain that all about us is random, and right down to the DNA molecule there is no such thing as information, you have your null hypothesis intact. But if you acknowledge information, then Someone has been tinkering with biology, physics, and chemistry. That same Someone has established information that reduces the factors associated with uncertainty, eliminates the dizzying number of useless possibilities, and powerfully pays a hefty dissipation bill on the front end.

Therefore, you must abandon the quest for the black rose, accept the intelligence of an Informer, and reject the null. More than that, if new species have indeed appeared throughout the ages, and quite suddenly as the fossil record indicates, then the Informer—"God" in the English language—has remained active from the start. It is now up to you to ascribe your chosen name to the Giver of Information, and decide the true nature of the Informer. This means that our existence requires accepting that a "miracle" was performed—several of them, in fact, and right up to our present geologic time—and miracles make scientists uneasy. But since science itself renders natural evolution impossible, you might as well begin your earnest search for God.

The following quote has also been attributed to Sir Peter Medawar.

> I cannot give any scientist of any age better advice than this: the intensity of a conviction that a hypothesis is true has no bearing over whether it is true or not.

I have met many natural evolutionists whose beliefs were "front-loaded" back when they were children. They now aggressively fight against an unthinkable alternative they have rejected their entire lives. I have also met many spiritual people who in the same fashion have grown up with the concept of "God," or found Him through a personal search. (I use the term *spiritual* as opposed to *mechanically religious,* and *spiritual* as opposed to *fanatical, narcissistic,* or *self-serving*—which describe all too many in the "business" of religion.)

I believe Medawar's quote calls all of us to allow these core beliefs to undergo honest scrutiny. Perhaps we should define our basic interpretation of the origins issue with the null hypothesis, and then set out not to prove what we want to believe, but to *disprove* it if possible.

In my case, I remember reading a criticism that there has been no scientific testing of the fourth law, therefore to declare that the conservation of information is valid and an active Informer must exist is hubris of the highest degree. And yet, does not the world abound with data that discards the null hypothesis? In like manner, my null has been thrown out many times over as I continuously and honestly examined physics, astronomy, geology, paleontology, molecular biology, and genetics—even mathematical probabilities—which continue to hold their individual knives to the throat of "self-made" at every turn.

This unavoidable presence of a Designer also leaves no wiggle room for those who believe we can still all act like fully civilized humans without a superior intelligence—because God is here! In fact, do not our bodies themselves cry out God's presence? I like Psalm 139:14, which says, "I will give thanks to You for I am fearfully and wonder-fully made; wonderful are Your works, and my soul knows it very well." You know, if I were "self-made," I would wave the white flag of surrender. So join me, as well as these fields of science and the truth of Scripture, and declare the title of this book to be valid.

PART FOUR

CONCLUSION

15

TODAY'S INFLUENTIAL DARWINISTS

Old and Young

Professor Emeritus Ernst Mayr of Harvard University published 25 different books, wrote innumerable articles, and received a list of accolades too long to mention. He recently died in 2005 at the age of 100, shortly after publishing his last book, *What Makes Biology Unique?: Considerations on the Autonomy of a Scientific Discipline*. Ernst Mayr was a giant in biological science. He was already an icon when I began my collegiate work in the early 1970s, and there have been no contenders for his status since as the global leader in the field.

Mayr had many biological specialties such as taxonomy (classifying) and ornithology (birds). But he was also known as the most eminent evolutionary biologist of the century. For example, Mayr's theory of *peripatric speciation* ultimately rose above the *allotropic, parapatric,* and *sympatric* alternatives as the most accepted evolutionary method for the random production of new species.* Mayr proposed many other evolutionary explanations that have more or less become "law" for the

---

* *Peripatric speciation* is said to have happened when an isolated small group of a newly altered species suddenly appears on the periphery of an existing related population. After the new variety carves out its own niche, it may grow to a population that rivals its relatives. From there it could drive the "less fit" forerunner species into extinction, or interbreed with it to produce a hybrid. See *Reclaiming Science from Darwinism*, chapter 23, for more details on the problems with this theory.

Darwinists. This includes dividing the whole theory of "self-made" into five different categories for an individual's acceptance or rejection, which are "general evolution," "common descent," "gradualism," "populational speciation," and "natural selection." No doubt about it, the man was on the cutting edge of evolutionary thinking and believed in what he taught—even calling Charles Darwin "my hero."

And here's where I will again tip my hat. In all my readings of Mayr, and in all the printed discussions of the work he so believed in, never once did I encounter him attacking or belittling people of faith. Why? First, the man never came across as arrogant or self-centered. He was an honest investigator who confined his thinking to the issue at hand. But more importantly, I believe Mayr did not secretly doubt evolution to the point he had to prove it to himself by attacking others and desperately proselytizing. I think he was secure enough in the belief that evolution held all the cards, and therefore he did not have to deal with closet fears over such weighty matters as the soul.

Final Words

What did Ernst Mayr believe at the end of his life? As he reflected on over 80 years of study at the highest level, what was his final take on the origin of humans? In is final book, *What Makes Biology Unique?* he devoted a section in chapter 2 to what he called "Biology as a Historical Science." In this section, the 100-year-old biology guru reveals what has to be his best strike-out pitch. Is it a condensation of the finest theories of evolution? Is it the powerful results of painstaking laboratory research? Is it the most fine-tuned details that explain the lingering questions about the natural origin of life? No. Rather, Mayr gives the world as his legacy "historical narratives." He explains them this way:

> There is no way to explain these phenomena by laws. Evolutionary biology tries to find the answer to the "why?" questions. Experiments are usually inappropriate for obtaining answers to evolutionary questions. We cannot experiment about the extinction of dinosaurs or the origin of mankind. With the experiment unavailable for research

in historical biology, a remarkable new heuristic method has been introduced, that of "historical narratives." Just as in much of theory formation, the scientist starts with a conjecture and thoroughly tests it for its validity, so in evolutionary biology the scientist constructs a historical narrative, which then is tested for its explanatory value.

Don't you find this statement absolutely extraordinary? I do, and when I read these words (and the rest of the book), my esteem for Mayr rises further for his complete honesty. Here, when it comes to a general academic discipline he wholly supports and has made the center of his life—and a make-or-break issue within that discipline—he basically says that hard science such as laboratory experiments are at best a poor avenue for verifying the mechanisms of evolution. And I assume that includes all the past experiments he's seen and done in his long life, which Darwinists constantly say have "proved" evolution.

What does Mayr say you should do—whether you believe in *"general evolution," "common descent," "gradualism," "populational spe-ciation,"* or *"natural selection"?* Well, read his paragraph above one more time. To me it sounds like Mayr says, "Consider what you need to have answered, and make something up that sounds good!" In other words, fashion your own conjecture, write it up with a lot of fancy sounding words, and then test it for its explanatory value—but not with scientific experimentation, mind you! (Then how do you test it? I guess you try it on your colleagues as you shoot the breeze over a cup of coffee.)

The "Historical Narrative"

I have to believe Mayr's final stance must drive the true Darwinists batty. There is no doubt from this quote, or from the rest of his book, that we are talking here about philosophical science as opposed to empirical science because there's a lot of debate in his pages—but not a single photo, sketch, chart, graph, or diagram from an experiment. Bottom line? Mayr offers no solid proof, and doesn't even pretend to, for Darwinism's weakest link—explaining human existence.

Let me also add that it's easy to see why Charles Darwin is Mayr's hero. In all the information we know about Darwin, there is not one bit of evidence that he did a single scientific experiment—not one! No, Darwin did what I believe all adherents to strict evolution do, "make it up as you go"—like his statement that a fish bladder could have been the forerunner of mammal lungs. (Darwin said that in *Origins*.) The difference is that Darwin had enough sense (early on, anyway) to express grave doubts about the validity of his own "historical narratives."* Before we go on to one recently published historical narrative by a young, up-and-coming biologist, let's be sure we understand what Darwinian evolution actually purports and how it applies to the past.

First, I will start as many Darwinists do—with the assumption that a preexisting, fine-tuned universe with metabolizing life is already present on Earth. (That's an immense assumption, isn't it?) Allowing life is already present, then Darwinism says nature constantly throws out a variety of genetic accidents in present species. These accidents are caused either by random mutating agents (ultraviolet radiation, thermal heat, lightning, and so on), gene mixups during hybrid mating, or chromosomal aberrations during routine DNA duplication.

Of course most of these mutations leave the organism unfit to survive (deformed limbs, stunted growth, damaged flowers, and so on) and they immediately die out of the population, taking their damaged genes with them. However, a few invariably turn out to be "good" accidents where the altered species is actually better than the ancestral species. Then since all life is in competition for a limited amount of resources, and all species produce more offspring than can possibly reach maturity, nature selects the improved mutated species as more fit to survive, allowing it to reproduce and increase its presence in the gene pool, often at the expense or even extinction of other competing species.

Therefore over long periods of time, the "good" accidents add up, and allow organisms to occupy new niches and produce more diversified food webs—and more importantly, carry life forward in

---

* Read the appendix on the life of Charles Darwin in *Reclaiming Science from Darwinism*. I believe it sets the record straight.

complexity. In due time, this complexity went through sea life, land invertebrates, fish that became amphibians and reptiles, reptiles that became birds and mammals—and mammals that became lower primates that became apes that became hominids that became humans. And if this seems unduly lucky, well, given all the places in the vast universe where this could happen, and a few billion years of time here on Earth where it did have time to happen, the improbable became reality.

Got it? Good. Then let's apply this reasoning to perhaps the most well-known historical narrative—the classic origin of those elegant long necks on giraffes. According to theory, way back in the distant past of the Cenezoic era (starting 65 mya to present), nature threw out giraffes with differing neck lengths from some common ancestral stock. In the struggle for food in the savanna where trees are scarce, only the longest-necked variety could reach sufficient leaves for food in the upper branches, and all other giraffes with any shorter version of neck length starved to extinction. In short, accidents of nature provided new genetic combinations, and then natural selection removed the genes less fit. Call it a case of "Mother Nature giveth, and Mother Nature taketh away."

The Recipe for a Svelte Neck

Even if the classic Darwinian explanation for the development of the giraffe's neck length is acceptable, the problems with that creature are just beginning. You have to account for bread-loaf-sized neck vertebrae, a two-foot-long heart, blood pressure so high it would kill other mammals (to reach eight feet up to the brain), pressure sensors in the neck to prevent aneurysms when the animal is bending to drink, and tiny capillaries with red blood cells one-third the size of normal.

Furthermore, you have to add special adaptations in skin, lungs, and trachea, as well as other subsystems that are necessary to support these highly specific main systems. Once again, how do you account for such an incredible quantity of new genetic information—coming *all at once*?

No New Details

In the course of being questioned about my first book, I was often asked my opinion of the biggest indicator that Darwinism was a failed theory. My answer was usually the same. I would say something like, "The main voices of evolution in the twentieth century have passed on, and there are no new young and brilliant Darwinists coming out of science to carry the theory forward by fleshing out more of the intricate details of how life made itself." Now, I am not saying science currently fails to produce any new brilliant Darwinists. Our educational system is still turning them out because the old watchdogs that want to maintain evolution's monopoly on the education and research systems are still exerting an influence—even though they are still tethered to the same old doghouse with the same short rope.

What I'm saying is that no new young minds are unraveling more of the missing *details* of how life made itself, or extending currently held evolutionary mechanisms into new territory. And to me there's no greater indication that Darwinism has hit a brick wall—that evolution is a dead-end theory—than when they use historical narratives for their explanations when good hard science is required. And here is my case in point.

Bioligist Sean B. Carroll is undoubtedly a highly educated individual. A professor and budding author out of the University of Wisconsin, I would also consider him one of the bright minds to come out of science, a member of the next generation of researchers who will lead us further into the twenty-first century. Since he is also a Darwinist, I'm sure many would cite Dr. Carroll as a reason my previous words about "no new brilliant evolutionary scientists" are grossly untrue. But remember, the "kicker" above is not that science can't produce smart people, but that nobody currently coming out of science is carrying the details of evolution forward. To put it clearly, nobody is explaining details that have been repeatedly asked for, ever since movements like Intelligent Design began asking the tough questions.

A Historical Fish Tale

In its Fall 2006 issue, a magazine called *Skeptical Inquirer* included an article by Dr. Carroll with an intriguing title: "The Bloodless Fish of Bouvet Island—DNA and Evolution in Action." The article begins with verifiable documentation from actual on-site journal writers, rather than historical narration of what is only imagined but never seen. Carroll tells of the mystery of Bouvet Island in the cold reaches of the far southern Atlantic Ocean, which in the early days of global circumnavigation was seldom found and is still seldom visited. With Bouvet Island being over 1500 miles from the nearest major landmass, and averaging below freezing temperatures that sustain an ice cover several hundred feet thick, it's not a very hospitable place. However, a biology student who visited there as early as 1928 reported catching and examining a curious specimen called a "white crocodile fish," described as transparently "bloodless." This fish legend, kept alive by whalers and other explorers, was finally caught and thoroughly studied in 1953, and it still continues to amaze researchers with the absence of hemoglobin in its blood.

Without a doubt, the article is filled not only with verifiable history but also good hard science. Dr. Carroll explains how every vertebrate ever known (animals with backbones) possesses the oxygen-transporting protein hemoglobin in red blood cells, and mentions other fish in these extremely cold waters that are nonetheless red-blooded. Furthermore, in explaining how the icefish is able to survive, he covers oxygen solubility related to water temperature, microtubule formation (a cell's inner structure) below 50 degrees F., and the unique amino-acid sequences in the icefish's biochemical "antifreeze." Extremely scientific, extremely educational. However, Dr. Carroll's main reason for writing the article, and ostensibly the reason for the magazine's printing of such—based on its name—was to explain how the totally natural processes in evolution could produce such an oddity. And here's where historical narrative is used to replace verifiable science. It reads like this, as if someone had been there videotaping it:

> Over the past 55 million years, the temperature of the Southern Ocean has dropped, from about 60 degrees (F) to less than 30 degrees in some locales. About 33-34 million years ago, in the continual movement of the Earth's tectonic plates, Antarctica was severed from the southern

tip of South America, and became completely surrounded by ocean. Ensuing changes in ocean currents isolated the waters around Antarctica. This limited the migration of fish populations such that they either adapted to the change, or went extinct (the fate of most). While others vanished, one group of fish [200 species of icefish in family Nototheniodae] exploited the changing ecosystem.

Though this narrative is obviously full of guesswork, it reads to me as if all this ancient history was actually observed—you know, like an embedded news reporter who took notes during a recent war event as the action unfolded. I have no problem at all with the extreme age of the Earth, the slow breakup of the supercontinent Pangaea, and new currents generating new climate changes. However, I have an *extreme* problem with the additional historical narrative Carroll adds to explain the mechanism that actually made this fish arise from its ancestors. Here are the words:

> In these amazing fish, the two genes that normally contain the DNA code for the globin part of the hemoglobin molecule have gone extinct. One gene is a molecular fossil, a mere remnant of a globin gene—it still resides in the DNA of the icefish, but is utterly useless and is eroding away just as a fossil withers upon exposure to the elements. A second globin gene, one that usually lies adjacent to the first in the DNA of red-blooded fish, has eroded away completely. This is absolute proof that the icefish have abandoned, forever, the genes for the making of a molecule that nurtured the lives of their ancestors for over 500 million years.

DNA Comes, DNA Goes...

As far as I can see, the phrase that speaks of DNA of red-blooded fish "eroding away just as a fossil withers upon exposure to the elements" can mean one thing, and only one thing—cold water slowly wore away the blood-producing genes of ancient fish. Isn't that how it reads? I see a poorly disguised version of vintage comments such as, "Giraffes got long necks by stretching them to reach leaves," or "Mice babies will get shorter tails if you shorten those of the parents." Even astute middle schoolers realize that environmental factors like extremely cold water cannot, by themselves, change DNA patterns. It's a strong whiff of that Lamarckian odor, and you can tell because the mutating agents always touted by Darwinists that theoretically might change genes (lightning, UV rays, and so on) are not cited. Furthermore, Carroll offers no evidence for this claim—either present or fossilized fish subspecies where the DNA can be shown to be partly eroded away.

This is made-up science that doesn't even follow Darwinism. To make the historical narrative at least follow Darwinian thought, you should read something like "Several million years ago, ultraviolet radiation, perhaps refracted by the prismatic effect of the thick ice, suddenly altered the genetic code in one red-blooded female fish ovum to disable the globin gene, and a new species appeared." Or, "A male fish swimming too close to the surface was struck by lightning and the shock altered all of the globin alleles in his sperm cells." Or, "Two separate species managed to mate, and in the chromosomal scramble, new genetic codes for globin were produced in the adapted offspring."

However, you'd better add to the narrative that you get *two* similarly mutated offspring (also, they'd better not both be males), that they manage to survive all sorts of perils such as pedation, and that they somehow find each other within the expanses of the ocean so they can mate as mature fish and produce a stable population. Of course the Darwinists can't be specific on how the new genetic codes were produced because "a fish being struck by lightning" truly sounds like a make-it-up-as-you-go approach. Therefore, the implication of environmental influences is flirted with, so perhaps unaware readers will jump to the full conclusion that cold water made this fish.

Dr. Carroll adds another piece of excellent biological information that nonetheless becomes a major scientific betrayal to the historical narrative. He describes in detail the amazing adaptations made by the icefish to survive without red blood, including extra large gills for maximum oxygen absorption, a scaleless body to allow some oxygen osmosis right through the skin, and cell organelles that form at body temperatures normally prohibitive to this. And to this list Dr. Carroll adds enlarged capillaries, a bigger heart, and increased blood volume.

But the impression I get in this article, one ever present when Darwinists begin to explain adaptations, is that these variations came about piecemeal (by the cold again?) as the fish lived out their lives. So how many of the six adaptations above (new gills, skin, organelles, capillaries, heart, and blood) did the fish need in order to cross the threshold of bloodless survival? Three out of six, or half of them? Then those three had better appear *simultaneously* because only two means a dead fish. But if you understand the way biological systems work, you would be correct to say that all six adaptations are absolutely critical or you get a dead icefish. However, if they indeed came about piecemeal, what do the other five adaptations do while waiting for the sixth to be mutated into place? Call it, "Nothing works until everything works."

But the biggest nonsense lies ahead. When the UV rays hit, or when the lightning struck, or the genetic scramble occurred when two incompatible species still mated, how did all this new and improved genetic *information* get created? What type of nitrogenous base pair alterations in DNA coding would have had to fantastically fall together to account for larger gills? And take the loss of scales to produce a smooth skin. It is truly bizarre to think that millions of years ago, reconfiguring forces hammered one poor fish (okay, two), and somehow did a wholesale beneficial rewrite of his present chromosomes to produce so much new and unique genetic *information*. (See the previous chapter of this book.)

This is why I firmly stand on my previous statement that no new young and brilliant Darwinists are coming out of science *to carry forward the further intricate details of evolution*. Sure, I'd call Dr. Carroll new on the scene. I'd even call him brilliant. But his message is just a glorified form of the same tired theory that's been around for over 100 years—a theory that is at a complete dead end. This is also why I believe Ernst Mayr—being the honest and introspective man that he was—promoted "historical narratives" at the end of his life, instead of presenting us with photos, sketches, charts, graphs, and diagrams that, as we've seen, could essentially prove nothing.

Ernst Mayr's Last Bequest

Back to Ernst Mayr one more time. In the very end of *What Makes Biology Unique?* he covers a question central to this book: "Where did humans come from?"

I think he might empathize with the unidentified scientist I quoted in chapter 8, who said of the latest hominid find, "They ought to put it back in the ground." Mayr basically says what every paleoanthropologist says, the theory of hominid evolution is in complete disarray. Here is his very first sentence in the chapter "The Origin of Humans":

> The study of the evolution of human ancestors is at present in considerable turmoil, after a period of some forty or fifty years of relative stability.

I can tell you where the initial stability and the subsequent instability came from. Back in Louis Leakey's day, when we had so little hominid evidence, it was easy to imagine at will. But now that more hominid finds continue to be made, they just refuse to support that "stable" theory that humans were made by natural processes. But since the Darwinists can't change the theory, they are doomed to stay in turmoil.

Here's another pertinent point. I was surprised—no, amazed—that after Mayr wrote the bulk of the chapter about hominid evolution, he admitted his words *might already be invalid* based on a recent find that may cause yet another "drastic revision" of the monkey-to-man theory. His words were, "What I present here is the picture we had *before* the discovery of Sahelanthropus"(emphasis mine). Then at the end of the chapter, Mayr includes a very short appendix that admits that *Sahelanthropus*—though having to be considered a more advanced branch of *Australopithecus*—lived approximately 2 million years *earlier* than its supposed less complex ancestors. Adding this to the material of chapters 8 and 9, we now have the foremost biologist in all the world also saying that the hominid fossil record just doesn't stack up as it is always conveniently portrayed in textbooks.

However, my favorite part of Mayr's human evolution chapter, in fact of the whole book, is Mayr's "historical narrative" of how humans came to be. Again, no photos, sketches, charts, graphs, or diagrams. I say Mayr gives us just more stretched giraffe necks, cut-off mice tails, and fish that had their blood taken away by cold water. First, he starts off the section on the supposed transition of *Australopithecus* to *Homo* with these exact words:

> Not having any fossils that can serve as missing links, we have to fall back on the time-honored method of historical science, the construction of a historical narrative.

Back in chapter 8, I allowed that at least 4 percent of the hominid evidence—approximately 200 specimens—came from the 4.5 to 2 mya time period. But Mayr allows none at all. (Actually, I suppose this benefits the Darwinist because, if there is no possibility of contradictory evidence, now they can write any scenario they care to fabricate.)

Mayr on ET Life

"Is there life on other worlds?" is one of the questions Ernst Mayr addresses in *What Makes Biology Unique?* He follows a quite sequential train of thought—until his summation—with observations such as the following:

- "No"—life on other planets doesn't have to mean intelligent aliens. It could mean simple bacteria or other types of molecular aggregates.

- "No"—the universe doesn't give us that many possible places for other life-forms after all. Astronomy is finding that solar planets that could sustain some form of life are actually quite an exceptional find.

- "No"—life on our planet doesn't vary from one basic molecular code (read "design"). If the random origin of life was so easy, why didn't we get more forms of life based on different molecular codes?

- "No"—complex life doesn't come easy. An eye on one organism did not come from an eye on another. Natural selection gave us eyes at least 40 different times, bioluminescence 26 different times, and so on, and all were acquired independently. (Correct—Mayr says such complex features were "acquired independently." Check it out.)

- "No"—human intelligence doesn't come easy. There is only an infinitesimal chance that it happened here.

- "No"—communication with ET life doesn't seem possible after you've multiplied together all the prohibitive factors of probabilities and the vast distances in space.

But then...

- "Yes"—despite all of his own observations, this doesn't keep Mayr from believing intelligent life developed here on its own, or that there is a high probability of life on other worlds.

Mayr's Narrative

Here is a condensed version of the events in Ernst Mayr's historical narrative on hominid evolution. It begins in Africa, because Mayr correctly observes not a single hominid fossil older than 2 million years has been found outside of that continent. Note that you may read nothing new in the following because these points are rather standard-issue for a Darwinist. Maybe the real thing to remember is that these are the final beliefs of the man most in the know.

- The first australopithecines live in trees as creatures that walked on, and grasped with, all four legs. However, climate changes caused Africa to become more arid and many of the trees died off, depriving australopithecines of their retreat to branches for safety. Now exposed to predators in the bush country, their arms shortened and their legs lengthened as they transitioned from quadrupeds to bipeds for speed of escape.

- Ingenuity from increasing brain size aided in survival. It allowed the incorporation of fire for protection and warmth, and the discovery of flaked-stone tools for construction of shelters and processing tough food.

- Decreasing tooth enamel in the emerging *Homo* species reduced their ability to eat the tougher savannah plant foods, so they gravitated toward a carnivorous diet, perhaps first by scavenging the carcasses of other carnivores. Later, the use of tools for hunting, and fire for cooking the kill, helped accelerate the switch to the more versatile omnivorous diet.

- The result of this increased protein in the diet due to hunting led to a rapid increase in body size. While australopithecines were approximately 3.5 feet tall, the earliest *Homos* were about 4.5 feet tall and Neanderthals 5.5 feet tall. The accompanying increase in physical strength allowed hominids to migrate out of Africa and disperse to other continents.

- Increasing upright stature set a limit to the size of the mother's birth canal that in turn limited fetal brain size. So the growth of a baby's brain was shifted more to the postpartum age, making hominid newborns increasingly backward and helpless compared to ape babies.

- As newborns became more helpless, instinctual maternal "stay-at-home" care from females had to improve, as did the need for more permanent shelters. While this reduced sexual dimorphism because of the need for more gender equity in strength to carry infants and build structures, it also increased the division of male and female duties. Eventually this led to a growing social structure in stone-age clans that in turn produced the first ancient civilizations (Sumerians, Israelites, Egyptians, and so on) based on patriarchal domination—ancient civilizations from which all our present day ancestries developed.

On the surface, this could be believable. These packaged narratives do make history seem to flow before your eyes—at first glance, that is. But stand back and see if once again you don't have environmental factors constantly improving genetic codes. That just can't happen. Yet many, many highly intelligent people are perfectly willing to entrust their physical existence, and even if only by default their spiritual existence, to the theory of self-made life.

From my experience, it's always been the approach of ardent Darwinists to not encourage you to take a second look. First, they tell their tale with a lot of scientific-sounding words like "peripatric speciation" so that the average or uninformed person feels inadequate to engage them in debate. Then, if you ask them to back up their narratives with hard data, they do it mostly with artists' drawings—such as the human-looking monkey faces we've all seen on the pages of publications like *National Geographic*. And the most important plank of Darwinism? Never, *ever,* entertain scrutiny of opposing theories or allow others to tell the other side of the story.

The Other Side

In *Reclaiming Science from Darwinism* and *Exposing Darwinism's Weakest Link,* I have told the "other side" over and over. Now, here comes your last set of either-or decisions in this book. Below is a condensation of challenges to natural evolution. Either all statements are wrong, and an active God is not, and has never been, a part of creation. Or else, any one statement is correct (or perhaps all), and natural evolution is in complete collapse. You decide whether each is true, or not.

T   F

_____   _____   1. Accounting for "molecular evolution" before cellular evolution is an abject impossibility. There are no provable mechanisms for how molecules could increase in complexity without cells to produce and utilize them. For example, you cannot assume proteins before you have the DNA that codes for them. Furthermore, there is no "survival of the fittest" operating in molecular evolution. The larger the unprotected molecule, the more vulnerable it is to denaturing.

_____   _____   2. The second law of thermodynamics says all systems go to disorder and silence and never become more ordered and dynamic. This immovable rock of physics prohibits many times over the random increase in pre-cellular or post-cellular complexity.

_____   _____   3. The odds of producing the order in the universe, the perfection in our own solar system, and the precision on our planet all stretch the limits of luck beyond believability. Someone tinkered with physics.

_____   _____   4. Searching for extraterrestrial life has yielded nothing but failure, including finding no presence of even the simplest bacterial forms on our neighboring planet Mars, where conditions are marginally suitable. As far as we know—and we know a lot—life is still a miracle, not a statistic.

_____   _____   5. The Darwinian form of gradual natural evolution is absolutely betrayed by the fossil record, which provides woefully inadequate transitional forms; and theories of evolution where large leaps supposedly were made has no basis in fact. The fossil record provides us with no species undergoing true transition, just a broad assortment of immutable life-forms.

_____   _____   6. Supposed examples of macroevolution in the past, and proposed examples of microevolution in the present, all fail the acid tests of believability and testability. The standard "icons" printed in biology textbooks for 100 years are all in various states of disbelief, disrepute, fraud, and collapse.

7. The scientific backdrop of our planet—not just the necessities but all of the "bells and whistles"—is perfect for our species. It is as if Someone was anticipating our arrival.

8. Certain miraculous features of our universe, such as the water molecule that—fortunately—breaks all the rules of chemistry, once again stretch the limits of luck beyond the breaking point.

9. The supposed straight and unbroken pathway of evolution from monkey to man is in complete disarray. Though the theory is still printed as if it's nicely sequential, it's actually replete with contradictions, reversibilities, retrogressions, deceptions, and fraud. And the more evidence is exhumed, the more impossible the "self-made" explanation for *Homo sapiens* becomes.

10. Other scientific aspects of human development—vestigial structures, vestigial behaviors, language development, and so on—constantly betray evolution rather than support it.

11. Universal standards in the areas of good versus evil and right versus wrong—as well as other societal values—transcend cultures and individuals. However, as common and undeniable as they are, their existence has no biological explanation.

12. The story in the Garden of Eden—as fact instead of allegory—is the only suitable explanation for the origin of spiritual humanity. The reliability of the book of Genesis is verified by

scientific and historical data, and there simply is no reasonable substitute story for the basis of the "soul" in other religions or legends. Furthermore, other details in the chapters of Genesis are easily blended with the best of what science has learned about the creation of our world, and Bible and science can certainly co-exist.

_____ _____ 13. Information theory without question sweeps away all "random" explanations. You simply cannot have the complexity and harmony we observe without the input of a guiding intelligence. There truly is no free lunch.

_____ _____ 14. In all of the above scientific objections, math is constantly cited as part of the impassible barrier to self-made life. Universal probabilities show that even all the time and space in the universe will not contain the odds to overcome blind luck, and phenomena like the divine proportion show that the creation cannot possibly be accidental.

The above list, with the exception of statement 12 and perhaps 11, is strictly scientific information. To me, it completes the picture of Design compared to Darwinism.

Over my years in public education I have taught both Design and Darwinism views to my students as neutrally as possible—and have also done so with my own children—so that everyone can decide for themselves. But if these 14 statements are so fraudulent, why in the world wouldn't a Darwinist *welcome* them into the science classroom and laboratory where they could be properly exposed. No—strict Darwinism is dead. And as the wise old cavalryman advised, "When the horse is dead…dismount."

16

Postscript

For the Spiritually Adventurous Only

The deed of life was done. And humans are here as well. But there were no eyewitnesses to record exactly how the deed was done. So to identify the perpetrator, Darwinists combine the sketchy circumstantial evidence with extensive guesswork, and after a short sequestration, issue the verdict in the form of historical narratives that describe their godless convictions of an accidental process. Fair enough. Then I can offer my own historical narrative for the "un-accidental" existence of humans.

- In the beginning, out of the void God spoke into existence the exploding flash of quantum packets that began the universe. These produced energy in the form of light and electromagnetic forces, as well as the subatomic particles that eventually produced the elements of the cosmos. At this moment in creation, God established the principles of physics, chemistry, and math on which He would build the rest of His works—ultimately intending the final product to be a home for us, spiritual entities in a biological body whom He foreknew.

- Despite its nondescript physical location in the universe, God designated our planet as the focus of His creative energy. He established the Earth in the perfect location, made it with just the right size, shape, and tilt, and equipped it with the perfect geological, chemical, and climatic conditions. Spiritually, Earth is the center of the universe.

- As part of the planet's settling process, God separated land and water through intended and directed geologic processes. As volcanic mountains rose and valleys sank, water could collect into oceans and lakes, and the water cycle could begin to generate a permanent atmosphere.

- As soon as the planet was stable, God introduced the genetic information necessary for life. Single-celled creatures such as bacteria, algae, and protozoans, first prokaryotes and then eukaryotes, soon filled the waters. Plant forms were established on land, and more oxygen was added to the stabilizing atmosphere.

- After single-celled life and plant life were successfully established, there was another infusion of genetic information that we now call the Cambrian explosion. In a very short span of geologic time, God genetically introduced all of the approximately 24 interdependent animal phyla that have since inhabited the planet. After this "biological big bang," there has not been any need—or any room—for any other animal phyla.

- After the Cambrian explosion, the passage of geologic time saw plant and animal life moving forward in planned complexity. Long periods of genetic stability were followed by short sudden surges as God first maintained or removed present species, and then rapidly introduced species with new genetic information. God's repeated use of long stability and then short surges is the reason "missing links" remain missing.

- After many millennia of advancing biological life *(nefesh)*, God chose to introduce to the world a spiritual man and woman *(neshama).* Though physically patterned closely after the hominid primates—and still bearing some of their physical and behavioral vestiges—these two beings were nonetheless unique in all creation. After giving this couple the right of choice, a conscience to discern right from wrong, and a spiritual destiny based on obedience, God then placed them in a divinely protected portion of the long functioning world. There they stayed for an unknown number of years until they finally violated the one command given them. This led to their expulsion from paradise, and they began to age and later die as all mortals now must do. However, their offspring eventually populated all the Earth, giving rise to today's civilizations.

Not long ago I was sitting at a pricey restaurant with my wife and two dear friends eating the best steak I have ever had in my life. We were out on the patio just after dark, and though the weather was somewhat cool, these big overhead heaters kept us quite cozy. Across the street, beautiful fountains swayed to the gentle sounds of soothing music. There we were, away from the daily grind, and no deadlines the next morning to keep us from sleeping in. It was truly as if the whole world revolved around us, and time felt like it was standing still. What's more, I never once though about the fine-tuned biology, chemistry, and physics that made it all possible—I just relaxed and soaked it all in.

And you know what's really cool? I get to enjoy such contentment as this at other times. What comes to mind is trout fishing in a remote wilderness river with a whole day to burn, spending time with that "electrifying someone," or taking the time to cook a "farmhouse breakfast" for my children on a lazy Saturday morning—with all the bacon they can possibly steal before the eggs are done. In each of these cases, almost like heaven.

But isn't life terrible at times? As a lifelong public school teacher, I've repeatedly seen misery and sorrow at a depth impossible to describe.

I'm not so much talking about hunger, illness, or physical danger either—threats to the body—as I am abandonment, heartbreak, and grief—threats to the soul. Of course the other dangers are out there too, such as unchecked famine, pandemic diseases, and senseless bloodshed. And when all the latter happens to the young among us, we know how sorrowful that is.

But even if you've never faced true starvation, terminal illness, or roving assassins, you've still had sorrow. We have all experienced that "Down on your knees, no place to turn" type of fear and pain from which we think we may never recover. I'm convinced Jesus understood all this, and much better than I ever will. In the incident where He healed Lazarus from the dead comes the shortest verse in the Bible, the universally known "Jesus wept." But why was He crying? Surely not for Lazarus. The man was about to be restored to life. Was He moved to tears by His own impending death on the cross in just a handful of days? No, just before He took His last breath He was still praying for His enemies. I'm convinced that when Jesus saw the sorrow all around Him, He also felt the sudden rush of all the pain and agony of the past, present, and future of all humanity, especially the self-induced forms caused by the evil to which people succumb.

Finding Perspective

That's the problem. Life is hard enough when you make good choices, and people don't commit suicide just because they think they are going through a "rough phase." But what's weird is that people (with faith or without) still try to perfect this life as if that were doable. (As one ex-drug user once described it, "I was in the chase for the never-ending buzz.") I'm not immune. Sometimes I think if I could just get that last car problem fixed, pay off those braces, find that secret hunting spot, get the second mortgage paid off—maybe even get my wife to start acting right—I could finally sit back and enjoy life on "cruise control."

But there's no such thing, is there? As an extreme example, I actually had a middle-aged professor friend who mapped out what he thought was his last 20 years of employment. He had every advancement and raise he hoped to earn, every class he hoped to teach, and every book he hoped to write and promote through travel. He also had every major vacation planned for 20 concurrent summers. He even planned several fishing and hunting adventures per year, including locations and approximate dates, as well as the types of boats and vehicles he expected he would have to buy or replace during this time period to complete these adventures. Not only that, he also had a plan to accelerate his mortgage payoff based on projected salary raises so that he could ease into retirement debt-free, after which he would plan the next 20 years. As a 47-year-old Darwinist, I'd say my friend had an extreme amount of faith that life would continue on as per normal. However, pancreatic cancer four years later had other ideas.

However, let's say my friend had lived his next 20 years as planned, and then 20 more in similar fashion to make it to age 87 and beyond. Would he say that he found the meaning of life in any of these pursuits, or would he still need 20 more? I remember a preacher once saying that you know people are meant for something bigger than what can be found on Earth, because nothing on Earth *ever* fully satisfies.

Looking back on my life, and the lives of so many others, I couldn't agree more. I can't think of one thing I pursued—sometimes desperately—that once achieved had a payoff that was all I expected it to be. Take the guy I knew who devoted his life to raising koi, those expensive Oriental carp that look a lot like big goldfish to me. His life was defined by attending koi conventions, reading koi magazines, getting together with his koi buddies, and putting more and more money into koi breeder tanks and accessories. Is that the meaning of life? Can true fulfillment be found in carp? I'm not judging this man or anyone else either because…what am I still chasing that I will never catch?

Futility Is the Rule

Jesus tells the parable of a man who decided to build bigger buildings to store his increasing wealth, thinking then it would be his turn to put his life on "cruise control." Even if you never heard the story, you can guess the outcome. Didn't happen. And why not? Because Romans 8:20-21 says that's impossible. I see these key verses as a powerful scientific statement that puts perspective on spiritual people who must navigate an altogether biological world. The verses begin with, "The creation was subjected to futility."

Left alone, ecology is a fine-tuned arrangement built on self-maintenance and total recyclability. But remember, the system is based on death. Every creature must reproduce more offspring than can possibly survive to adulthood so that every life-form has the "opportunity" to be eaten—as well as to eat, of course. And that can have a violent and dismal appearance.

When the three-foot corn snake in my biology class would eat, it was disturbing to many students. The snake would smell the unsuspecting mouse with flicks of its tongue, and edge up on it as the class watched. Then as a true constrictor, in the blink of an eye it would grab that mouse, wrap it up in about three coils, and squeeze the life out of it at both ends—literally. Then, when through his body the snake could feel the mouse's heart had stopped, it would leisurely uncoil and swallow the mouse—headfirst. Every time the tail was the last thing to disappear.

It was rough for some to watch, but the scenario was no worse than when an owl would swoop out of the night and grab such a snake with its powerful talons, or no worse than when a slaughterhouse would butcher a live cow to provide the hamburgers my squeamish students so readily ate.

This constant recycling of dead plant and animal bodies underscores the word *futility* used in Romans. For example, we are never immune from at least the possibility of starvation, and our other biological necessities like warmth and sleep take constant maintenance lest they fall below minimum. And, of course, our eventual demise is unavoidable no matter what we do or how much we ignore it. Furthermore, all creation was subjected not to just the biological constraints of the second law of thermodynamics, but to mechanical futility as well. Therefore, all our "toys," from I-Pods to SUVs are in some state of degradation on the path to complete breakdown. Finally, the second law also says even our sun has a limit to its life, as do all burning objects in the cosmos, if time goes that far. *If...*

If you add the rest of Romans 8:20-21, you get this:

> The creation was subjected to futility, not willingly, but because of Him who subjected it, in hope that the creation itself also will be set free from its slavery to corruption into the freedom of the glory of the children of God.

"In hope." I like that. Ever since we all lost Paradise by the actions of the original two, it's been an unwinnable struggle. But the promise is there that we will be reclaimed, and all this futility will be conquered by a plan set in place before time.

Permit me one final example. A recent feel-good movie called *Facing the Giants* begins with a high-school football coach having a rough life. Money's tight, the car keeps breaking down, and due to complications in his body, he and his wife have never been able to conceive. Meanwhile, the team's perennial losing record shows no sign of turning around, his better players are transferring to other schools, and there is talk of him being fired. The coach is a man of faith, and in his prayers of desperation he keeps asking God "Why?"

At that point, an older and wiser friend tells him of two farmers who prayed for rain. Afterwards, one farmer sat and waited while the other went out and began to prepare his fields. The moral of the fable was "Which farmer had the better faith?" and the question to the coach was "Which man are you?" The coach began to realize that coaching and playing football was not ultimately about football, but about serving in the kingdom. As he began to ask the players to give their best in all areas of life, a transformation began to take place in all their lives, and the rededication began to spill over to other students and even other parents. (At one point, a particularly difficult boy went to his father to ask for forgiveness for his rebelliousness, and the overjoyed father bought the coach a new truck.)

You can probably write the rest of the script from here. They began to play as a team, made it to the state playoffs, and won the championship in a thriller. In the final scene of two years later, the coach is sitting with his baby son, and his wife, obviously pregnant again. Then he walks by the mantel, where *two* championship trophies are on display.

From the theme of the movie, and the final look on the coach's face, I get the impression he would be just as content if his wife were still barren and he was selling vacuum cleaners door to door. Look at it like this. We can all agree that finally getting two championships and two children would not be the end of life's challenges for the coach. There will be plenty of disappointments yet to be had, such as in upcoming football seasons and throughout a life of parenting. The point again being that material possessions, public accolades, and even fatherhood join the list of every earthly thing (including koi) that can never bring total fulfillment in this life that can, and will, end all too soon. Therefore, we must be meant for a life beyond this one.

Though we perhaps are locked in bodies 98.4 percent like common chimps, our uncommon spiritual destination is spelled out in Hebrews 11 that describes us as exiles passing through a strange land who are heading for our true home. It's just like the words of the Southern Gospel song that says, "This world is not my home. I'm just a-passin' through."

Not everything that can be counted, counts. And not everything that counts can be counted.

AFTER ALBERT EINSTEIN DIED IN 1955, PEOPLE WERE CLEANING
OUT HIS OFFICE AT PRINCETON UNIVERSITY. HERE THEY FOUND
A SMALL CARD WITH THESE WORDS, BUT NO AUTHOR CITED.
THOUGH THEY ARE USUALLY ATTRIBUTED TO EINSTEIN, TO THIS
DAY NOBODY KNOWS IF THEY WERE REALLY HIS WORDS.

FOR FURTHER
CONSIDERATION

A Proposed
Reconciliation of Timelines

Combining Genesis and Geology

I believe it doesn't take much effort to reconcile every valid scientific theory about the Earth being approximately 13.7 billion years old with every fact in Scripture. There is a way to blend geology—Earth's story told in rocks and fossils—with Genesis—God's story told in the Bible. Forthcoming is an explanation I think you will find understandable, reasonable, and workable.

First, I'm going to ask you to permit me four major suppositions. They are listed here and then explained.

First supposition	Allow time to be interpreted much as an infinite being would interpret it
Second supposition	Accept the below-defined steady-state model of the universe
Third supposition	Allow theological information, primarily from the book of Genesis
Fourth supposition	Do not hold rigidly to a *day* in Genesis being 24 hours long

First Supposition: Time

Allowing a more open interpretation of the normally held notion of time is extremely difficult because our lives are filled with stopwatches, clocks, and calendars. Even using analogies, as we must, it's nearly impossible to grasp the passage of time as God sees it. Whereas our lives are sandwiched between a birthday and a funeral with a ridiculously short time in between, neither microseconds nor millennia have any bearing on His activities. I would say a sequence of activities can be constructed from God's point of view—such as events thought to be before creation (Ezekiel 28:11-19) or after creation (Revelation 20:11-15). However, unless mortal human history has to be factored in, no act of an infinite God can be "too long" or "too short," evaluated from our finite perspective.

Second Supposition: Model of the Universe

From science's multiplicity of choices, accept only the steady-state model as I define it here for the origin and duration of the universe.* This model says that our present reality had one definite starting point (the big bang, if you insist), and since then the expanding universe has been on a one-way entropic path to total death and complete confoundedness that must be reached someday unless God intervenes. (For review, see chapter 11 of *Reclaiming Science from Darwinism*, "The Long Arm of the Law," on thermodynamics.) The diagram below shows our universe beginning with a burst of maximum energy, but if left to its own devices, eventually dissipating into an end of utter silence.

Steady-State Model of the Universe

Beginning .... End

Understand that the steady-state model is in contrast to other theories. The *static-state model*, seen below, once held by the ancients, has

---

* To avoid confusion, note that many use the term *steady-state model* to designate what I call the *static-state* model, which is explained shortly.

no basis in physics. This theory says that the natural laws governing our present reality had no beginning, have no end, and remain unchanged over the passage of time. Reason itself should discard this view.

Static-State Model of the Universe

No beginning .... No end

⬅━━━━━━   ━━━━━━➡

There are two other theories of the status of our universe, seen below, with which reputable physicists have dabbled. The first is the *progressive/regressive-state model.* It adds a second phase to the steady-state model. This theory says that if the total mass of our currently expanding universe is insufficient, the spreading apart of celestial objects will eventually reverse. Then the universe will collapse back on itself like a tape on rewind and end in a final cataclysm equal to the big bang at the beginning.

The second theory, the *oscillation-state model,* is more or less an extension of the progressive/regressive-state model. In this view, the universe has been in a constant state of expanding and collapsing, expanding and collapsing, for untold years—with no possible way to assess a beginning or an end. (You can imagine it as a variation of wave mechanics, as discussed back in chapter 7, where our present reality is on the rising side of yet another crest that is among countless other crests and troughs.) In both these last two theories, the time frame in which we live is obviously an unimaginably minuscule portion of all of time itself.

Progressive/Regressive-State Model of the Universe

Beginning ....

End ....

Oscillation-State Model of the Universe

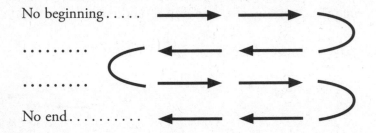

Again, the steady-state model says our universe had one beginning and faces a single end, even if it's uncertain what that end is. While this view has been called "painfully traditional and unimaginative," most physicists hold to it because it fits all the laws of thermodynamics.

Now if I'm allowed my opinion, anything other than a steady-state model is unbelievably unscientific or based on wild speculation. Interpretations of the universe that add such scenarios as reversals, slingshots, and sidesteps, as seen above, in my view are conjured by minds hoping to obfuscate the obvious. To these speculations you can add the notorious ideas of parallel universes, time warps, multiple realities, and so on. To borrow a thought from George Gilder, believers in such notions first invent *philosophic* concepts, and then use today's *scientific* concepts to demonstrate, diagram, and detail them as if they were already reality. Gilder calls this the "silliest stratagem in the history of science."

I fully agree. So why generate such fairy tales, which are in essence untestable? I have a suspicion that the real reason people search for any alternative to the steady-state model is because it sounds too much like the biblical account of creation—one beginning, one end. And most of us know how the universe ends in *that* story.

Third Supposition: Theological Information

For a religious interpretation of geologic time, allow me to only use the creation story in the first few chapters of Genesis. Here's why. The five major religions of the world—Buddhism, Christianity, Hinduism, Islam, and Judaism—account for about 95 percent of the world's population.

Then, with respect to Buddhism and Hinduism, there's no consistent "creation story" in either. Buddhists are much more concerned with the here and now. They meditate and promote self-denial in this life, but primary origins or final destinations are not a central concern. Hindus, of course, have reincarnation. Here souls have been traveling indefinitely through time—improving or regressing in the next life depending on earned karma—in a system that seems to have no beginning or end.

So that leaves Christianity, Islam, and Judaism, and all three of these religions accept the Biblical account of creation in Genesis, at least up through the story of Abraham.

Fourth Supposition: The Length of a Day

With respect to the times listed specifically in Genesis chapters 1 and 2, allow that a *day* is not something like one 6:00 PM to the next 6:00 PM. In fact, it is only in the minority of instances that the biblical use of the word *day* means 24 hours. The ancient Hebrew word for day is *yom,* and it literally means "a period of natural light" of any duration.

Yom is used over 1250 times in the Old Testament, and 85 percent of the time it refers to something other than a daily cycle. For example, *yom* can mean a *duration,* such as when Jacob set a marker over his wife Rachael's grave that is there "to this *day*" (Genesis 35:20). It can also be a *metaphor,* such as when Jeremiah's tears flowed "*day* and night" (Lamentations 2:18). Or it can be an *event,* such as when Joshua said, "Choose for yourselves this *day* whom you will serve" (Joshua 24:15).

Yom can even be used simply as meaning an *alternative to darkness,* such as when God gave the Israelites a cloud to lead them by *day,* and a pillar of fire to lead them by night (see Exodus 13:21). Even Jewish observances have a broad usage for *yom,* such as the Day of Atonement (better known as the ten-day purification process of *Yom* Kippur) and such concepts as a "*day* of retribution" or a "*day* of service."

If you still struggle with the "24 hours always equals a day" concept, at least remember that the timekeeping devices for our calendar—the sun, moon, and stars—were not made until Day Four (Genesis 1:14-19), when creation was already more than halfway done.

Now on to the chart. But first, let me once again list these four important suppositions with which to assess its content.

First supposition   Allow time to be interpreted much as an infinite being would interpret it

Second supposition   Accept the above-defined steady-state model of the universe

Third supposition   Allow theological information, primarily from the book of Genesis

Fourth supposition   Do not hold rigidly to a *day* in Genesis being 24 hours long

Timeline Combining Genesis and Geology

mya = million years ago; bya = billion years ago

Genesis Time	Geologic Time	Elapsed Time	Events, Additions, Separations
DAY ONE *Let there be light.*	(Starting about 13.7 bya) From 10^{-43} sec. to 10^{-33} sec.	10^{-10} seconds	The start of the big bang; gravity and electronuclear forces appear; quarks and antiquarks annihilate each other to produce *light*.
DAY TWO *Let there be an "expanse" and let "vapors" separate.*	From 10^{-33} sec. (13.7 bya) up to 4.6 bya	9.1 billion years	Subatomic particles appear; helium and hydrogen nuclei are formed, followed by heavier nuclei; dust clouds separate, and begin to condense; clouds with sufficient mass will eventually ignite into stars, those insufficient will become planets; Earth's atmosphere starts to form.
DAY THREE *Let the waters be gathered together, and let dry land appear. Let Earth sprout vegetation.*	Precambrian eon begins 4.6 bya and ends at 543 mya. This covers the Hadean (800 my), Archaean (1300 my), and Proterozoic (1957 my) eras.	4057 million years	Earth has sufficient matter to be called a planet; volcanic activity raises mountains; violent storms force water into forming valleys; oceans and seas fill with water; simple algae cells appear in seas, followed by more complex algae and protozoans; moss is established in shore areas; ferns appear inland, later to be followed by cycads, true trees, and later flowers.
DAY FOUR *Let two "great lights" appear; one to rule the day and one to rule the night. Let the stars appear also.*	The first stars were thought to appear about 200 million years after the big bang.	(Spanning Day Two to Day Six)	The formation of stars and planets is a continuing process, still being observed today in space by powerful telescopes, like the Hubble. Our own sun and moon take full form in the latter half of the 13.7-billion-year history of our universe.

Genesis Time	Geologic Time	Elapsed Time	Events, Additions, Separations
DAY FIVE *Let the waters teem with swarms of living creatures, and fill the waters in the seas. Let the birds fly above the Earth.*	Phanerozoic eon begins with the Paleozoic era (543 mya), ushered in by the "Cambrian explosion" and extends into the Mesozoic Era (about 227 million years into the Triassic period).	316 million years	Multicellular marine organisms in all 30 phyla present today suddenly explode around the world. In the subsequent Cambrian, Ordovician, Silurian, Devonian, Carboniferous, and Permian periods, populations in the sea advance from sponges and jellyfish to worms, mollusks, jawless and cartilaginous fish. Rich growth in plants and microorganisms produce coal beds and oil fields. Toward the end of the Paleozoic era amphibians appear, and the first primitive bird forms appear in the Triassic period but do not greatly diversify until later in the Cenozoic era.
DAY SIX *Let the Earth bring forth living creatures after their kind; cattle, creeping things, and beasts of the Earth. "Let us make man in our image."*	Begins with the second half of the Triassic period (about 227 mya) of the Mesozoic era through all of the Cenozoic era, 65 million years to present.	227 million years	Reptiles appear in the second half of the Triassic period and expand into the diversity of dinosaurs in the Jurassic and Cretaceous periods. The first mammals have arrived and appear rodentlike, but dinosaur domination keeps mammal and bird populations limited. Then all dinosaurs go extinct, and mammals and birds flourish throughout the Tertiary and Quaternary periods. The first true hominids appeared in the Pliocene epoch (5 mya), become stone-age clans by the Pleistocene epoch (1.5 mya), and become civilized during our present Holocene epoch (less than 10,000 years ago).
DAY SEVEN *He rested from all His work.*			Creation has ceased; general laws of thermodynamics now apply.

I interpret the above as a type of ongoing "separation" process. The sequence of separation, covering time periods known well to only God, should go something like this.

- First, light was *separated* from darkness.
- Then "waters" were *separated* from "waters" (subatomic particles separating into distinct atoms and then molecules).
- Then "water" was *separated* from dry land.
- Then nonliving (inorganic) material was *separated* from living (organic) organisms.
- Then plants were *separated* from animals.
- Then plant and animal species were *separated* from each other (each reproducing "after its own kind").
- Then spiritual creatures (true humans) were *separated* from all other animal life.
- Then man was *separated* from woman.
- And finally, God *separated* Himself from His work (on the seventh day, He rested).

Separation theme aside, is the above chart completely correct? I doubt it, because there are too many variables to account for and too little data available from such an immense time frame. However, did you find the general approach sound? Could you improve the sequence of events if you tinkered with it yourself? If you let the four suppositions serve as a guide, I think you'll like your final product.

Those of you who find the chart agreeable will find that it reinforces part two of this book: The math, the chemistry, the physics, and the geology of our world make for the perfect setup not only for all of life, but for that which makes us distinctly human. Moreover, the chart also provides a consistent backdrop for part three, which demonstrates that Darwinism can in no way account for that which makes us distinctly human.

Possible Expanded Scenarios for the Six Days

If you are interested in more of the possible scientific details in each of the six days, in the following pages I analyze each day in a bit more depth.

Additional Information for Day One

The prominent astrophysicist Stephen Hawking is everyone's expert on the science of "In the beginning..." He has investigated the sequence of events in the big bang, and in some cases he has charted them down to the tiniest fractions of time. This quote from his book *A Brief History of Time* gives his explanation for what happened during that first fractional tick of the geologic clock.

At the big bang itself, the universe is thought to have had zero size, and so to have been infinitely hot. But as the universe expanded, the temperature of the radiation decreased. One second after the big bang, it would have fallen ten thousand million degrees. This is about a thousand times the temperature at the center of the sun, but temperatures as high as this are reached in H-bomb explosions.

As I see it, Hawking could just have easily used the phrase "Let there be radiation," whereas God used the phrase "Let there be light."

Additional Information for Day Two

According to the chart, the passage of one second of time has already carried us from Day One in Genesis 1:3 (the creation of radiation, or light) into Day Two, where nuclei are forming that will become the lighter atoms...that will become the heavier atoms...that will become the molecules...that will become the raw materials from which stars and planets are formed. How accurately does Genesis describe this? A bit of ancient Hebrew might help.

On Day Two, God called for a *rajia*, Hebrew for an "expanse" (or "firmament" in some translations) to fill the void. And what filled the expanse? God called forth *mayim*, translated as "waters" or, more accurately, "vapors." Why is the distinction of "vapors" important? Because it denotes more chemistry than just H_2O. And this is compatible with Genesis 1:7, which ends by saying that the "vapors of the heavens above were separated from the vapors of the Earth below," signifying that the chemistry of the Earth was becoming a recognizable location within the chemistry of the rest of the expanding universe. Furthermore, the *mayim* of just the Earth were also separating to form the gases of our planet's atmosphere above the surface below. (You know, when the apostle Peter says that "the Earth was formed out of water and by water," I believe he was revealing much more chemistry than is usually understood at first glance.

So now at the end of Day Two we finally have our Earth, some 4.6 bya. And its originally inhospitable surface is settling down and being readied for life. We can now begin to look at geologic timelines that document the history of our planet and the way they are constructed. Though I've never seen two timelines that were the same, most tend to break down Earth's 4.6 billion year history into the four divisions listed below.

- **Eons**—These are the first major divisions that span all of Earth's time, and there are only two that basically divide the primitive Earth from the complex Earth. Perhaps the best known is the second—the Precambrian eon said to have begun 543 mya—where life on Earth was thought to be more complex than mere single-celled bacteria.

- **Eras**—These are major subdivisions that break down eons. Perhaps the best known—the Mesozoic era, said to be from 248 mya to 65 mya—is also called "The Age of Dinosaurs."

- **Periods**—These are lesser subdivisions that further break down eras. Perhaps the best known—the Jurassic period, said to be from 206 to 144 mya—was made famous by the original *Jurassic Park* movie (arguably the best dinosaur film of all time).

- **Epochs**—These are the smallest subdivisions that break down periods. One of the most critical epochs in this book—the Pliocene epoch, from 5.3 to 1.8 mya—is when Darwinists say nonhumans supposedly made that miraculous transition into full humans.

Personally, I see the construction of such geologic timelines to be one of the most tenuous, least agreed upon, and sometimes most fraudulent representations to come out of evolutionary science. You do not have to dig very far beneath the surface to see that the criteria for these divisions are highly speculative, and that proof for their transitional boundaries is in some cases so sketchy as to resemble fairy tales. Also, almost every timeline I've ever seen never bothers to show how horribly skewed the comparative time percentages of many divisions are. Among other delusions, this prevents the casual observer from realizing that life has to come "crashing in" in the last few ticks of the evolutionary clock.

In the next appendix I present my own abbreviated geologic timeline, drawn as most evolutionary scientists would endorse, and then I describe the myriad of problems with this standard approach. For now, consider that science says we modern humans are living in…

The *Holocene epoch* (10,000 years ago to present)
of the *Quaternary period* (1.8 mya to present)
of the *Cenozoic era* (65 mya to present)
of the *Phanerozoic eon* (543 mya to present)
of the e*ntire history of the Earth* (4.6 bya to present)
of the *entire history of the universe* (13.7 bya to present).

I would say these words constitute a mouthful.

Additional Information for Day Three

Now that we have a stable Earth, the Genesis account of Day Three says dry land is now distinct from oceans, and we get vegetation—plant life. Can this be squared with valid scientific facts? Well, science says after the first 800 million years of Hadean Era settling, we find the Earth a much quieter place with warm seas filled with roiling minerals and nutrients—sort of a chemical broth, which a Russian scientist of the 1920s named Oparin termed a *prebiotic soup,* more commonly called *primordial soup.* Geology says this sets the stage for the Archaean era, where a miracle just happened—life is now in the ocean!

What kind of life? Evolutionists say it most certainly had to be the simplest of all life we know today, a prokaryotic cyanobacteria that is also known as "blue-green algae." Blue-green algae are photosynthetic organisms, which utilize the same autotrophic process as all other plants. Their fossilized presence is left in the form of hardened mats called *stromatolites*—often termed the most ancient of all fossil remains. (Taxonomists no longer consider algae to technically be plants, but how many scientific details is Genesis obligated to provide in a handful of chapters?)

The succinctness of Day Three in Genesis fits right into the science scenario. What doesn't fit is the evolutionary delusion that a fully functioning metabolizer—such as a blue-green alga with its myriad of micromachines—can suddenly appear from an inorganic primordial soup as soon as conditions permit. (For a further explanation of the absurdity of the sudden appearance of life, read about the Proterozoic era in the next appendix.)

Additional Information for Day Four

This day takes some careful interpretation. To be clear on the wording, here is the exact text of Genesis 1:14-18 (NIV):

> Then God said, "Let there be lights in the expanse of the sky to separate the day from the night, and let them serve as signs to mark seasons, and days and years; and let them be lights in the expanse of the sky to give light on the earth." And it was so. God made two great lights—the greater light to govern the day and the lesser light to govern the night. He also made the stars. God set them in the expanse of the sky to give light on the earth, to govern the day and the night, and to separate light from the darkness. And God saw that it was good.

You read it right. Sun, moon, and stars on Day Four, after half of creation is already accomplished. How is this possible? Well, we have light from Day One, a planet on Day Two, and land and seas with plants on Day Three. I would say it is time to set up solar and lunar seasons. And accounting for stars fits as well here as anywhere else. Physicists studying the big bang say star formation is an ongoing process, with the initial ones appearing "soon" after the big bang in the first

200 million years. And as astronomers have shown, using telescopes like the Hubble, stars appear to still be condensing and igniting in present time. So it seems reasonable to mention their presence in Day Four with the other celestial objects.

Now, how can such important objects as the sun and moon, and such massive and innumerable objects as stars, appear after so much work has already been done? Why does all the rest of the cosmos seem like such a "fourth-day afterthought" compared to the first three days of intense focus on our tiny little outpost in space?

Here's the way I see it. The Earth may not be the physical center of the universe, but it is undoubtedly the spiritual center of Genesis. Earth may be physically dwarfed by our sun, and pitifully insignificant compared to black holes and such, but these "lights" were created for the benefit of our planet, not vice versa.

Later on, when these "signs and seasons" allow the tremendous diversity of plants and animals, we get that amazing physical backdrop introduced in chapter 3 of this book. And as I detailed in all of part two, this physical backdrop also sets the stage for the comfortable provisions enjoyed only by *Homo sapiens.*

In sum, the Earth is the crown jewel of creation, and the rest of the cosmos is just window dressing provided on the fourth day. And when I examine the whole set-up, I can only agree that it is "good."

Additional Information for Day Five

According to Genesis, at the end of Day Four two-thirds of creation is already finished, and all we have on Earth is plant life—probably beginning with nothing more than photosynthetic blue-green algae. Obviously there's a lot to finish in the short time left. But Genesis indicates that animal life explodes on the oceanic scene, and science agrees. The Cambrian explosion of about 543 mya, a term endorsed by actual paleontologists but dreaded by Darwinists, says all 30 present-day animal phyla—all the way to chordates—suddenly appear in the marine fossil record.

Call it an explosion of genetic information—a "biological big bang" if you will—for which evolutionary science has absolutely no answer. And the explosion of life took place not just in one locale but in the same geologic level of almost every water-deposited stratum world-wide. It truly looks as if someone said, "Let the waters teem with swarms of living creatures," and boom—we got sponges, jellyfish, starfish, clams, oysters, snails, octopi, and all manner of fish—perhaps even protists and aquatic worms and insects. I'd say, let's give God a round of applause! Then Genesis says at the end of Day Five we also get some birds, the primitive ones of the Triassic period if you wish, and now the stage is set for the Day Six—the last day, where the beasts of the Earth appear in rapid fashion.

Additional Information for Day Six

If the opportunity ever presents itself, don't pass up a visit to Dino-saur National Monument in extreme northwest Colorado. From the parking area, trolleys take you along a riverbed, where you will see life-sized dinosaurs peeking at you from among the trees. When you reach the visitors' center, you will find the south half of the building filled with the expected fossil exhibits and informational displays. However, the north half is an ongoing excavation site where from a balcony you can actually watch paleontologists working on partially exposed dinosaur skeletons imbedded in a deep, cut-away bank. Very educational!

Even the parking-lot barrier is educational. The wooden rails on the semi-circular border are marked off as a geologic timeline (such as the chart found in this book's next appendix), and to go left to right takes you from Earth's big bang to modern time. There is nearly nothing marked on the rails—except the appearance of the first cell about a third of the way around—until you get to the last eight feet or so, and then you go from fish all the way to humans, as complexity comes crashing in the last few steps you walk. So says science. So also says Genesis.

In Genesis 1:24-27, the Day Six description says that now the Earth finally gets its "creatures, creeping things, and beasts." This is in perfect alignment with geologic timelines, where paleontology says we get a sudden progression of those legged land animals—the amphibians, reptiles (including the dinosaurs), more advanced birds, and every mammal, as well as arachnids and insects. Evolutionary science says these all appeared from about the middle of the Mesozoic era, which geologic timelines show as the last 5 percent of all of Earth's time. All this complexity in just 5 percent of all time? I would call that quite a "day's" work.

Once again, no basic conflict here over the scientific and the biblical accounts. Fossils and faith go hand in hand, and the title of the chart above, "Combining Genesis and Geology," is not a stretch at all.

Oh, yes. One minor detail—humans. Day Six of Genesis grandly culminates by saying that after all other life is created, man is fashioned from the "dust of the ground." Paleontology also says that, as the most advanced animal, *Homo sapiens* appeared last as "stone age people" in the Pleistocene epoch, which began about 1.8 mya. If you do the math based on a 4.6-billion-year-old Earth, that's a very skinny .0388 percent of all Earth's time—which I would call the very end. And of course our physical bodies obviously have no special chemical elements other than what you find in the dirt to which they return. ("Ashes to ashes, dust to dust.")

Abbreviated Geologic Timeline

Mya = million years ago

EON

I. *Precambrian eon*—When life was absent or not complex
(4600 to 543 mya—88.2 percent of all Earth time)

ERA

A. *Hadean era*—Hot, forming, boiling planet; no life
(4600 to 3800 mya—17 percent of all Earth time)

B. *Archaean era*—Cooling planet, but still not able to support life
(3800 to 2500 mya—28 percent of all Earth time)

C. *Proterozoic era*—Stable planet; single cells appear in primordial soup
(2500 to 543 mya—43 percent of all Earth time)

II. *Phanerozoic eon*—When life was now complex
(543 mya to present—11.8 percent of all Earth time)

D. *Paleozoic era*—Ancient complex ocean life; worms, armored fish, amphibians, and so on
(543 to 248 mya—6.4 percent of all Earth time)

E. *Mesozoic era*—Age of dinosaurs; also earliest birds and mammals
(248 to 65 mya—4 percent of all Earth time)

PERIOD

1. *Triassic period*—Late amphibians, early simple dinosaurs
(248 to 206 mya—1 percent of all Earth time)

2. *Jurassic period*—More advanced dinosaurs, early birds
(206 to 144 mya—1.3 percent of all Earth time)

3. *Cretaceous period*—Most complex dinosaurs; ends in
dinosaur extinction
(144 to 65 mya—1.7 percent of all Earth time)

F. *Cenozoic era*—Age of advanced life; bony fish, birds, mammals
(65 mya to present—1.4 percent of all Earth time)

4. *Tertiary period*—Continental drift over, flowering plants,
birds and mammals
(65 to 1.8 mya—1.36 percent of all Earth time)

EPOCH

a. *Paleocene epoch*—Beginning of great advancement of
birds and mammals
(65 to 54.8 mya—0.22 percent of all Earth time)

b. *Eocene epoch*—Add ungulates (grazing animals) and
early horse forerunners
(54.8 to 33.7 mya—0.46 percent of all Earth time)

c. *Oligocene epoch*—Add primitive elephants, bronto-
therium, and early whales
(33.7 to 23.8 mya—0.21 percent of all Earth time)

d. *Miocene epoch*—Add large predatory birds, rhino and
hippo forerunners, later whales
(23.8 to 5.3 mya—0.4 percent of all Earth time)

e. *Pliocene epoch*—Add saber-tooth cat, prehistoric hominids, and later genus *Homo*
(5.3 to 1.8 mya—0.07 percent of all Earth time)

5. *Quaternary period*—Hominids join the planetary complexity
(1.8 mya to present—0.039 percent of all Earth time)

f. *Pleistocene epoch*—Add mammoth, cave bear, and Stone age *Homo sapiens* (1.8 mya to 10,000 years ago—0.0388 percent of all Earth time)

g. *Holocene epoch*—Add civilized *Homo sapiens* (10,000 years ago to present—0.0002 percent of all Earth time)

The graphic above is termed an *abbreviated* version of a geologic timeline because some charts contain much more detail. Some versions take the various *epochs* and further reduce them to *stages* or *ages* that can be less than a million years in duration—an eyelash of time—that give you more of a "snapshot" of what the person constructing the chart thinks was happening at that particular moment. And that begins my list of criticisms over the inherent falsity of geologic timelines—falsities that are necessary to maintain the illusion of natural evolution.

Proposed progressive sequences are never uniform. This is a classic case of "the devil is in the details." The closer you inspect the various subdivisions, the less the supposed transition is documented, the more the imagination is obviously at play, and the less agreement you find among paleontologists. To put it simply, just like the supposed progressive evolution of any one animal cannot be documented (like the evolution of whales or horses in *Reclaiming Science from Darwinism,* chapter 18), neither does the whole sequence of evolution "stack" like always depicted.

As proof, put two different versions of the timeline together and see how much disagreement you find in division names, times, and species as you zoom on to smaller durations of time—and how much someone's imagination takes over. For example, the Paleocene epoch of the Tertiary period of the Cenozoic era offers almost no transitional examples when birds and mammals supposedly "exploded" into the diversity of the coming Eocene epoch. But the wording on every chart I've ever seen attempts to underscore that progression still can be endorsed, and drawings attempt to document what actual fossils do not. It's a classic case of "circular reasoning," and having your mind made up going in, and finding a theory to fit it.

The skewed nature of the timelines is not explained. Only in rare instances will chart designers mention how complex life must come tumbling in at the last minute. For example, take my chart above. About 75 percent of the space of the page covers the Phanerozoic eon which is only 11.8 percent of all time. Of course it would be a waste of paper to proportionately depict the 88.2 percent of the Precambrian eon with very little on it, but it also conveniently hides the fact that evolution believes virtually mountains of new and improved genetic information were randomly generated in virtually no time at all. That's another reason the Cenozoic era needs so much detail because so much of how we define animal life on Earth didn't mysteriously arrive until the last 1.4 percent of Earth's time.

In *Reclaiming Science from Darwinism,* chapter 10, I examined the effect of crunching Earth's time into a 365-day calendar year, and how an abundance of dinosaurs would not hit the scene until about December 18, while our diversity of mammals wouldn't show up until about December 27. Later again, in chapter 18, I mentioned how 22 families of very slow-breeding cetaceans (from whales to dolphins) would have to mutate from only one potential ancestor (*Ambulocetus natans)* starting on about December 30. Then with monkeys turning into humans? Get out your stopwatch because it happened in split seconds. In my view, the skewed nature of geologic timelines is one of Darwinism's most tightly guarded deceptions.

The first cell is an unwarranted assumption. A prominent evolutionary biologist named Lynn Margulis has said that to go from inorganic molecules to bacteria is a greater probabilistic hurdle than to go from bacteria to people. And yet today's geologic timelines toss in that living metabolizer almost as soon as conditions permit. This ignores the myriad of cellular micromachines, metabolic processes, and organelles that are obviously useless taken individually, but somehow patiently wait in the "soup" until they can all assemble and begin to function. (The buzzard of spontaneous generation, now so snickered at because of the seventeenth- and eighteenth-century scientists who believed it, has come home to roost in geologic timelines.)

The Cambrian explosion is the vexation of Darwinism. Here is one fully documented mystery that is actually included in some versions of geologic timelines, and yet one likely to get you in trouble in public schools if you explain the dilemma. Around that magical time of 543 mya when evolutionary science says we stepped from the Precambrian eon to Phanerozoic eon—when life went from simple prokaryotes (asexual reproducers) to complex eukaryotes (sexual reproducers)— we got it all in the Cambrian explosion. By that I mean all 30 or so animal phyla alive today, including chordates, made a sudden appearance all over the Earth with no viable theory to account for this burst of complexity. Some scientists say at this point the gene pool became immediately interactive and required no additional body plans to complete the web of life. Mention this in your classroom at your own risk.

Finally, **Darwinism's weakest link** is its inability to explain human evolution using its supposed change mechanisms in the impossibly short time allotted with the nearly unworkable fossil evidence at hand. That's why I wrote this book, isn't it?

A List of Relevant Resources

*My Comments on Some of the
Books Mentioned in This Text*

Science and Medicine

Burgess, Stuart. *Hallmarks of Design.* Day One Publications, 2000

The stable order and beauty in nature, and the compatible way humans fit into this order, are obvious products of intent and not accident, says Burgess. For example, Darwinists commonly say that similarities in species are due to natural variations from common stock. But Burgess says that just as similarities in our man-made products are indications of the reusing of good design, so are similarities in nature due to the reuse of proven intelligent constructs. And in his opinion, "God" is the only reasonable explanation for the source of these intelligent constructs.

Cuozzo, Jack. *Buried Alive.* Master Books, 1998.

Cuozzo, a licensed orthodontist, tells his personal experiences in his quest to examine actual samples of prehistoric hominid skulls. He explains how tightly guarded such samples are, and how the caretakers generally refuse to let objective researchers examine the evidence. In the few instances he was given permission to examine skull fragments, Cuozzo tells of how often jawbones were incorrectly placed with skulls, how often evidence was intentionally altered to fit a preconception, and how often unexplained bone features and their impossible locations were swept "under the rug." Finally, the author also tells of harassment and threats from evolutionists whenever his Christian background became public knowledge, and how some researchers worked to discredit findings that were well within his area of expertise, but outside of theirs.

Darwin, Charles. *The Origin of Species.* John Murray Publishers, 1859.

Darwin wrote this book, universally credited with starting the theory of evolution, early in his life. It was his attempt to explain how small variations in species could naturally arise from those immutable forms made during the Creation. It was only later that some of Darwin's contemporaries took his ideas such as natural selection and expanded them to account for large-scale changes by which species would vault into completely new forms. Darwin's original book appears poorly understood, partly because his writing style is rather awkward, and partly because people have not fully investigated his work to compare it with what is now so commonly accepted.

Darwin, Charles. *The Descent of Man.* Prometheus Books, 1998.

Written 20 years after *The Origin of Species,* this volume includes much more evolutionary philosophy than Darwin's previous work. Here Darwin now asserts that humans have obviously descended from lower species by natural processes. Through almost exclusive use of his theory of "sexual selection," he explains how courtship and mating practices in lower animals have evolved into similar practices in modern humans. As in *Origins,* Darwin uses no experimentation to test his views, but still makes sweeping generalizations on how time and chance have established in *Homo sapiens* such traits as mental prowess, language, and societal fabric.

Dembski, William. *No Free Lunch.* Rowman & Littlefield Publishers, Inc., 2002.

In a book of rigorous science and math, Dembski shows how the complexity and compatibility we see in life and the cosmos could never have been "purchased" without the expenditure of intelligence. His "no free lunch" theorems demonstrate how the odds of luck creating order are quickly exhausted, and how "random" can never create complex specified information. Proposing a "fourth law of thermodynamics" to explain the "conservation of information," Dembski shows that the assortment of accidental processes credited by Darwinists with creating humanity could never have done the job.

Geisler, Norman L., and Frank Turek. *I Don't Have Enough Faith to be an Atheist.* Crossway Books, 2004.

The main premise for this book is that accepting the myriad of explanations necessary to support evolution takes much more belief in the unseen than that required by any religion. Citing undeniable examples of scientific difficulties inherent in Darwinism, the authors show time and again that the grounds for accepting a natural explanation for the origin of life provide much more tenuous footing than the grounds for accepting a spiritual one.

Hawking, Stephen. *A Brief History of Time.* Bantam Books, 1996.

Hawking, probably the most acclaimed expert on the scientific origin of our universe, explains the ancient phenomenon now widely known as the big bang. He details the initial explosive origin of quantum particles such as light, and goes on to explain the subsequent generation of subatomic particles, atoms, and finally molecules. These substances then separate and collect to form galaxies, solar systems, and planets, which in turn allows planets to further settle, stabilize, and (at least in the case of Earth) set the stage for life. It can be shown that, while Hawking's division of events is naturalistic and involves time frames from microseconds to billions of years, his account faithfully follows the abbreviated version of the first chapter of Genesis (if one allows flexibility with the time element inherent in the biblical word *day*).

Lubenow, Marvin. *Bones of Contention.* Baker Books, 1992.

Lubenow examines the human fossil record from a faith-based point of view. He feels that if you study the hominid evidence without a preconditioned mind-set that it supports evolution, you will find "monkey to man" to be a science inexact to the highest degree. By examining the many suppositions built around *Homo neanderthalis, Homo erectus, Homo habilis,* and the like, Lubenow feels an objective person can immediately see the inconsistencies, reversals, and anomalies preventing any type of the fossil sequencing that Darwinists so completely accept. Lubenow also clearly explains how in most cases only very small bone fragments exist, and yet evolutionists still use the scanty evidence to imaginatively build elaborate prehuman societies.

Mayr, Ernst. *What Makes Biology Unique.* Cambridge University Press, 2004.

This book is the final work of arguably the most prominent and respected Darwinist in American science. Writing at the age of 100, Mayr summarizes much of what biology now purports, especially in the area of evolution and natural rise of the human race from lesser primates. This volume is surprisingly much more philosophic than scientific, and Mayr readily admits how much of evolutionary theory is thinly supported by today's proposed evidence. As an example, instead of citing hard data, experimental results, and painstaking research, Mayr promotes "historical narratives" (individual musings on how life made itself) as a valid approach to explain how gradual changes occurred, such as monkeys leaving the trees to eventually walk on their hind legs.

Medawar, Peter. *The Limits of Science.* Oxford University Press, 1988.

Medawar forcefully explains what many professionals are reluctant to admit—that science falls far short of explaining much of our existence. A transplant surgeon by profession, Medawar describes how, even with the best of our efforts (such as in organ transplants), humans can never improve on—and most often fall short of—imitating what "nature" has already perfected. He believes that much of what science studies lies beyond natural processes, which necessitates intelligent involvement from outside of the system to introduce such fine-tuned information.

Simmons, Geoffrey. *What Darwin Didn't Know.* Harvest House Publishers, 2004.

An MD with nearly 40 years of experience, Simmons carefully explains how the theory of evolution is over 150 years old but has had very little authentic updating since that time. As proof of the need to reexamine the theory, Simmons cites the amazing complexity of the human body's systems and the many intricate subsystems necessary to support them, which science has only lately begun to understand. He also examines some of the highly complex human biological processes at the microscopic level, processes that also can be fully researched only with the aid of modern technology. Simmons says that if such information had been known back in Darwin's time, his whole theory might have been discarded at the outset.

Stove, David. *Darwinian Fairytales.* Encounter Books, 1995.

Stove, a man who professes no religion of any kind, nonetheless forcefully challenges the idea that humans evolved according to today's accepted Darwinian mechanisms. By directly refuting the science promoted by those such as Richard Dawkins, Stove, with humor and candor, is unrelenting in exposing evolutionary inconsistencies. For example, he believes that to simply open a dictionary and read from A to Z is to find a treasure trove of human attributes (*altruism* to *zealotry*) that most certainly must lie beyond a natural explanation.

Culture, Religion, and Science

Brown, Dan. *The Da Vinci Code.* Doubleday, 2003.

Brown does a commendable job of weaving fact with fiction to produce a highly readable novel. Taking some truths from the biblical account of the life and times of Jesus and combining them with a modern-day secret society that he expands into a conspiracy lasting several hundreds of years, Brown creates a tale that to the uninformed would seem 100 percent true. However, by recasting many of the verifiable facts in the New Testament in a way that reduces the divinity of Jesus, this book gives many skeptics a reason to dismiss other biblical constructs and concepts that would otherwise define the true spiritual nature of humans.

Coulter, Ann. *Godless.* Crown Forum Publishers, 2006.

With her well-known biting wit, Coulter explains how certain political beliefs predispose people to adopt an atheistic view of life and humanity, which in turn becomes its own form of religion. Coulter goes on to explain how a blanket acceptance of evolution leads these same people to values and behaviors that cause many of the societal ills afflicting our schools, homes, and places of work. As for the science portion, Coulter devotes an entire chapter to explaining the scientific problems with Darwinism, and she forcefully challenges the assumption that humanity is here by one big accident.

Dawkins, Richard. *The God Delusion.* First Mariner Books, 2006.

Arguably the last of the vocal atheists from the end of the twentieth century, Dawkins vehemently reaffirms that totally natural scientific processes are all that are needed to account for our existence. In trying to prove this thesis, Dawkins constantly ridicules the beliefs of faith-based people by portraying them as being duped into theology by their own weaknesses and fears. He also debates the attributes people ascribe to "God," and explains that if these attributes are true, God exhibits some of the worst behaviors of the human race.

O'Reilly, Bill. *Culture Warrior.* Broadway Books, 2006.

Reporter O'Reilly examines how many in today's political environment are discarding the bedrock values on which our country was built. These values are being replaced by a nebulous type of "situation ethics" that attack and discard the long-standing Judeo-Christian traditions that once brought our country the success and stability now being threatened. Coining the term "secular progressives" ("S-Ps"), O'Reilly believes that this movement is to our nation's detriment, and because of these misguided people, the phrase "under God" is now "under review."

INDEX OF SELECTED TERMS AND NAMES

INDEX OF SELECTED KEY INDIVIDUALS

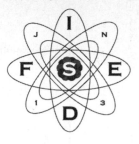

An Invitation to Connect with
the Professional Consultancy Called the...

INTERNATIONAL FOUNDATION FOR SCIENCE EDUCATION BY DESIGN

DR. KENNETH POPPE, SENIOR CONSULTANT

www.IFSED.org

Our Mission

To promote excellence in non-evolutionary science, math, and spiritual education through cutting-edge instructional materials and guest speakers.

Our Vision

To partner with home schools, private schools, public schools, colleges, and church organizations that believe that the current monopoly evolution holds in science and social education is unwarranted.

Please contact www.IFSED.org about the following:

A. *FREE* downloadable and reproducible student exercises:
1. A 5-page student exercise, "History of Religion and Faith vs. Science"
2. A 5-page math assessment tool, "Pre-Test—Basic Math Skills"
3. A 5-page student exercise, "Evolving the Giraffe"

B. Books for bulk order at reduced cost
1. *Reclaiming Science from Darwinism*: A Clear Understanding of Creation, Evolution, and Intelligent Design

2. *Exposing Darwinism's Weakest Link: Why Evolution Can't Explain Human Existence*

C. Math materials for order

1. A 58-page student math crash-course tutorial that explains, develops, practices, and assesses all the basic math skills through pre-algebra

2. A 10-page student exercise, "The Exponential Function" and "The Laws of Probability," which challenges current Darwinian explanations for the origin of life

D. Science materials for order

1. A condensed course, "Biology and the Life Sciences," which covers scientific classification, food webs, molecular biology, cell theory, genetics, plant and animal characteristics, and the ten classic human body systems—all from a non-evolutionary perspective

2. A condensed course in *chemistry* that covers atomic theory, subatomic particles, the periodic table, compounds and mixtures, reactions, inorganic chemistry, organic (life-related) molecules, and supposed chemical evolution—all from a non-evolutionary perspective

3. A condensed course in *physics* that covers energy vs. matter, kinetic vs. potential energy, Newtonian laws of motion, the laws of thermodynamics, steady and variable change rates in moving objects, Einstein's theories of relativity, nuclear physics, and quantum mechanics—all from a non-evolutionary perspective

E. Church study materials for order

1. A student study guide for Bible groups, Sunday schools, or individuals on *Reclaiming Science from Darwinism: A Clear Understanding of Evolution, Creation, and Intelligent Design*

2. A student study guide for Bible groups, Sunday schools, or individuals on *Exposing Darwinism's Weakest Link: Why Evolution Can't Explain Human Existence*

F. Guest speaker and consultation services

1. *For educators:* High-energy public presentations and staff training seminars on scientific challenges to evolution, and how to incorporate this information in classrooms and district standards

2. *For church, parent, and civic organizations:* Engaging and humorous presentations for conducting public forums, launching lesson/sermon series, or educating any group of constituents on the many problems with natural evolution

3. *For media, political, and legislative groups:* Technical support and advice for newsrooms, courtrooms, legislatures, and school boardrooms, where the issue is academic honesty and freedom of speech to explore the weaknesses in evolutionary theory.

Contact information:

Dr. Kenneth Poppe, Senior IFSED Consultant
PO Box 578
Firestone, CO 80520
www.ifsed.org

Also by Kenneth Poppe

RECLAIMING SCIENCE FROM DARWINISM

A Clear Understanding of Creation, Evolution, and Intelligent Design

Where's the Science?

The concern that haunted Charles Darwin—and has dogged Darwinism for 150 years—is now an inescapable conclusion: *The science is not there.*

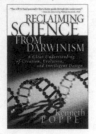 Today, we have mountains of evidence that relates to the origins of life. *Reclaiming Science from Darwinism* shows you why that evidence indisputably supports purpose and design in the cosmos...and decisively exposes Darwinism's failures. Using enlightening analogies, pointed examples, and clear explanations, Kenneth Poppe digs into these issues and more:

- mind-sets that undermine objectivity in both science and religion

- the impossibility of the first cell coming about by blind luck

- the mathematical *im*probabilities of random improvement in species

- scientists' fantasies regarding extraterrestrial life

- unsupported assumptions about bridging the gaps in the fossil record with "good" mutations

Up-to-date, straightforward, and spiced with humor as well as helpful graphics, this resource offers you solid information so you can judge for yourself where the science really is.

Excellent for students and parents,
as well as educators who want to present a
complete picture of origins science

To read a sample chapter, go to www.harvesthousepublishers.com

WHAT DARWIN DIDN'T KNOW
Geoffrey Simmons, M.D.

"A marvelous, entertaining, physician's-eye
view of the intricate functioning of the human body."
Dr. Michael Behe
bestselling author of Darwin's Black Box

What Darwin didn't know lies at the tips of your fingers... and everywhere else in your anatomy.

The founder of evolutionary theory didn't know that the function of every cell and every system in your body follows an intricate DNA blueprint. In fact, he didn't know much about the human body at all.

Drawing on the most recent research as well as years of clinical work, Geoffrey Simmons tells the real story about your amazing complexity:

- *The brain* resembles a continent swept by electrical hurricanes and chemical tidal waves that somehow makes sense out of reality

- *A fertilized egg* makes a journey as complex as the path of a golf ball that rolls 30 miles and lands precisely in the 18th hole of a course it's never seen

- *The immune system* contains multiple defenses that confine trillions of microorganisms to your skin, like passengers innocently sunning themselves on the deck of a cruise ship

What Darwin Didn't Know pictures the wonders of the human body in their true context—a marvelous system fashioned by an infinitely wise Designer.

To read a sample chapter, go to www.harvesthousepublishers.com

BILLIONS OF MISSING LINKS

A Rational Look at the Mysteries Evolution Can't Explain
Geoffrey Simmons, M.D.

"A well-researched and open-minded analysis."
Stephen Meyer, PhD
Director of the Center for
Science and Culture, Discovery Institute

No preceding links, no subsequent links, no "sideways" links

From the blue whale to the virus, from the macro to the micro, current scientific evidence reveals Darwinism's most fatal flaw—the billions of "missing links" in the story of chance development of life.

Dr. Geoffrey Simmons reveals how interdependent structures and systems—massive complexity upon massive complexity—apparently came about all at once, whole and entire. There are no precedents, no "in-betweens," no mistakes, no "first tries." He lifts the lid on dozens of Darwinian dilemmas:

- the fossilized reptile with feathers that supposedly changed into a bird able to take off, fly, land safely, build nests, and lay eggs that don't fall to the ground

- the walking fish that, while still in the sea, came up with a way to find food on land—as well as keep from drying out and burning its tender feet on hot sand

- the unlucky skunk ancestor that had to try out different scents until it found one that worked to chase off predators

The picture is crystal clear...and the conclusion, rational: Only the intelligence and purpose of an infinitely wise Designer can explain the intricate creatures, connections, and "coincidences" you observe everywhere.

A superb resource for students and parents,
as well as educators who want to present the "full picture."

To read a sample chapter, go to www.harvesthousepublishers.com